ENGAGING
—*the*—
CIVIL WAR

Chris Mackowski and Brian Matthew Jordan, Series Editors

A Public-History Initiative of Emerging Civil War
and Southern Illinois University Press

TURNING POINTS
OF THE AMERICAN CIVIL WAR

Edited by Chris Mackowski and Kristopher D. White
Foreword by Thomas A. Desjardin

Southern Illinois University Press
Carbondale

Southern Illinois University Press
www.siupress.com

Cover illustration: High Water Mark monument at Gettysburg National
    Battlefield. *Photo by Chris Mackowski*

Library of Congress Cataloging-in-Publication Data
Names: Mackowski, Chris, editor, author. | White, Kristopher D.,
    editor, author.
Title: Turning points of the American Civil War / edited by Chris
    Mackowski and Kristopher D. White ; foreword by Thomas A.
    Desjardin.
Description: Carbondale : Southern Illinois University Press, 2017. |
    Series: Engaging the Civil War | Includes bibliographical references
    and index.
Identifiers: LCCN 2017011803 | ISBN 9780809336210 (cloth : alk.
    paper) | ISBN 9780809336227 (e-book)
Subjects: LCSH: United States—History—Civil War,
    1861–1865—Campaigns.
Classification: LCC E470 .T87 2017 | DDC 973.7/3—dc23 LC record
    available at https://lccn.loc.gov/2017011803

Printed on recycled paper. ♻

This paper meets the requirements of ANSI/NISO Z39.48-1992
    (Permanence of Paper) ∞

Chris: *To Vince Kohler and Mark Van Tilburg*

Kris: *To Len and Terry, the best in-laws a guy could ask for*

Jointly, we dedicate this book
to our colleagues at Emerging Civil War

Contents

Illustrations

Foreword: Gettysburg—*The* Turning Point of the Civil War?

Thomas A. Desjardin

In my years at Gettysburg giving tours of the battlefield and Soldiers' National Cemetery, I got a sense of how visitors connect to the place. Among the common themes was the need for people to get as close to the "most important" site as possible. For example, one of the most common questions asked by tourists who took part in a tour of the cemetery—other than "What time does the four o'clock tour start?"—was, "Where exactly did Lincoln stand?"

The answer to this question was most often met with great disappointment. Lincoln did not deliver his speech from within what is now the national cemetery at all but rather stood a few dozen yards beyond the iron fence inside the privately owned Evergreen Cemetery ("and no, you cannot go over there"). Occasionally, the disappointment was diminished slightly by the description of the staging on which dignitaries sat and by the fact that Lincoln stood upon it about five feet above the ground. Still, the need to connect with Lincoln by placing one's feet exactly where his were planted for that historic moment is a powerful draw.

These kinds of encounters with pilgrims to historic battlefields are not uncommon, and they reveal the desire within us to be as close as possible to an actual historical, noteworthy moment, even if only geographically. The greater the importance of the event, the greater the desire to stand near its most significant location. The booth above the stage at Ford's Theatre, the room in Independence Hall where the Declaration of Independence was signed, and the parlor of Wilmer McLean's former home at Appomattox Courthouse all draw us to be physically "present" at great moments in history.

The town of Plymouth, Massachusetts, owes most of its annual tourism revenue to a rock that has no actual connection to the first settlers there. Thousands upon thousands visit the town so as to stop at the enormous shrine built over an otherwise nondescript boulder that probably never fell under the eye of a single passenger on the *Mayflower*. Standing at the actual spot where the first settlers stepped on the shores of our nation is a compelling urge. Never mind that the 1620 settlers were far from the first arrivals even to what is now New England. Plymouth Rock is famous for its mythical image, and people want to see it due to its contrived meaning, not for its factual historical importance.

All too often, the place where something significant occurred has derived that significance not from what actually occurred there—often we don't agree on the details of what did happen—but rather as a result of a process by which we as a collective society have designated it so. Cementing these places in our public imagination, we label them historic sites and national parks and over time spend enormous amounts of money on monuments, museums, and staff to help reinforce the importance and remind people of it.

Battlefields, particularly older sites where conflicts were fought within smaller areas, tend toward this idea. Finding the one square yard where the most significant moment of the Battle of the Bulge occurred, for example, is a fool's errand. But if one could find or create a story and raise it to a level of importance by convincing the world populace that something that occurred at that exact location was crucial to the Allied victory, the nearest little village would soon need many new hotels, restaurants, and gift shops in order to capitalize on that story.

Nothing captures the imagination of historic travelers like standing near—or better yet, touching—some historical object that was the original source of enormous importance. Just ask those responsible for the care of the Liberty Bell in Philadelphia who had to stop allowing tourists to touch the crack running up its famous side lest the thousands of rubbing fingers wear away the metal. The fact that the bell itself has very little actual historical significance or connection to the Founding Fathers is a story for another day.

This desire invades even the most cynical among us. During a visit to Vienna, Austria, decades ago I was thrilled to visit the museum exhibit that holds the car in which the archduke Franz Ferdinand was assassinated, igniting the First World War. I often start my stories about that visit by saying that I got to stand next to the car that caused the deaths of more than ten million people. This, of course, is a preposterous statement to make, but it provides an entrée into a conversation about how that war began and is evidence of our desire to boil it down to a momentary event.

Millions of soldiers and sailors fought in the Civil War. Over four years, these combatants engaged one another across an expanse that reached from Portland Harbor in Maine to Picacho Peak in what is now Arizona. To hold up one moment of this vast conflict occurring at one location as the pivotal event that decided the outcome of the war may be just as preposterous as blaming the First World War on a car. Nevertheless, there is something within us that seeks to refine great events down to one narrow, even pinpoint occurrence.

There is an old fable about how the loss of a single nail in the single shoe of a single horse cost a king a battle and thus his kingdom. "But for the loss of a nail" the horse would not have thrown a shoe, its rider would have delivered the crucial message that turned the tide of battle, and the king would have won the battle and saved his kingdom. If only one blacksmith had taken just a moment to secure one nail in one horse's shoe, the world would be dramatically different. This, of course, is simply not how great events are decided, but something in our individual and collective psyches as humans makes us want to refine enormous happenings down to the simplest act. Having done so, we and generations that follow us can visit the exact spot where great things were decided.

When it comes to the American Civil War, this psychological search for "The Moment" or "The Act" most often settles on what many consider the greatest battle of the war—the three days' fighting at Gettysburg in July 1863. This is not necessarily because of any special military advantage that was brought about by the outcome of this event that was recognized at the time; rather, as is often the case, the importance of this event above all others is the result of forces that played no part in the fighting. For this reason, the story of Gettysburg and its importance has been shaped far more by those who have sought to memorialize the battle after the fact than by those who manned musket, shell, and saber on the field itself.

The importance of Gettysburg in the American mind is the result of many nonmilitary factors that few who visit the field or study it casually ever consider. First, the battle occurred closer to the media center of New York City than any other. Geography provided relatively easy access by train; reporters, photographers, sketch artists, and others could reach the field soon after the fighting and some even while the conflict still raged.

As the largest and most significant battle fought in the Eastern Theater of the war, Gettysburg stood out to participants and observers alike as the only major battle, from Bull Run to Appomattox, in which the Union forces could claim an outright victory. It is little wonder then that Union veterans of the East focused on this particular fight as the one on which to dwell, reminisce, and heap greater attention and importance, particularly when compared to the Western Theater, where Union forces seldom lost a fight. By refining the war's importance down to Gettysburg, eastern veterans focused a disproportionate share of attention on their one great victory.

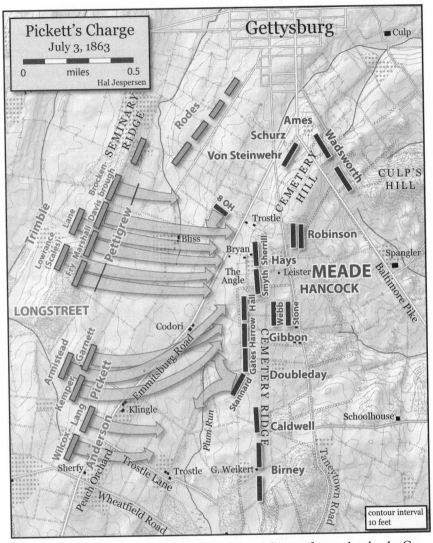

Pickett's Charge
July 3, 1863

0   miles   0.5

Hal Jespersen

Gettysburg

Culp

Rodes

SEMINARY RIDGE

Brockenbrough
Davis
Marshall
Fry

Trimble

Lowrance
(Scales)
Lane

Pettigrew

8 OH

Bliss

Ames

Schurz

Von Steinwehr

CEMETERY HILL

Wadsworth

CULP'S HILL

Trostle

Robinson

Spangler

Bryan

Hays

Smyth
Sherrill

Leister

MEADE

Baltimore Pike

The Angle

HANCOCK

LONGSTREET

Codori

Gates
Harrow
Hall

Webb
Stone

Emmitsburg Road

Gibbon

CEMETERY RIDGE

Armistead
Garnett

Pickett

Kemper
Lang

Anderson

Wilcox

Klingle

Stannard

Doubleday

Schoolhouse

Plum Run

Caldwell

Taneytown Road

Sherfy

Peach Orchard

Trostle Lane

Trostle

G. Weikert

Birney

Wheatfield Road

contour interval
10 feet

Pickett's Charge. As the climactic action of the war's most famous battle, the Confederate attack on July 3, 1863, has assumed mythic importance. The nominal focus of that attack—the Federal position along Cemetery Ridge—became the focus of John Bachelder's postwar efforts to memorialize the battlefield and shape the narrative of the battle. *Map by Hal Jespersen*

While it is rare that momentary events considered stoically and on cold, hard, sometimes boring facts and statistical analysis can be found to have played a deciding role in far larger events, particularly enormous military conflicts, occasionally a single person can have the effect of changing for all time the perception of an incident that most of us hold. Public perception of great events is often shaped not by long, drawn-out factual analysis but rather by novels, paintings, poems, and films. Most of us know about Paul Revere's ride because of Henry Wadsworth Longfellow's epic poem. We may not know the century in which the Battle of Balaclava was fought or by whom, but most of us have heard of the Charge of the Light Brigade, thanks to the poetry of Alfred Lord Tennyson. Each of these great descriptions of a moment in time lends itself to the need in our minds to refine great events down to the actions of a few people or, better yet, a single person.

While there is no great poem that elevated Gettysburg to literary immortality nor one great act by a single soldier that turned the tide of battle and thus the war, there was one single individual who had more of an impact than anyone else on what most people know today as the story of Gettysburg. More remarkable, this one person was not present at the battle, never served in combat of any kind—if one exempts letter writing—and had no real military background.

John Badger Bachelder was a painter of landscape scenes and a lithographer in New England in the 1860s. When the war broke out, he decided he might make his fortune by painting *the* iconic moment of the war and selling reproductions of it to a wide audience. It was not until more than two years into the epic struggle that an opportunity presented itself. Bachelder arrived on the field at Gettysburg just a few days after fighting ceased, and he immediately began questioning everyone he could about the events that had occurred there.

In his search for the iconic moment and location that a static painting requires, Bachelder decided that Gettysburg must provide the subject matter. Thus convinced, he spent the next year making maps; interviewing veterans, both in hospitals and among the army still in the field; collecting information; and searching for the specific episode for his intended painting. Thanks to his efforts, and to the fact that others who might have served such a purpose were still fighting the war, Bachelder became recognized as a key authority on the history of the battle. In time, he parlayed this into a huge $50,000 contract direct from Congress to write the definitive history of the battle. Perhaps more important, he managed to get himself appointed as the official "Superintendent of Tablets and Legends" for the battlefield, a position that gave him authority over every word inscribed into every monument and marker on the field. In this role, he had a profound effect on how people perceived the battle, an effect that lingers strongly even today.

For his painting to become a commercial success, however, Bachelder needed to convince his audience that Gettysburg was the decisive battle of the war and that somewhere among the many subconflicts that made up the larger whole of the battle there was a key moment that decided the overall engagement. Thus, his artwork could focus on the moment when the entire war was decided in an instant and in such a way that it could be captured as a single moment on canvas.

In all of his work shaping the story of the battle to his whim, it was not until several years after the war had ended that he finally found the moment and the specific place that would serve as the subject for his long-planned artwork. That this location and event centered on a small group of trees created more of an attraction to a landscape painter.

As he later recalled it, his concept began in that summer of 1869 as something of an epiphany.

Congress tasked John Bachelder with writing the first official history of the battle of Gettysburg. His efforts produced extensive notes and maps, such as this one, that make up one of the most important—and influential—documentary collections about the war. However, he never completed the actual written history. *Library of Congress*

Soon after the close of the war I met Colonel [Walter] Harrison at Gettysburg, who was General Pickett's assistant general, and was with him at the battle. I invited Colonel Harrison to visit the battlefield with me, and we spent several hours under the shade cast by the copse of trees, when he explained to me what an important feature that copse of trees was at the time of the battle, and how it had been a landmark towards which Longstreet's assault of July 3d 1863 had been directed. Impressed with its importance, I remarked, "Why, Colonel, as the battle of Gettysburg was the crowning event of this campaign, this copse of trees must have been the high water mark of the rebellion." To which he assented, and from that time on, I felt a reverence for those trees.[1]

Having thus concluded that the war had been decided at a spot that had received little attention from visitors or veterans before that time, Bachelder gave the place an iconic name that represented the importance he desired to portray. Years after, he admitted as much when he took credit for recognizing and perpetuating the importance of the site: "The thought of naming the copse of trees the 'High Water Mark of the Rebellion,' and the idea of perpetuating its memory by a monument, was mine."[2]

What Bachelder had set out to do—and later succeeded at—was literally shape the battlefield to prove his own point. If he could attach to just one small area of the field the absolute significance of being the exact spot where the entire Civil War was lost and won, then surely people would come to view this battle as the decisive event of that war, as he had concluded for himself back in 1863. In the vast fields of corn, hay, and wheat that now made up the surrounding scene, a small clump of trees provided a natural landmark upon which he could focus his idea. This small grove of trees, conveniently located at the geographic center of the battlefield as a whole, could represent the exact location where the greatest nation on earth was saved, and Bachelder set out to enshrine that location.

While Bachelder is not solely responsible for elevating Gettysburg as the ultimate turning point of the Civil War, he certainly played an enormously significant role at a critical time. Much of what we believe today about the overall importance of the battle is in some way linked to and influenced by his efforts.

The question remains, *was* Gettysburg the turning point of the Civil War? The many answers to this question are as elusive as the motives of those who make the arguments. There is no way to statistically analyze any military battle and come to an irrefutable conclusion. History is not mathematics. The answer to "What is one plus one?" is concrete and immovable. A definitive answer to the question of whether Gettysburg was the decisive event of the war is impossible to prove by any scientific method. It is left instead for us to endlessly debate the point without ever reaching an unassailable conclusion.

And after all, is this not what keeps the story of Gettysburg alive and makes it so enjoyable to study?

Notes

1. John B. Bachelder, report to Col. C. H. Buehler of the Gettysburg Battlefield Monument Association, February 1, 1894, Bachelder Papers, Gettysburg National Military Park, Pa.
2. Ibid.

Acknowledgments

Our foremost thanks go to Sylvia Frank Rodrigue, who made this book possible in many ways. We thank her and her colleagues at Southern Illinois University Press for their support of Emerging Civil War, the Engaging the Civil War series, and this volume in particular.

Turning Points of the American Civil War gathers a collection of emerging and experienced voices, and we're grateful for the contributions they made to this volume: Dan Davis, Stephen Davis, Tom Desjardin, Ryan Longfellow, Jim Morgan, Rob Orrison, Kevin Pawlak, and Rea Redd. We owe a particular thanks to Greg Mertz, a longtime mentor and friend.

Emerging Civil War's Chris Kolakowski, Meg Thompson, and William Lee White also offered assistance with this volume. Cartographer Hal Jespersen once more provided us with excellent maps. Doug Crenshaw assisted with research, placing the location of Johnston's wounding on the map on page 109.

Most especially, we thank all of the authors involved with Emerging Civil War, who make not only this book but also all of our many projects possible.

CHRIS: My first thanks go out to Kris, who always challenges me to keep looking at the war in new ways and to be the best historian possible. As my best friend and writing partner, he's the yin to my yang. I would like to thank Dr. Pauline Hoffman, dean of the School of Communication at St. Bonaventure University, as well as Suzzane Ciesla, Kathy Boser, and the staff of work-study students who contributed logistical support. Thanks finally go to my family for their ongoing moral support—particularly my children, Steph, Jackson, and Maxwell, and my wife, Jennifer.

KRIS: First and foremost, I have to thank my coeditor and best friend, Chris Mackowski, who goes above and beyond the call of duty to get our titles to press (and to deal with me). And I have to thank my entire family for all their support: my dad, who always looks forward to my next project; my wife, Sarah, who endures the countless hours of research, writing, and editing that go along with any project of this size; and my research assistants, Dobby and Mosby.

A Note about Sources

Many of our authors draw from some of the same standard reference materials. For the sake of convenience and clarity, those works are abbreviated thus in the notes.

Battles & Leaders   Robert Underwood Johnson, ed., *Battles and Leaders of the Civil War*, 4 vols. (New York: Century Company, 1887; New York: Castle Books, 1956; New York: Thomas Yoseloff, 1956; New York: Fairfax Press, 1979). Editions used are indicated in the notes.

OR   Robert N. Scott, ed., *The War of the Rebellion: A Compilation of the Official Records of the Union and Confederate Armies*, 128 vols. (Washington, D.C.: Government Printing Office, 1880–91). All citations are from the first series unless otherwise noted.

ENGAGING
——*the*——
CIVIL WAR

For additional content that will let you engage this material further, look for unique QR codes at the end of each chapter. Scanning them will take you to exclusive online material, additional photos and images, links to online resources, and related blog posts at www.emergingcivilwar.com.

A QR scanner app is readily available for download through the app store on your smartphone.

Turning Points of the American Civil War

The "Copse of Trees" and John Bachelder's massive "High Water Mark" monument fix Gettysburg in the public imagination as the turning point of the Civil War. *Photo by Chris Mackowski*

❄ Introduction

Chris Mackowski and Kristopher D. White

The massive bronze book in the middle of the battlefield might as well say, "You are *here*." In actuality, it lists the different units that fought along Gettysburg's Cemetery Ridge on July 3, 1863. The book itself measures eight by ten feet and sits, flanked by two cannon, on a platform that measures eighteen by forty-eight feet. Just beyond the open book, a small cluster of trees—the "copse" of trees—obscures what would otherwise be a view across a mile of open ground. Confederates crossed that space, supposedly aiming at these trees, trying to write history.

In different decades, as kids visiting the battlefield, the two of us each stood before the bronze pages, captivated, as though the book of history itself lay open before us. Chris first came here in 1979 with his third-grade class from Hershey Elementary School; Kris first came in 1984 after his father went to a car show in nearby Carlisle, Pennsylvania. Millions of other schoolkids just like us, over the course of a dozen decades, have stood where we stood. Perhaps you have stood there, too.

The bronze book, historian John Bachelder would have us all believe, marks the turning point of the American Civil War. "The thought of naming the copse of trees the 'High Water Mark of the Rebellion,' and the idea of perpetuating its memory by a monument, was mine," Bachelder claimed in 1894.[1] American memory has largely adopted this view.

Tom Desjardin touched on Bachelder's story in this book's foreword, but Tom gives the topic extensive treatment in his marvelous book *These Honored Dead: How the Story of Gettysburg Shaped American Memory*. Tom's book should be required reading for any serious student of the Civil War because it sheds invaluable light on what we know versus what we *think* we know. Most important, it deconstructs *how* we know what we know and why.

1

Were it not for Bachelder's ceaseless public relations efforts on behalf of his own version of the Gettysburg story, would we still view Gettysburg as the turning point?

We are all tempted to pose that question with italics: *the* turning point. Or maybe with capital letters: The Turning Point. The battle's convenient occurrence at approximately the chronological midpoint of the war adds to the appeal of that narrative. The story of the war prior to the battle was one of Confederate ascendance and afterward one of decline—or so the popular understanding goes, even though it's total rubbish. Even the most cursory look at the war's overall narrative shows the Western Theater as a string of Union victories all the way through September 1863, moving inexorably forward again after the Federals broke the siege of Chattanooga that November. Even if one takes into account the Confederate advance into Kentucky in the fall of 1862, the near-crippling of the Union army during its victory at Stones River, and Major General Ulysses S. Grant's many delays getting into Vicksburg, the overall narrative arc still points forward and upward for the Union. Consider that many modern historians believe the war was actually won in the West; if so, then the story of Gettysburg largely becomes moot.

Even if one were to look only at the Eastern Theater, Chancellorsville—not Gettysburg—marks the "High Tide" of Confederate fortunes, as one of the essays in this volume explains. After Chancellorsville, it was all downhill for the Army of Northern Virginia, which would never again win an offensive battlefield victory. That context does not make the Army of the Potomac ascendant by default, though. Midway through the fall campaign of 1863, as General Robert E. Lee consistently bedeviled his Federal counterpart, Federal commander Major General George Gordon Meade admitted, "This was a deep game, and I am free to admit that in the playing of it he has got the advantage of me."[2] Two weeks later, after the Federal victories at Rappahannock Station and Kelly's Ford, a surgeon in the 121st New York Infantry saw *that* as the turning point. "Heretofore, the tide has been uniformly against us," Dr. Daniel Holt wrote, "but *now* the tables are turned, thank fortune."[3] The indomitable Confederate position along Mine Run at the end of the month would argue otherwise, however, forcing the Federals to withdraw and settle into winter camp.

So, let's assume for a moment that Gettysburg was not *the* turning point. That leaves us with two options: (1) some other event served as *the* turning point, or (2) Gettysburg was just *a* turning point, not *the* turning point.

The convenience of option 1—and also its inherent problem—is that it fits more squarely with the way we construct narratives: introduction, rising action, climax, falling action, conclusion. Literary theorists call this "Freytag's Pyramid" because action rises to the point of climax and then falls. German novelist Gustav Freytag first proposed this idea in 1863—coincidentally the same year as the battle of Gettysburg—although it has its roots deep in Western tradition. Our cultural storytelling tendencies bias us toward it. We're always looking for that climactic moment to arrive, that lightbulb to go off, that turning point to turn.[4]

Narratives have become a deeply effective way to tell history. We have all heard countless people lament that "history is boring" because they've had to memorize a litany of facts: names, dates, and places. Perhaps you have had a similar experience. Fortunately, we've also heard people tell us about a teacher, a tour guide, a park ranger, or a writer who "made history come alive." Those historians tell good stories and, in doing so, connect people with their history.

Such stories are intentional constructs, though, inclusive of certain facts and exclusive of others, intentionally organized in a particular way. One of our mentors, historian Greg Mertz—who has a contribution in this volume—once said when he taught us about giving tours of the Fredericksburg battlefield, "You can't tell everything about the battle in thirty-five minutes." You have to pick and choose what you can fit in that time frame. So it goes with telling any story: you have to strategically decide what to include in order to achieve the result you want.

"It's not a question of twisting the facts into a narrative," explained Shelby Foote, author of *The Civil War: A Narrative,* in a 1999 interview with the *Paris Review.* "It is absolutely true that no list of facts ever gives you a valid account of what happened. The bare-bone facts are what you use to shape your description of what happened," which also involves knowing "how to develop a character, manage a plot."[5]

And so it goes with the larger story of the war. With that in mind, and with the traditional narrative structure as context, it's little wonder that John Bachelder's interpretation of Gettysburg as *the* turning point proves convenient and attractive.

Native American and Eastern storytelling traditions give us a different lens through which to view events, though. "To those used to the patterns of European fairy tales and folktales, Indian legends often seem chaotic, inconsistent, or incomplete," explain folklore scholars Richard Erdoes and Alfonzo Ortiz. "Plots seem to travel at their own speed, defying convention and at times doing away completely with recognizable beginnings and endings."[6] The narrative structures don't seek to build a story toward a particular climactic moment; rather, they unspool a sequence of events and leave it to the listener/reader to interpret meaning. The plotline looks much more like a continuum of events, one following the next following the next, rather than a sequence of rising action that builds one incident on top of the next. In Native American narratives, there's not even necessarily cause and effect to be discerned in those events, just as our real lives often consist of disconnected occurrences that still somehow add up to create our own individual stories.

This collection of essays assumes that the Civil War unfolded as a continuum of events with several major turning points, one leading to the next leading to the next. There is no enforceability of the Emancipation Proclamation if the Federals don't score a battlefield victory. There is no invasion of Pennsylvania if Lee doesn't first take command. There is no Grant in the Wilderness if he is not first unleashed by his win at Vicksburg. In the essays in this book, our historians show why the war was significantly different after each turning point than it was before. As you'll see, the ripples from one "turn" carry forward and create circumstances that lead to the next.

Many of the events we cover here aren't traditionally considered turning points because they're often remembered with other hooks. Through labeling, monumentation, writing, and even development/preservation, public memory has come to see some of these incidents not primarily as "turns" in the war's larger narrative but in other imagination-capturing ways. In the introductions to each essay, we'll discuss these more traditional ways of remembering before situating the events into their historical context as turning points. Our goal is to help you see those events from new perspectives.

A hallmark of Emerging Civil War is the variety of voices, styles, backgrounds, and approaches of our authors. You'll see some of that diversity on display here as each author explores one of the critical moments in the war. There might be other turning points we've not included in this book. For instance, historian Albert Conner Jr. credibly argues in *Seizing Destiny: The Army of the Potomac's Valley Forge and the Civil War Winter That Saved the Union* that Major General Joseph Hooker's resuscitation of the Army of the Potomac between February and April 1863 was the war's single most important non-combat military turning point.[7] Stephen Sears contends a Confederate strategy meeting on May 15, 1863, "easily qualifies as a pivotal moment in Confederate history," which, by extension, implies a pivotal moment in the war.[8] Writer Jack Hurst characterized the 1862 fall of Forts Henry and Donelson as "the campaign that decided the Civil War."[9] Even novelist Harry Turtledove posits through his fiction the loss (or not) of Lee's Special Order 191 in September 1862 as a war-changing event.[10] Our collection of historians encourages you to use this volume as a starting point to explore your own perspectives on the war's key moments. As you do, we hope you'll better appreciate the overall continuum of the war and its many ripples.

It's not uncommon to talk of "the flow of history." Ironically, John Bachelder's big bronze book defies that idea with pages that don't actually turn. Instead, frozen open to a single two-page spread, it fixes on one moment in time at one specific spot. As compelling as that moment was and as handsome as the monument remains, we should not read too much into that magnificent, immovable book. Here, we offer you one in which the pages of history still turn.

NOTES

1. John B. Bachelder, report to Col. C. H. Buehler of the Gettysburg Battlefield Monument Association, February 1, 1894, Bachelder Papers, Gettysburg National Military Park, Pa., quoted in Thomas A. Desjardin, *These Honored Dead: How the Story of Gettysburg Shaped American Memory* (Cambridge, Mass.: Da Capo, 2004), 98.

2. George Gordon Meade, *The Life and Letters of George Gordon Meade, Major-General United States Army* (New York: Charles Scribner's Sons, 1913), 2:154.

3. Daniel M. Holt, *A Surgeon's Civil War: The Letters and Diary of Daniel M. Holt, M.D.*, ed. James M. Greiner et al. (Kent, Ohio: Kent State University Press, 1994), 157.

4. For a more modern take on storytelling structure and technique, see Robert McKee's *Story: Substance, Structure, Style, and the Principles of Screenwriting* (New York: Regan Books, 1997). Although ostensibly writing about screenwriting, McKee is widely recognized as one of the great modern teachers of storytelling techniques.

5. Shelby Foote, interview by Carter Coleman, Donald Faulkner, William Kennedy, "The Art of Fiction No. 158," *Paris Review*, no. 151 (Summer 1999). Available online at http://www.theparisreview.org/interviews/931/the-art-of-fiction-no-158-shelby-foote.

6. Richard Erdoes and Alfonso Ortiz, eds., *American Indian Myths and Legends* (New York: Pantheon, 1984), xii.

7. Coauthored with Chris Mackowski (El Dorado Hills, Calif.: Savas Beatie, 2016).

8. Stephen Sears, *Gettysburg* (New York: Houghton Mifflin, 2003), 1.

9. Jack Hurst, *Men of Fire: Grant, Forrest, and the Campaign That Decided the Civil War* (New York: Basic Books, 2007).

10. Harry Turtledove, *How Few Remain: A Novel of the Second War between the States* (New York: Ballantine Books, 1997).

1. Bull Run

Editors' Introduction

Manassas National Battlefield protects the site of the first major engagement of the American Civil War, but the battlefield itself came late to the party. While other Civil War battlefields received federal protection as early as 1890, Manassas was not officially designated a national park until 1940. Prior to that, various preservation and conservation efforts protected different parcels of land.

On Henry Hill, where the climax of the battle took place on July 21, 1861, the Sons of Confederate Veterans (SCV) set aside 130 acres, at a cost of $25,000, in 1921. Their vision: Manassas Battlefield Confederate Park, which would "serve as the 'supreme battlefield memorial' to all Confederate soldiers," writes historian Joan Zenzen in the park's official administrative history.[1] *The SCV "wanted to give voice to the South's 'distinct, wonderful, equally thrilling, all-important story.'"*[2]

In 1933, the SCV's Manassas Battlefield Committee made overtures to the National Park Service (NPS) about the possibility of taking over the property. The NPS, interested, "wanted Bull Run to become a point of historic interest of the same caliber as Gettysburg," Zenzen writes.[3] *"Park Service personnel exchanged correspondence reflecting varying titles for the proposed battlefield park, using both Bull Run and Manassas as possible names."*[4]

Federals traditionally called the clash the battle of Bull Run, drawing the name from a stream that marked the eastern edge of the battlefield. Manassas, the Confederate name, came from the nearby town and railroad junction.

Popular legend has it that Federals consistently named their battles after the closest body of water or other natural feature while Confederates named their battles after the nearest settlements. "I've often thought that that's because towns were unusual to settlers, who lived rurally, so they named them after the nearest town," explained author Shelby Foote in Ken Burns's The Civil War*—an answer that has since become almost axiomatic.*[5]

The convention does not always work, however. It certainly holds for Bull Run/Manassas as well as for Antietam/Sharpsburg and Stones River/Murfreesboro,

A massive bronze statue of Confederate general Thomas J. Jackson dominates the landscape at Manassas National Battlefield's Henry House Hill. Jackson earned his nickname, "Stonewall," during the battle of First Manassas—one of the best-known stories from the battle. *Photo by Chris Mackowski*

but the Federals never called Fredericksburg "Rappahannock" or Vicksburg "Mississippi," and everyone called Gettysburg "Gettysburg." Federals used "Shiloh" and "Pittsburg Landing" interchangeably for the same battle.

Another popular legend says that the NPS, when naming battlefields, adopted the name used by the winning side. Again, no evidence suggests that is true, at least not formally. When the NPS settled on "Manassas National Battlefield," it may have had more to do with placating the land donors than anything. "While [the name] was not a formal stipulation made by the SCV," says NPS historian Jim Burgess, "it is likely the government, in its diplomatic efforts to acquire the Henry farm, did not want to alienate the SCV either and deliberately adopted the Southern name to acknowledge the Confederate victory here."6

But "Bull Run" and "Manassas" have not always necessarily been assigned to North and South, respectively, as commonly believed. There once existed a Bull Run Chapter of the United Daughters of the Confederacy and a Manassas Picket Post of Union Veterans, for instance.

Discrepancies over how to remember Bull Run/Manassas extend beyond naming rights. Bull Run is often cited as the first battle of the Civil War. Historians, though, are quick to qualify that as the "first major battle" because the first infantry engagement actually took place in what is now Philippi, West Virginia, on June 3, 1861. First Manassas also tends to overshadow Second Manassas in the historical memory—even though the second battle, August 28–30, 1862, involved more than twice as many men, saw nearly four times the casualties, and covered four times as much ground.7 There's even controversy over Stonewall Jackson's nom de guerre, bestowed at First Manassas: was it a compliment offered for steadfast immovability or an insult hurled at dunderheaded immobility?

The fog of historical memory is symbolic of the fog of war that hovered over the battlefield itself on July 21, 1861. Mismatched uniforms of every color and style made it difficult to differentiate sides; inadequate maps sent marching men wayward; plans of attack pinwheeled in opposite directions; poor discipline led to slow, disorganized marching and frustrated coordinated movement on the battlefield. "We got mixed up with many strange troops, apparently in panic," one Confederate said.8

Federal commander Brigadier General Irvin McDowell worried about just that kind of chaos. His men had not yet been trained enough, he argued when Lincoln pressed him to confront the Confederate forces amassing near Manassas Junction that hot summer. The president nonetheless urged McDowell onward. "You are green, it is true," Lincoln conceded; "but they are green, also; you are green alike."9

The combined armies totaled slightly more than 60,000 men: 28,450 Federals and 32,230 Confederates. While the Federal force arrived all at once (with the exception of stragglers), Confederate forces arrived piecemeal, with fresh reinforcements trickling onto the battlefield throughout the day, ultimately proving to be the deciding factor. They turned an apparent Federal victory into a rout.

A handful of picnicking spectators, out from Washington to watch the spectacle as if it were some sporting match, found themselves under fire by battle's end. "These gentry," sneered Confederate correspondent Peter Wellington Alexander, "including a corps of correspondents and telegraphists from New York and Washington, were provided with horses, buggies, carriages, liquors and cigars, and indeed with a full outfit for a dainty taste of camps life in the 'rebel provinces.'"[10]

The number of civilians present for the battle, says historian John Hennessy, "has been exaggerated by moviemakers, novelists, and historians alike."[11] While he estimates the number of spectators at fifty or so, the civilians have nonetheless assumed a prominent supporting role in the story of Manassas because their presence was a unique component of the battle not known elsewhere—one more way in which memory has clouded history.

The presence of the civilians is something we want to remember because it underscores what we know about the popular assumption of the time: the war would be a quick affair. One swift blow would end it. Boy soldiers worried the war would end before they had the chance to even get into the fight and win their share of glory. War was romantic, a jaunty thing to be treated like a spectator sport. "But the battle field presented a horrid spectacle—men and horses butchered in all sorts of ways," veteran John Coxe soberly discovered. "Never afterwards did the horrors of any battle field impress me so unfavorably."[12]

Such was the fulcrum of July 21, 1861: "A great and cautious national official predicted that it would blow over 'in sixty days,' and folks generally believed the prediction," Walt Whitman recalled. But in the aftermath of First Bull Run, "a mixture of awful consternation, uncertainty, rage, shame, helplessness, and stupefying disappointment" settled in.[13]

Aside from these changed attitudes—what historians have called an "end to innocence"[14]—perhaps the most important result of the battle was the change in the Federal army itself. As Robert Orrison explains in the following essay, that change came about due to one man: Major General George Brinton McClellan, whose rise to prominence was a direct result of the battle. The transformation he wrought on the army makes the first battle of Manassas the first major turning point of the war.

Confidence Renewed:
Surviving Bull Run and the Birth
of the Army of the Potomac

Robert Orrison

"Our men are not great soldiers," wrote Colonel William T. Sherman to his wife soon after the battle of First Bull Run on July 21, 1861. "It will take a long time to overcome these things, and what is in store for us in the future I know not."[15] Before the battle, Sherman was one of the few in the Federal army who realized the army was not ready for serious action. After the debacle along the banks of Bull Run, his sentiments summed up his worst fears of the volunteer army. An army that was created mostly from three-month enlistment volunteers, with little training and high hopes, was hardly an army at all.

Now political leaders and citizens of the Federal capital were worried about a possible Confederate attack. The morale of the men was at an all-time low, which would surely affect citizen support for the war. As Abraham Lincoln said frankly, "It's damned bad."[16] The next few days, weeks, and months were critical to the effort to preserve the Union. A new mentality of professionalism was needed, as was a dynamic leader. The new commander had to mold a professional army out of citizen volunteers. He also had to do this in the shadow of the political storm that was Washington, D.C.

The organization of the army improved, a more rigid training regimen began, and an overall esprit de corps formed. From the defeat on the heights of Judith Henry's farm came the genesis of an army that not only would save the Union but also would free millions of enslaved African Americans.

"The First Battle of Bull Run, Va., Sunday afternoon July 21, 1861," with a subtitle that reads "Panic among the teamsters and civilians and general stampede towards Arlington Heights." *Library of Congress*

"Driven the enemy before him"—that phrase came as part of the encouraging telegram that Lieutenant General Winfield Scott, general-in-chief of the U.S. Army, received from Brigadier General Irvin McDowell at 4:00 p.m. on July 21.[17] It was the first word Scott and President Lincoln had heard from their army commander that day; he had left Washington a few days before to confront the Confederate forces amassed around Manassas Junction, nearly thirty miles away. As Scott and Lincoln nervously awaited more news, both knew that today a major battle was sure to happen.

The telegraph went eerily silent.

Soon another message arrived: "The day is lost. Save Washington and the remnants of this army, all available troops ought to be thrown forward in one body."[18]

This was not what either Scott or Lincoln expected.

McDowell's plan had been a good one: feint an attack in the area around Blackburn's Ford and Stone Bridge while moving the bulk of his force around the unprotected Confederate left flank. But the follow-through by the army's leadership, coupled with the army's inexperienced troops, doomed the Northern forces. The Southern army was equally inexperienced and ill prepared, but as defenders on the battlefield, their role in battle was less complicated. Both Federal and Confederate armies made mistakes that day. The deciding factor was the inability of Major General Robert Patterson in the northern Shenandoah Valley to keep the Confederate army under General Joseph Johnston from reinforcing the Confederates at Manassas Junction. The fresh Confederate troops constantly arriving at the battlefield proved decisive.

All of these factors became hot topics for armchair generals and the Lincoln administration on the evening of July 21. But for those in the field, that night would be long remembered. Notable war correspondent William Howard Russell was part of the retreat that night and wrote that "a disgraceful panic and confusion had attended the retreat of a portion of the army."[19]

By 5:00 p.m., the entire Federal army was put to retreat. Many of the units south of Bull Run were in mass confusion, but there were still organized units near Centreville, Virginia. These men, under Colonel Dixon Miles and Major George Sykes, held a defensive line. As the routed units cleared Centreville, calm slowly came over the army. Top officers held a council of war to determine if they should stay or retreat to the defenses of Washington. Though there were men willing to fight, the majority of the army refused to remain at Centreville and continued their confused march eastward along the Warrenton Turnpike. The Federal commanders had no choice but to move with them.[20]

When McDowell reached Fairfax Courthouse, he sent a message to Washington: "The larger part of the men are a confused mob, entirely demoralized." He continued in a following telegram: "Many of the volunteers did not wait for authority to proceed to the Potomac, but left on their own decision." McDowell admittedly explained that he had little control over his defeated army.[21]

Most of the men who made that evening march had been up since 2:00 a.m. Delirious and tired, they trudged on to relative safety along the heights of Arlington. As Sherman wrote, "The retreat was by night, and disorderly in the extreme. The men of different regiments mingled together." Some men disobeyed orders and crossed the bridges into the city and began to visit the hotel bars and taverns. By Monday morning, most of the army was back in Washington.[22]

In assessing the damage to the army at Bull Run, the disaster that took place became more real. Nearly five hundred men were reported killed, with one thousand wounded and another seventeen hundred missing and probably captured. In the history of the nation, this was one of the bloodiest days ever.[23]

The Federal medical staff was not prepared for such bloodshed, and neither were the civilians within the capital. Many, like Mary Henry, were shocked to see bloodstained men enter the city and amazed at how "weary and exhausted" they looked. Charles Haydon wrote on July 22 how terrible it was "to see the wagons coming in last night loaded down with dead, cut, torn and mangled in every possible manner." War was no longer a matter of pomp and circumstance.[24]

Another sign of total defeat: the amount of equipment the Federal army left behind in its hasty retreat from the field. The Confederates reported capturing twenty-five cannon of various sizes, four thousand muskets, and five hundred thousand rounds of small arms ammunition. Even twenty-seven hundred camp messes and seven hundred blankets were left behind by McDowell's army.[25]

Scott quickly took control of the city and began to calm Lincoln's fears about the safety of the capital. The general ordered the forts on the Virginia side of the river strengthened. He also kept the regulars at the front in Arlington and shifted units that were not at Bull Run across the river to Virginia to bolster McDowell's army.

Rumors abounded that the Confederates were close behind McDowell. Reports came in that Confederates were near Fairfax Courthouse and could possibly be under the command of Confederate president Jefferson Davis. Many feared Washington would be under attack—but Scott knew he had the artillery and men to stop any such Confederate assault. He continued to pull men from other areas to bolster the defenses of the city.[26]

By the end of July 22, Secretary of War Simon Cameron reported that the lines near the city were being bolstered and the troops were in better condition than previously thought. "There is no danger of the capital nor the Republic," he wrote. But the army was still disorganized, many were missing from their units, and officers were still spending a lot of their time in the bars and saloons.

One thing that needed the biggest lift was the morale of the Northern populace. No one expected a disaster of the likes of Bull Run. Lincoln needed something to turn around the confidence of the people, or the nascent war effort was doomed. Prolific writer George Templeton Strong summed up many Northerners' thoughts in late July when he wrote of "total defeat and national disaster on the largest scale."[27]

On July 22, Scott wired thirty-five-year-old Major General George B. McClellan in West Virginia: "Circumstances make your presence here necessary. . . . Come hither without delay." McClellan would turn into one of the most controversial leaders of the Civil War. But in late July 1861, the administration, army, and Northern populace saw him as a savior, and he relished that role. Over the next few months, he would take an army of amateurs and turn them into one of the most formidable military organizations in the history of the world.[28]

As McClellan settled into his new position as commander of the Military District of the Potomac, he wrote his wife, "I seem to have become the power of the land."[29] By that time, McClellan was already a popular military figure. A foreign observer that year said "his look was piercing, his voice gentle, his temper equable, his word of command clear and definite."[30]

McClellan graduated second in his class at West Point in 1846 and served with distinction as an engineer during the Mexican-American War. After the war, he served at various posts with the Corps of Engineers and was selected to be an official observer for the United States in Europe during the Crimean War.

In 1857, he resigned from the army and served in various positions, including engineer, vice president, and president with the Illinois Central Railroad and then with the Ohio and Mississippi Railroad. As one of his friends wrote, "He was a leader and organizer, natural born."[31] During this time he married his wife, Mary Ellen Marcy, who would be a lifetime confidant and whose correspondence still provides historians with a wealth of knowledge.

As the Civil War began, McClellan at the young age of thirty-four was a much sought after man to lead Northern troops. In April he took command of the Ohio state militia as a major general but by the next month was commissioned into U.S. service as a major general and commander of the Department of the Ohio, a vast region from western Virginia to Missouri.

He quickly organized volunteers and began to protect the critical B&O Railroad that connected Baltimore and Washington with the West. He oversaw a small invasion of western Virginia, which played a major role in the politics of the region. Winning victories at Philippi and Rich Mountain, he was seen as the most successful military leader in the field for the Union thus far.

McClellan reveled in his new celebrity and accepted his nickname "Young Napoleon." The *New York Herald* enhanced his status by dubbing him "the Napoleon of the Present War."[32] He appreciated the aristocracy of the South and was a devotee of a patrician way of life. He was one for dramatics and self-aggrandizement—and it would be his personality most of all that would lead others to detest him.

With his political connections, youth, and ambition—and being the only true military hero available—McClellan was the obvious choice to Lincoln and Scott as the man to turn around the army in Washington.

McClellan saw his mission as twofold. First, he was to create a large and organized army that could end the rebellion in a broad stroke. Second, Washington, D.C., must be properly fortified and defended. He worked with vigor to accomplish these goals.[33]

Upon his arrival in the capital, everyone from Scott to Lincoln to congressional leaders deferred to his judgment. The pretentious McClellan was confident that he was the man to save America. He would take no time to start changing how the army around Washington was organized, trained, and operated.

McClellan's assignment as division commander was to oversee all the Federal forces in and around the capital city. This included the Departments of Washington and Northeastern Virginia as well as the Army of Northeastern Virginia under General McDowell. McClellan outranked McDowell already, so this new arrangement would not include a demotion for McDowell, just a reassignment in the new army structure.[34]

One of the first things McClellan had to do was get the army back as a cohesive unit and restore proper discipline. Scott had secured the safety of the capital after Bull Run, but the army had "degenerated into an armed mob."[35] Delinquent officers and men filled the city streets. The city's taverns were supposed to be off-limits, but many were packed with men from McDowell's army, a persistent problem before and after First Bull Run.

On McClellan's second day in Washington, he began to inspect the camps and positions of the army. He was not impressed. Many were in poor condition and unorganized. What entrenchments had been built in Arlington had been sloppily built and were wholly inadequate. McDowell agreed with McClellan's assessment that the men in the army around Washington were in low spirits and had no confidence in success. In somewhat of an exaggeration, McClellan believed he had to create everything from "foundation" up.[36]

On July 30, McClellan appointed Colonel Andrew Porter as provost marshal over the city and declared martial law. Assigned to Porter were regular army units, and Porter was to report directly to McClellan. Porter took the role seriously. McClellan also issued orders canceling all visits to the city unless approved in writing by the brigade commanders. Soon, most enlisted men vanished from the streets of Washington.[37]

In years after the war, much was written about the lack of discipline among the men during and after Bull Run. But one must also take into consideration the lack of preparedness of those men. The common volunteer soldier was not used to giving up individual freedom and control; however, to be a cohesive unit, following a commanding officer's orders was a necessity.

McClellan, with the help of other professional soldiers such as Sherman, began to deal with unruly and mutinous regiments. One notable occurrence involved the Seventy-Ninth New York Infantry. The unit fought well at Bull Run, but the men had become disgruntled over leadership and a revoked request for leave. In defiance, they began to smuggle in liquor, and then the rank and file began to disobey orders. When Brigadier General Daniel Sickles was named their brigade commander, many of the men refused to serve under him because of a reputation tarnished by a prewar extramarital affair and his acquittal in a murder trial.[38]

McClellan dealt with the disobedient unit swiftly. He ordered Porter to take several companies of regular infantry, cavalry, and artillery to the Seventy-Ninth New York camp, surround it, and arrest the ringleaders. Porter was authorized to "use force" to put down the mutiny, and McClellan ordered that the unit's colors be taken.[39]

The army was also full of unqualified officers. Many of these were politically appointed or state-appointed men with little training. Furthermore, many of the enlisted men saw their officers as their equals, not as their superiors. This led to disobeying orders and issues of protocol. As newly arrived Brigadier General George Meade wrote, "The officers, as a rule, are ignorant, inefficient and worthless. We have been weeding out some of the worst."[40]

McClellan sought to remove ineffective officers through a congressionally approved military review board. McClellan appointed officers to the board, which then examined all officers of the army. The process began to slowly remove many incompetent officers. The better the officers, McClellan rightfully believed, the better the discipline, morale, and competency of the men they commanded.

Through strong discipline, the army began to transform into a systematic force. The volunteer soldiers were expected to be professional soldiers, and, through the efforts of veteran officers, they began to look the part.

It did not take the new general long to put his personal mark on the army's organization. By August, McClellan was implementing his army organizational plan with the new commanders. The army up to this point had been organized into brigades of nearly four thousand infantrymen. Of course, this had been a sufficient structure when the army was relatively small; the prewar army had numbered only sixteen thousand. However, the army McClellan proposed to create would reach two hundred thousand men—too unwieldy for each brigade to report to the army commander. McClellan proposed combining several brigades to create a division. This larger force (up to ten thousand men) would eventually be combined into corps (composed of two to three divisions).

By July 29, McClellan offered to Lincoln his proposed list of six regular army and twenty-six volunteer general officers. Most significant, after only two days in Washington, McClellan was already bypassing Scott, his superior, to go directly to the president.[41]

For his commanders, McClellan relied heavily on West Pointers and men he trusted, including such notables such as Edwin Sumner, Fitz John Porter, Joseph Hooker, and former army commander Irvin McDowell. Of his dozen division commanders, seven had attended West Point. Several he had served with during the Mexican-American War. These infantry divisions formed the basis of McClellan's army organization. The other two branches, artillery and cavalry, were to be divided among the divisions and were to report directly to the division commanders.

When it came to cavalry, McClellan saw its role as subsidiary to the other two branches. Unlike the real Napoleon, the "Young Napoleon" did not understand the merits of a consolidated cavalry corps. Rather, McClellan divided the cavalry among the divisions, where they served as couriers, pickets, and cover for wagon trains. Each cavalry command placed under an infantry division was subject to that commander's orders. This kept the cavalry from acting as a cohesive unit on offensive and scouting operations. McClellan appointed Brigadier General George Stoneman as chief of cavalry, but this was more of a title than a position of organizational strength. The early organization of the cavalry put the Federals at a disadvantage compared with the Confederate cavalry, which was organized as a separate branch of the Confederate army.[42]

Finally, McClellan spent considerable effort organizing the artillery. He appointed the highly qualified Brigadier General William F. Berry as chief of artillery. Berry was an experience artilleryman and organizer before the war. He proposed using the several regular army batteries in the army as a core for new volunteer artillery units. This required pulling many units from the western forts and replacing them with new volunteer units. The regulars would then assist in training the new units. The regular batteries were also spread out among the various divisions, which allowed for veteran experience and leadership with the artillery in each division.[43]

On August 20, McClellan consolidated the Division of the Potomac into the Army of the Potomac—the army that would come to signify the Northern war effort and that would sometimes be called "Lincoln's Army." With the consolidation, McClellan's authority covered a wide swath of land from eastern Maryland to the Shenandoah Valley.

McClellan first set up his staff, much larger than previous army staffs, growing from sixteen to nearly sixty officers. He appointed a chief medical director, chief quartermaster, chief commissary, and chief engineer and topographical engineer, among many more. He relied on his staff to enforce the new army guidelines to make the army more disciplined and effective.[44]

Scott opposed many of McClellan's changes to the army structure, including the consolidation, as he preferred the smaller geographic departments. He also believed brigades were sufficient to manage the army and that the regulars should be kept whole as a unit to back up the volunteers, not dispersed through the army. In most cases, though, McClellan won his argument with the president, and he began making decisions without Scott's advice or permission.

McClellan's ability for self-promotion and his sensational attitude toward the defense of Washington—and toward everything relating to his image as well—began to rankle his superior. It was clear to many that McClellan's ambition drove him and that he coveted Scott's job. Scott was the general-in-chief of all U.S. armies, and McClellan should have reported to him. Avoiding proper military protocol, however, McClellan conferred with Lincoln and Secretary of War Cameron directly. McClellan had a direct line with congressional leaders, as well. Scott issued official orders to remind officers—specifically McClellan—about the official chain of command in all communications: all information was to go through Scott before being given to civilian authorities. McClellan acknowledged the order but generally ignored it like many others Scott made.[45]

Lincoln was just as much at fault as McClellan for allowing this to happen. At the first cabinet meeting McClellan attended, Lincoln overlooked inviting Scott—a bad portent of what was to come. McClellan had no faith in Scott and privately questioned the old Virginian's patriotism. He wrote to his wife that "that confounded old General always comes in the way. . . . He is a perfect imbecile."[46]

Scott was much offended by McClellan's continued assessment of the military situation after Bull Run. Scott did not buy into McClellan's initial assessment of the condition of the army and saw it as an "affront" to his leadership. He also did not accept McClellan's estimation of Confederate strength in and around Centerville, which the Young Napoleon put at one hundred thousand rebels. McClellan's constant fear for Washington's safety began to wear on the veteran Scott, who had confidence that the city was more than safe.[47]

Both men had their defenders, but the sentiment of those in power was that Scott should retire. As newspaper journalist James Riggs wrote in

A cartoon by Alfred Waud shows Uncle Sam with an arm on Major General George B. McClellan's shoulder. Beneath a sign that says "War Department," Winfield Scott, Abraham Lincoln, and Edwin M. Stanton prepare for the show: "Every day this week onward to Richmond by a select company of star generals." *Library of Congress*

August 1861, "McClellan has done more in ten days towards organizing the advance than Scott did in ten weeks." That summer would see a once-cordial relationship deteriorate into outright insubordination by McClellan—and Scott's retirement that fall.[48]

Organizing the army was important, but probably more important was training that army to become efficient and lethal. Originally Lincoln's call for seventy-five thousand three-month volunteers was thought by Scott and Lincoln as sufficient, but it soon became clear that more men were needed and for a longer term. This was a product of the initial naïveté of the government about how long the war would last and how hard the South would actually fight to leave the Union.

The short enlistments had directly affected the recent campaign. In the northern Shenandoah Valley, many of the Federal soldiers under Patterson had spoken openly about leaving since their enlistments were about to expire—thus, in Patterson's opinion, tying his hands in his failed effort to keep Johnston in the valley.[49] Furthermore, the push for McDowell to move against the Confederates in July had partially been due to the fact that many men in his army could possibly leave in late July when their enlistments expired. For example, on July 20, the men of the Fourth Pennsylvania Infantry and Eighth New York Infantry denied requests to remain and went home when their enlistments ended that day.[50]

Lincoln was quick to recognize the problem with short-term enlistments and issued executive orders to call for forty-two thousand more volunteers to serve for a three-year term. On July 22, Lincoln and Congress authorized an additional call for five hundred thousand volunteers from the various states to also serve for three-year terms. Lincoln also increased the regular army to thirty-five thousand and hoped these professional soldiers would serve as the basis for leadership and training of the now-enlarged volunteer army.

Although many of the three-month units that stayed on past Bull Run began to leave the army, many reenlisted under the new three-year enlistment period. Other units remained in the army and began to find renewed confidence and energy. "Even the late battle has become an old story," wrote Elisha Hunt Rhodes of the Second Rhode Island Infantry on July 30. "I have recovered my strength and feel that I could make another campaign."[51]

As the three-month units left, in their place the new three-year recruits were arriving. These men would require proper drill and training. The experience of Bull Run gave credence to McClellan's commitment to give adequate time to train his army. This would be a tall task as there were, on average, ten thousand recruits arriving in Washington every week that summer. McClellan turned to professional soldiers he trusted—men such as Berry, Stoneman, and Brigadier General Silas Casey, who oversaw the camps of instruction for the rapidly arriving new recruits. All new regiments had to pass through these camps of instruction; only once they were deemed properly trained and outfitted were they sent to the Virginia side of the Potomac and assigned to brigades.

Drill sergeants taught everything from posture, marching maneuvers, and manual of arms to hygiene. McClellan worked tirelessly with his staff to make sure the new army would be the best in the world. Soldiers spent nearly five hours a day drilling with their units: at the company level, then at the regimental level, and then at the brigade level. Repetition was required to make these maneuvers second nature to them so they could conduct them under fire on the battlefield.[52]

Though many men in the army hated the monotony of drill, they began to respect its necessity. Chaplain Joseph Twichell of the Seventy-First New York Infantry wrote his father that "Gen. McClellan makes things go with a snap."[53] Men began to believe in McClellan, in their commanding officers, and in the army as a whole. This respect that his men started to show McClellan reiterated his belief in his paternalistic leadership style. His paternal affection for the army stemmed from his Whig political nature. As historian Ethan Rafuse wrote, "This paternalism permeated McClellan's efforts to build the Army of the Potomac."[54] This love for "his" army would become the basis of future battlefield criticisms of McClellan.

Men were also taught efficient camp layout and where to properly place company latrines. Lessons on how to correctly clean their weapons and accoutrements were drilled into each enlisted man's daily routine. Also, men were required to maintain physical training. As was discovered on the march to Bull Run, the common volunteer was not physically prepared for long marches on few rations while carrying heavy gear.

As summer turned into fall, the shape of the Army of the Potomac had vastly improved since July 21. The army was well supplied, equipped, drilled, and prepared for offensive actions. McClellan had expected it would take six months for his army to be properly prepared, but many of the units had responded much faster than that. By October, the army had grown from thirty-five thousand to nearly eighty thousand—with more recruits still arriving. But McClellan believed he needed even more men, and it became obvious to some that no major offensive operations would take place before 1862.

The days, weeks, and months after Bull Run were crucial to the survival of the Union. Though constituting only a portion of the entire Federal army, the military forces around Washington drew everyone's attention and interest. It was here, they believed, the nation would be saved or divided.

Most of McClellan's accomplishments during this time period are overshadowed by his tumultuous and insubordinate relationship with his commander, General Scott. Scott was not the man he once was; at over three hundred pounds, he fought bouts of gout and rheumatism. McClellan held blatant contempt for a commander he thought was too old and feeble to serve. McClellan's relationship with Lincoln and his cabinet began to chill, as well. He thought they meddled too much in the affairs of the army, where he believed they had no business. He regularly shared his distrust in letters to his wife, referring to Lincoln as a "well-meaning baboon" and Secretary of State William H. Seward as an "incompetent little puppy." McClellan's insubordination would lead to future issues with the army's commanders and the administration. A mistrust of the commanding general existed until Ulysses S. Grant arrived during the winter of 1864 to oversee the army's direction personally.[55]

How much of the army's recovery was attributed to McClellan, to others, or just to the passing of time is debatable. However, McClellan undeniably had a meaningful impact on the Federal army after Bull Run: he worked to clean the streets of drunken and disorderly soldiers, organize the various units, and instill an esprit de corps. Morale quickly turned around. His organizational skills were unmatched for his time. As journalist and Army of the Potomac historian William Swinton wrote after the war, "If other generals, the successors of McClellan, were able to achieve more decisive results than he, it was, again, in no small degree, because they had the perfect instrument he had fashioned to work withal."[56]

Unfortunately, McClellan exaggerated the condition of the army as he found it. He constantly overstated the bad condition of the troops, the army's logistics, and, of course, the enemy's intentions on attacking Washington. So in deducting just how much he transformed the army, one must look beyond his own writings on the time period.

In the years after the war, McClellan became an enigma and a controversial figure. After his removal from command in the fall of 1862 and then his ill-fated candidacy for president in 1864, he became unpopular among a number of Army of the Potomac veteran leaders and postwar writers. Many of these accounts try to discredit the direct impact McClellan had on the Union war effort in 1861. McClellan's own memoirs were so blunt that he left no bridge unburned. Also, as a Democrat, he was never endeared to the Republican Party, which was the party in power for much of the late nineteenth century. As Grant said years later as president, "McClellan is to me one of the mysteries of the war."[57]

But clearly McClellan was the right man to organize and prepare a large army for war, even if he was not the best choice to lead that army into an active campaign. He proved slow to commit his troops to an active campaign, and in the field he was slow to go on the offensive. His love of the army he created may have affected his ability to order it into battle.

McClellan had received strong support from the president and Congress to turn an army of short-term volunteers to a professional volunteer army. The men of the army who experienced this transformation came to admire and respect him, and, up to the point of his removal, he had their love. They called him "Little Mac" and cheered him whenever he reviewed them on parade or toured their camps. When other generals failed later in the war, there was always a subtle call for the return of McClellan. The veterans of 1861 remembered the work and admiration he put into the army, and they returned that admiration.[58]

Whether one believes the Federal army after Bull Run was in turmoil or just recovering from defeat, it cannot be denied that the time of July–October 1861 was critical in the Union war effort. The Northern political leaders and populace needed a boost in morale. The army needed to be professionalized for a war that was going to be long and bloody. The Confederates were serious about leaving the Union; after the defeat at Bull Run, the Federal army around Washington became serious about making sure their departure did not happen.

McClellan took an army that was thrown together and created one of the most formidable fighting forces in the world up to that time. He created a certain morale and esprit de corps that would allow the army to suffer setbacks but always bounce back after defeat. The organization and methods of training he implemented lasted the war and allowed for an effective management of an army that was larger than any in the history of the nation.

The enterprises that McClellan oversaw in the days, weeks, and months after First Bull Run to reinvent the most important army in the Union proved crucial. It would have long-reaching impact beyond the Army of the Potomac and the Civil War in general: the American military came of age that summer. As the *New York Herald* editorialized on August 1 about the condition of the Federal army around Washington, "Confidence Renewed."[59]

Editors' Notes

1. Joan Zenzen, *Battling for Manassas* (University Park: Penn State University Press, 1998), 15. The full text of the manuscript is available online through the National Park Service at http://www.npshistory.com/publications /mana/adhi/adhit.htm.
2. Ibid., 14.
3. Ibid., 20.
4. Ibid., 219n.
5. *The Civil War: A Film by Ken Burns*, episode five, "1863: The Universe of Battle" (1990), transcribed in the print companion: Geoffrey Ward et al., *The Civil War: The Complete Text of the Bestselling Narrative History of the Civil War* (New York: Random House, 1990), 222.
6. Jim Burgess to Chris Mackowski, e-mail, December 8, 2015.

7. Approximately 125,000 men (70,000 Federals and 55,000 Confederates) fought at Second Manassas, and 22,177 fell as casualties (13,824 Federals and 8,353 Confederates) (figures from the Civil War Trust).

8. John Coxe, "The First Battle of Manassas," *Confederate Veteran* 23 (1915): 26.

9. Testimony of General Irvin McDowell, December 26, 1861, in U.S. Congress, Joint Committee on the Conduct of the War, *Report of the Joint Committee on the Conduct of the War*, 2 vols. (Washington, D.C.: Government Printing Office, 1863), 2:38.

10. Peter W. Alexander, *Writing and Fighting the Confederate War: The Letters of Peter Wellington Alexander, Confederate War Correspondent*, ed. William B. Style (Kearny, N.J.: Belle Grove Publishing, 2002).

11. John Hennessy, *First Battle of Manassas: An End to Innocence, July 18–21, 1861* (Lynchburg, Va.: H. E. Howard, 1989), 156n.

12. Coxe, "First Battle," 26.

13. Walt Whitman, *Walt Whitman's Civil War*, ed. Walter Lowenfels (New York: Da Capo, 1960), 25.

14. The movie at Manassas National Battlefield's visitor center is titled *Manassas: An End to Innocence*, as is the park's guide for teachers (http://www.nps.gov /nr/twhp/wwwlps/lessons/12manassas/12manassas.htm). Historian Bradley Gottfried used the same term as the title of a 2011 article for *Hallowed Ground* magazine (http://www.civilwar.org/hallowed-ground-magazine /spring-2011/an-end-to-innocence.html?referrer=https://www.google .com/). See also the book by John Hennessy in n. 11.

Contributor's Notes

15. *Home Letters of General Sherman*, ed. M. A DeWolfe Howe (New York: Scribner's, 1909), 201–10.

16. Carl Sandburg, *Abraham Lincoln: The War Years* (New York: Harcourt, Brace, and World, 1939), 1:302.

17. *OR*, 2:747.

18. Ibid.

19. William Howard Russell, *My Diary, North and South*, ed. Eugene Berwanger (Baton Rouge: Louisiana State University Press, 2001), 464.

20. *OR*, 2:439.

21. Ibid., 316.

22. Ibid., 371.

23. Ibid., 327–28.

24. Diary of Mary Henry, Smithsonian Institution Archives, RU7001, box 51, folder 3, Washington, D.C.; Charles Haydon, *For Country, Cause and Leader: The Civil War Journal of Charles B. Haydon*, ed. Stephen Sears (New York: Ticknor and Fields, 1993), 58.

25. *OR*, 2:571.

26. Ibid., 758.

27. Ibid., 756; George Templeton Strong, *Diary of the Civil War, 1860–1865* (New York: Macmillan, 1962), 169.

28. *OR*, 2:753.

29. George B. McClellan to Ellen M. McClellan, July 27, 1861, McClellan Papers, Library of Congress, Washington, D.C.

30. Philippe, Comte de Paris, in *Battles & Leaders* (1979), 2:112.

31. *Forgotten Valor: The Memoirs, Journals and Civil War Letters of Orlando B. Willcox*, ed. Robert Scott (Kent, Ohio: Kent State University Press, 1999), 55.

32. *New York Herald*, July 15, 1861.

33. George B. McClellan, in *Battles & Leaders*, 2:161.

34. *OR*, 2:763.

35. Ibid., 755.

36. McClellan, *Battles & Leaders*, 2:161.

37. *OR*, 2:769.

38. Todd Williams, *The Seventy-Ninth Highlanders New York Volunteers in the War of the Rebellion, 1861–1865* (Albany: Press of Brandow, Barton, and Company, 1886), 62.

39. *OR*, 5:439.

40. *The Life and Letters of George Gordon Meade, Major-General United States Army* (New York: Charles Scribner's Sons, 1913), 1:231.

41. Russel H. Beatie, *The Army of the Potomac: Birth of Command, November 1860–September 1861* (Cambridge, Mass.: Da Capo, 2002), 427.

42. *OR*, 5:575.

43. Ibid., 579–80.

44. Ibid., 575.

45. Ibid., vol. 51, pt. 1, 492.

46. Editors, *Battles & Leaders*, 2:112.

47. Stephen W. Sears, *George B. McClellan: The Young Napoleon* (New York: Ticknor and Fields, 1988), 102.

48. James Riggs to Montgomery Blair, August 5, 1861, Salmon P. Chase Papers, Library of Congress, Washington, D.C.; George B. McClellan to Ellen

M. McClellan, August 8, 1861, McClellan Papers, Library of Congress, Washington, D.C.

49. U.S. Congress, Joint Committee on the Conduct of the War, *Report of the Joint Committee on the Conduct of the War*, 1:113.

50. *OR*, 2:745.

51. *All for the Union: The Civil War Diary and Letters of Elisha Hunt Rhodes*, ed. Robert Hunt Rhodes (New York: Vintage Books, 1992), 33.

52. *Gone for a Soldier: The Civil War Memoirs of Private Alfred Bellard*, ed. David Herbert Donald (Boston: Little, Brown, 1975), 15.

53. *The Civil War Letters of Joseph Hopkins Twichell: A Chaplain's Story*, ed. Peter Messent and Steve Courtney (Athens: University of Georgia Press, 2006), 65.

54. Ethan S. Rafuse, *McClellan's War* (Bloomington: Indiana University Press, 2005), 131.

55. Sears, *George B. McClellan*, 131–32.

56. William Swinton, *Campaigns of the Army of the Potomac* (New York: Smithmark, 1995), 67.

57. John Russell Young, *Around the World with General Grant*, ed. Michael Fellman (Baltimore: Johns Hopkins University Press, 2002), 264.

58. Sears, *George B. McClellan*, 97.

59. *New York Tribune*, August 1, 1861.

2. ✤ Ball's Bluff

Editors' Introduction

For most Northerners, the Civil War was a far-off affair that took place in ten thousand different places most people had never even heard of. While Confederates threatened the national capital after their victory at Manassas—or so Northerners worried—the fight otherwise seemed far away. Despite that geographic distance, though, the war made its presence known in other ways: empty places at the dinner table, telegraphs from the War Department, pine boxes at the train station.

In central Massachusetts, a poem appeared in a local newspaper, the Worcester Spy, that tried to articulate that intimate sense of loss. Published around Thanksgiving, the poem evoked a new poignancy for traditional family gatherings. "We shall meet but we shall miss him. / There will be one vacant chair," the poem said.

> When a year ago we gathered,
> Joy was in his mild blue eye.
> But a golden cord is severed.
> And our hopes in ruin lie.[1]

Written by Henry S. Washburn, "The Vacant Chair" was inspired by the death of John William Grout, a lieutenant with the Fifteenth Massachusetts who was killed on October 22, 1861, at the battle of Ball's Bluff. The following year, composer George F. Root set the poem to music, and the song became widely popular throughout the North and South.

Grout's body had washed down the Potomac River after the battle and washed up at Chain Bridge, Virginia, on the edge of Washington—some thirty-five miles from the battlefield—on November 5. Because Grout's name was on his clothing, authorities were able to identify his remains, which were sent back to Massachusetts.[2]

Grout was one of several soldiers whose corpses floated downriver, which was "strewn with bodies," said one of Grout's former comrades, Private Roland Bowen of the Fifteenth Massachusetts. One body made it as far as George Washington's Mount Vernon before washing up on the riverbank.[3]

Following the battle of Ball's Bluff, retrieval parties pulled the bodies of dead Federal soldiers from the Potomac River miles downstream. *Library of Congress*

Following the battle of Manassas the previous July, Washingtonians panicked at the thought of rebels at the gate of the capital. But in the wake of Ball's Bluff, in late October 1861, the war came to the very edge of the city, carried by muddy, bloodstained water.

The lament inspired by Grout's death tapped into the deepening gloom of mourning that war spread across both North and South, although no one yet had any idea of the full scale of the horror the war would eventually bring. By the end of the conflict, as many as 720,000 Americans would be dead. The battle at Manassas in July had banished ideas of a quick war, but it had not hinted at the eventual scope and scale of the battles to come. Thus far, battles consisted of a few thousand men on each side, often skirmishing rather than engaging in fully committed combat. In that regard, the small, accidental battle at Ball's Bluff was typical.

However, unlike other little fights in the war's early years, the battle at Ball's Bluff had implications that went well beyond either its size or its military significance. One of the other casualties of the battle was Colonel Edward D. Baker, a personal friend of President Lincoln's who was so close to the family that the Lincolns named one of their sons Edward Baker Lincoln. More important, Baker was a sitting U.S. senator. His death during the battle brought the war to the capital in an entirely different way than the river did, and, as James A. Morgan explains in the following essay, it would have far-reaching political implications for the rest of the conflict.

A monument now stands on the battlefield to commemorate Baker's death, although the marker is some seventy-five to one hundred yards from the exact spot of his wounding. A national cemetery containing fifty-four fallen soldiers buried in twenty-five graves—the third-smallest in the national cemetery system—sits nearby, surrounded by a stone wall. In 1984, the Northern Virginia Regional Park Authority established the Ball's Bluff Regional Park, protecting 221 acres of the core battlefield.[4] Seasonally, volunteers offer tours on the weekends.

The other lasting monument belongs to Grout. "The Vacant Chair" remains one of the most familiar Civil War–era songs. Occasionally, a modern artist will record an updated rendition, as relevant for today's far-off conflicts as it was in 1861:

> At our fireside, sad and lonely,
> Often will the bosom swell,
> At remembrance of the story,
> How our noble Willie fell.[5]

Unintended Consequences: Ball's Bluff and the Rise of the Joint Committee on the Conduct of the War

James A. Morgan

The small, accidental, early-war battle of Ball's Bluff, on the Potomac River just outside Leesburg, Virginia, had implications that went beyond either its size or its military significance. Indeed, it was not really a battle at all but a mere skirmish with seventeen hundred men on each side. Of military significance it had none. The relative positions of the contending forces on opposite sides of the Potomac were the same on the day after the battle as they had been on the day before. The only difference was that 259 men were dead.

Brigadier General Charles Pomeroy Stone, the Union division commander whose troops took part in the little fight, later described it as "about equal to an unnoticed morning's skirmish on the lines before Petersburg at a later period of the war."[6] That said, the battle's political ramifications were enormous and far-reaching as it led directly to the creation of the Joint Committee on the Conduct of the War. For that reason, Ball's Bluff may accurately be described as a "turning point."

In early October 1861, the popular song "All Quiet along the Potomac Tonight" accurately reflected the overall situation in northern Virginia. Union and Confederate troops, observing each other from across the river at Leesburg, generally maintained localized truces that allowed relatively unhindered communication and the easy fraternization that later became common.

This pleasant situation began to change at the beginning of the month when a five-thousand-man brigade under Colonel (and U.S. senator) Edward Dickinson Baker arrived in the vicinity of Poolesville, Maryland, General

30

Colonel Edward D. Baker became the only sitting U.S. senator to be killed in battle in American history. His death shook Washington in a way that thousands of deaths had not thus far been able to do. *Library of Congress*

Stone's headquarters, and became the third brigade in Stone's division. This jumped Stone's force from roughly seven thousand men to twelve thousand almost overnight, a fact that did not escape the notice of the Confederate commander, Colonel Nathan George Evans (dubbed "Shanks" by his West Point classmates because he was knock-kneed), in Leesburg. Baker's four-regiment brigade, styled the "California Brigade," arrived in Poolesville on October 3–4 and set up camp a few miles farther west near the confluence of the Potomac and Monocacy Rivers.[7]

The British-born Baker had been brought to America as a small child and grew up in Philadelphia. While practicing law in Illinois in the mid-1830s he met Abraham Lincoln, and the two became friends. Lincoln even named his second son, Edward Baker Lincoln, after him. Baker moved to California in 1852 and became active in Whig and then Republican politics, successfully stumping California and Oregon for Lincoln in 1860. That same year, he moved to Oregon and was named to the Senate from that state.

The First, Second, Third, and Fifth California Regiments had been recruited mainly in eastern Pennsylvania. They were the fruits of a plan by Baker and a few other high-placed men with West Coast connections to help secure California and Oregon to the Union by having a symbolic military unit under the California name serving in the Union army. As it would take months to transport actual California soldiers to the East (by which time most people assumed the war would be over), the recruiting was done first in New York and then in Philadelphia. As long as the name "California" was attached to this new unit, the origins of the men did not matter.

The original intention had been to recruit a single regiment, but efforts to raise "Colonel Baker's California Regiment"[8] were so successful that four regiments ultimately were organized. It might have been five, but administrative glitches apparently prevented the organization of what would have been the Fourth California, thus the curious numbering of Baker's four regiments. The soldiers were delighted with their California designation, though Baker himself reportedly referred to the project as a "pious fraud."[9]

On October 10, Colonel Evans received another shock when the twelve-thousand-man Union division of Brigadier General George McCall established a camp in Langley, about twenty-five miles from Leesburg. This put some twenty-four thousand Union troops within striking distance of Evans's brigade of fewer than three thousand, with the rest of the Confederate army still near Manassas, more than thirty miles away. Should the Federals attack his isolated force, Evans could not count on timely Confederate assistance.

Following some skirmishing near Harpers Ferry on October 16, Colonel Evans, fearing an attempted envelopment of his position by Union troops, withdrew his men several miles south of Leesburg. But he abandoned Leesburg without obtaining permission from General P. G. T. Beauregard, his immediate superior. Beauregard objected and chastised Evans, who, two days later, was back in Leesburg preparing to face what he assumed would be an overwhelming attack on his brigade.[10]

Evans's concern was reasonable but misplaced. Stone's "Corps of Observation" was simply living up to its name and observing, but Evans's sudden disappearance from the town led Major General George B. McClellan to order a reconnaissance-in-force to determine whether the Confederates were really gone. McClellan suspected a trap. The reconnaissance would not be by Stone from across the river but by McCall from Langley.

McClellan ordered McCall to move his division to Dranesville, about halfway between Langley and Leesburg, and then to probe westward in search of Evans. By the time McCall got to Dranesville and began his investigation, however, Evans had returned. This confusing situation led McClellan, on

October 19, to order McCall back to Langley the next morning. But McCall asked for an additional twenty-four hours to complete the road maps he had been making, and McClellan granted the request.[11]

Per General McClellan's suggestion on October 20, Stone conducted "a slight demonstration,"[12] which McClellan hoped would combine with Mc-Call's activities and result in Evans leaving Leesburg again. Stone positioned troops in sight of the Confederates, put boats into the river, and otherwise maneuvered to make Evans believe that the Federals were about to cross in strength. Evans recognized the feint, however, and did not respond. October 20 came to an end with nothing of significance having happened.

The story would have ended there had Stone not decided to send a small reconnaissance patrol across the river at Ball's Bluff that evening to see if anything had come of the day's maneuverings. This twenty-man patrol came from the Fifteenth Massachusetts, part of which was then occupying Harrison's Island, directly opposite Ball's Bluff.

Commanded by Captain Chase Philbrick, the volunteers crossed to Virginia at about dusk and then worked their way up the path to the top of the bluff. From there, they moved through a large clearing and some woods, eventually emerging into the fields where a subdivision is located today. Once there, Captain Philbrick saw what he thought were the tents of a Confederate camp. Without checking further, Philbrick returned to Harrison's Island and reported to General Stone that he had discovered an apparently unguarded Confederate camp. Philbrick's inexperience and the shadowy evening light, however, had confused him; the "tents" actually were trees.

What we would call a target of opportunity, General Stone called "a very nice little military chance." But it was the faulty intelligence from Philbrick that led, the next morning, to the battle of Ball's Bluff.[13]

General Stone received the patrol's report around 10:00 p.m. and responded to this opportunity to punish some apparently careless Confederates by ordering a raid on the camp. He immediately instructed Colonel Charles Devens, commanding the Fifteenth Massachusetts, to cross five companies of his regiment to the Virginia shore and, as soon as there was enough light the next morning, to move forward and attack the camp.[14]

Devens used three small boats to shuttle approximately three hundred men across the Virginia channel of the river, a few at a time. The effort, made more difficult by the fact that the river was high due to rain having fallen nearly every day in October, took several hours but was successfully completed shortly before dawn. Following behind these troops came about one hundred men of the Twentieth Massachusetts who would cover the bluff and protect the rear of the raiding party. After conferring with Colonel William R. Lee of the Twentieth to make sure that all was in order, Devens moved his men forward. Neither the commanders nor their men had any idea that this movement, a small-scale raid on a camp that turned out not to be there, would result in a disastrous battle only a few hours later.

It did not take long for Devens, guided by Captain Philbrick, to reach the site of the supposed camp and discover the error. Devens later defended Philbrick by stating that, even in daylight, "the trees gave very much the appearance of a row of tents." [15] With nothing for the raiding party to raid, however, he made the fateful decision not to return to the island but to deploy his men in a nearby tree line and send a messenger back to General Stone with an explanation and a request for further orders.

The messenger was Lieutenant Church Howe, the regimental quartermaster. He would have to go back to and down the bluff, some three-quarters of a mile distant, and then cross the Virginia channel of the river, Harrison's Island, and the much wider Maryland channel of the river before getting onto the C&O Canal towpath and riding some three miles downriver to Edwards Ferry, where General Stone was at that time. Several related events were taking place while Lieutenant Howe was making this trek.

As a diversion for the raiding party, Stone had ordered Major John Mix of the Third New York Cavalry to cross the river with thirty troopers at Edwards Ferry early that morning. Mix was to ride toward Leesburg on the Edwards Ferry Road and attract the attention of the Confederates. Having bought time for the force at Ball's Bluff to raid the camp, Mix was to retire back across the Potomac while the presumably successful raiding party was doing the same thing.[16]

Mix was doing this job as the raiding party was discovering the mistake about the tents, although of course he did not know that. After briefly engaging what probably was a part of the Thirteenth Mississippi along the Edwards Ferry Road, he retired back toward the river.

About 8:00 a.m., pickets from the Seventeenth Mississippi discovered and engaged the men of the Fifteenth Massachusetts in a brief firefight. Ironically, this occurred about the same time that Lieutenant Howe was reporting to General Stone that all was quiet. Hearing this new, and again incorrect, information, Stone decided to turn the raiding party into an expanded reconnaissance. He instructed Howe to return to Devens and inform him that the rest of the Fifteenth Massachusetts would soon be on its way to link up with him. On the arrival of these troops, Devens was to proceed toward Leesburg to gather what information he could about the whereabouts of the Confederates.[17]

Lieutenant Howe made the long trip back but, on reporting to his commander, was informed that the Massachusetts men had made contact with the enemy. Devens ordered a no doubt weary Howe to go back once more to General Stone and report on the changed situation.

As this was taking place, Colonel Baker arrived at Stone's headquarters and asked if he could be of any assistance. He knew of the morning's troop movements, but his own brigade had not been involved. Stone, unaware that fighting had begun, ordered Baker to proceed upriver to the crossing point, evaluate the situation, and decide whether to cross more troops over or recall those who were already on the Virginia side.[18]

At that point, around 10:00 a.m., Baker was heading upriver to take command of what he believed to be a large reconnaissance while Lieutenant Howe was on his way back downriver to General Stone to report that fighting had begun. The two men met, and Howe reported the new information to Baker, who said to him, "I am going over immediately with my whole force to take command."[19] Howe proceeded to General Stone and reported this conversation while Baker continued upriver and began ordering any troops he could find to cross over to Ball's Bluff.

The immediate problem was that no one had planned a major river crossing, and so the Federals were, as General Stone later reported to General McClellan, "a little short of boats."[20] Another problem was that Baker did not cross the river but remained on the Maryland side overseeing the scrambling search for more transportation.

All this time, Shanks Evans was watching events unfold, almost surely thinking that he was witnessing the very envelopment he had feared. Union troops were across the river at Ball's Bluff and Edwards Ferry while a full division was only a few miles away in Dranesville. Evans did not then know that the Ball's Bluff force was only a three-hundred-man raiding party, the Edwards Ferry force was a mere thirty-man cavalry diversion, and the division at Dranesville was about to turn around and leave the area. He did send additional troops to Ball's Bluff over the course of the morning to counter the slowly growing number of Union troops arriving in small groups as they could find boat transportation across both channels of the Potomac. Otherwise, Evans could do little but wait and watch.

Skirmishing continued off and on between Devens's Massachusetts men and the Virginians and Mississippians of Evans's brigade. Other Union troops were arriving at the bluff but made no effort to advance beyond it, though they surely must have heard the sounds of firing from only a few hundred yards away. With Baker still on the Maryland side of the river, no one was in overall command of the reinforcements at the bluff on the Virginia side. Colonel Lee of the Twentieth Massachusetts had the largest body of men there at the time but later said that he did not advance to the aid of Devens because he had no orders to do so.[21] One might be forgiven for wondering why he did not simply march to the sound of the guns.

When General Stone heard from Lieutenant Howe that fighting had begun and that Colonel Baker was going to cross over, he began crossing additional Union troops at Edwards Ferry. Today we call this prepositioning resources. McClellan never told Stone that he had ordered McCall out of the area, so Stone believed that McCall likely would be advancing on Leesburg from the east. Should that happen, Stone wanted to be prepared to link up with him. So he crossed several regiments to the Virginia side but had the men stack arms on the floodplain and wait. They waited in vain, though, as McCall was not coming.

Events at Ball's Bluff developed on their own. Colonel Devens, whose men had been doing all the fighting on the Union side, knew that other Federals were back at the bluff. He also knew that Baker was in command but had neither seen him nor received any orders from him during the day. Around 2:00 p.m., about the same time that Baker finally crossed into Virginia, Devens withdrew his men to the bluff.

There he encountered Baker, who ordered him to the Union right where he was to take up a concealed position in the tree line at a right angle to the line of the Federals already deployed. This alignment, resembling a backward capital *L*, covered the entrance to the open field, the only approach the Confederates could use, with what would prove a deadly crossfire.[22]

The continuous fighting began around three o'clock when Baker sent two companies of his First California forward to determine how many Confederates he faced. As these two companies advanced up the slope toward the entrance to the field, they were met by a portion of the Eighth Virginia (a local, mostly Loudoun County, unit) in a small but intense hand-to-hand encounter, which resulted in heavy casualties and both sides falling back. The Virginians were replaced by the Eighteenth Mississippi, which advanced across the field toward the Federals they could see and right into the crossfire from the ones they could not see. They were decimated by what Confederate soldier Elijah White, a Loudoun County resident serving as a guide for the

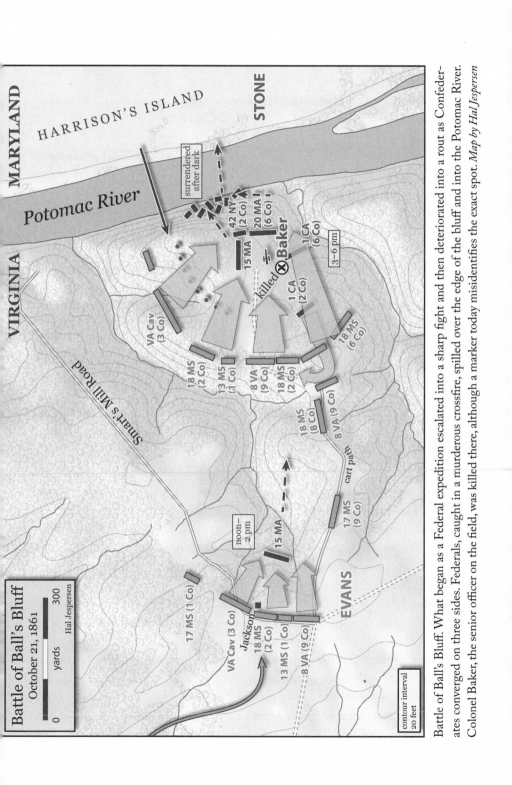

Battle of Ball's Bluff

October 21, 1861

0   yards   300

Hal Jespersen

contour interval
20 feet

MARYLAND

HARRISON'S ISLAND

STONE

Potomac River

VIRGINIA

surrendered
after dark

42 NY
(2 Co)

20 MA
(6 Co)

15 MA

1 CA
(6 Co)

killed ⊗ Baker

3–6 pm

VA Cav
(3 Co)

1 CA
(2 Co)

18 MS
(6 Co)

18 MS
(2 Co)

13 MS
(1 Co)

8 VA
(9 Co)

18 MS
(2 Co)

18 MS
(8 Co)

8 VA (9 Co)

cart path

Smart's Mill Road

17 MS
(9 Co)

noon—
2 pm

15 MA

17 MS (1 Co)

VA Cav (3 Co)

Jackson

18 MS
(2 Co)

13 MS (1 Co)

8 VA (9 Co)

EVANS

Battle of Ball's Bluff. What began as a Federal expedition escalated into a sharp fight and then deteriorated into a rout as Confederates converged on three sides. Federals, caught in a murderous crossfire, spilled over the edge of the bluff and into the Potomac River. Colonel Baker, the senior officer on the field, was killed there, although a marker today misidentifies the exact spot. *Map by Hal Jespersen*

Mississippians, called "the best directed & most destructive single volley I saw during the war."[23]

Not long after that, Colonel Baker was killed. He remains the only U.S. senator ever to die in combat, though the exact circumstances of his death are disputed.[24]

With Baker's death, there was some confusion as Colonels Charles Devens, William R. Lee, and Milton Cogswell (Forty-Second New York) sorted out the situation and determined what to do. Cogswell, the only West Pointer on the field, took command. He tried to organize a breakout from the constricted position on the bluff, telling his men, "We'll cut our way through to Edwards Ferry."[25] Unhappily for the Union troops, the breakout attempt quickly collapsed, and Cogswell ordered the men to hold long enough to save the wounded. With the bluff to their backs, minimal boat transportation, and a large number of wounded to deal with, the Federals did manage to hold back the Confederates for perhaps twenty to thirty minutes and successfully evacuate some of the wounded to Harrison's Island.

Then the bulk of the Seventeenth Mississippi, about six hundred fresh troops, arrived and sealed the Federals' fate. These men, with portions of the Eighteenth Mississippi and assorted other Confederates on their flanks, advanced across the field and broke the Union line, which simply melted into "one wild, panic-stricken herd."[26] With nightfall, the battle ended, but the controversy was about to begin.

Press, public, and political opinion quickly split into competing pro-Stone and pro-Baker camps. The focus at first was on the tragic battlefield defeat, but this quickly shifted to an emphasis on the political agenda of the more radical abolitionist members of Congress.

The pro-Baker camp based its support for him on the fact that Baker had been a popular antislavery Republican senator and a close friend of President Lincoln's and had died gloriously on the field of battle. Stone was none of those things, though General McClellan formally absolved him of blame three days after the battle when, as a result of his own investigation, he declared that "the disaster was caused by errors committed by the immediate commander, not General Stone."[27] This criticism did not sit well with many of Baker's Senate colleagues or their media supporters.

The first anti-Stone volley was fired on the very evening of the battle by Lieutenant Francis G. Young, quartermaster of the California Brigade. Inept or corrupt, and probably both, Young had been chastised by General Stone two days before the battle for questionable procurement practices, and he resented it.[28] This very junior officer first jumped the chain of command by sending a telegram directly to President Lincoln announcing Baker's death. He then sent another telegram to Lincoln that same night preposterously claiming that Baker had put him in command of a critical part of the battlefield and implying that Stone had been negligent in sending reinforcements. Young then accompanied Baker's body to Washington and was among the first to give his biased version of events to the press. His accounts of the battle were riddled with inaccuracies that clearly demonstrated that he had not actually been present on the field for very long, if at all.

Lieutenant Henry L. Abbott of the Twentieth Massachusetts wrote to his father and noted that Young, whom Abbott did not identify by name though the reference was clear, "was carried off the field to a place of safety about 15 minutes after the battle began, showing a slight scratch on his arm, but not showing his sword, which he left on the battlefield."[29] Lieutenant Colonel Isaac Wistar of the First California called Young "a coward + liar who was at no time within 2 miles of the battle field."[30]

But none of this mattered. Young's accounts were widely reported and became the basis for the accusations levied against General Stone by the press and, eventually, by the Joint Committee on the Conduct of the War (JCCW). Young himself testified before the committee on January 16, 1862, and became its star witness against Stone.

The JCCW evolved out of a December 3, 1861, resolution by Representative Roscoe Conkling of New York requesting Secretary of War Simon Cameron to furnish the House of Representatives with an explanation of the disaster at Ball's Bluff.[31] Two days later, Senator Zachariah Chandler of Michigan suggested that an official joint committee be formed to investigate the defeats at Bull Run and Ball's Bluff. Other members wanted to expand the scope of the committee's investigative power to include all military affairs and, in the somewhat ominous words of Maine's senator William P. Fessenden, "to keep an anxious, watchful eye over all the executive agents who are carrying on the war."[32] Congress authorized the committee on December 10. It first met on December 20, one year to the day after South Carolina seceded and got the ball rolling.

During the war years, the committee conducted a variety of investigations on different topics, including civilian and military contracting procedures, naval construction, medical treatment for wounded soldiers, and illicit trading with Confederates in Union-held areas, among others. But the underlying reason behind its creation was to change the war from one to preserve the Union into one to end slavery.

The committee would have seven members, three senators and four representatives, and would be dominated by the "Radical Republicans." Vice President Hannibal Hamlin, president of the Senate, chose the three senators: Benjamin Franklin Wade of Ohio as chairman, Zachariah Chandler, and Democrat Andrew Johnson of Tennessee. Speaker of the House Galusha Grow selected Representatives George Julian of Indiana, John Covode of Pennsylvania, Daniel Gooch of Massachusetts, and Democrat Moses Odell of New York. The two Democrats were chosen because they were "War Democrats" and not expected to seriously oppose the agenda of the Radicals. They were there largely to give the impression of bipartisanship. Odell, in fact, was fairly active and helpful.

Senator Johnson resigned early in 1862 to become the military governor of Tennessee. He had three Democratic successors on the committee during the war. But neither Joseph Wright (Indiana), Benjamin Harding (Oregon; Colonel Baker's replacement in the Senate), nor Charles Buckalew (Pennsylvania) played a very active role in the committee's business. Covode left Congress in 1864 and was replaced by Benjamin Loan of Missouri.[33]

As chairman, Wade was the key figure on the committee. A hard-core abolitionist, Wade had been a senator since 1851 and worked closely with Senator Charles Sumner of Massachusetts throughout the 1850s in opposition to fugitive slave laws and anything that would result in the expansion of slavery. His personal combativeness extended even to carrying a brace of pistols while on the Senate floor. Wade was one of the earliest advocates of voting rights for freed slaves.[34]

By the time the JCCW first met, attacks on General Stone were coming from Republican newspapers and various politicians, most notably from Sumner. Newspaper accounts, largely based on Francis Young's widely disseminated distortions, accused Stone of everything from ineptitude to treason. The charges were absurd given Stone's high West Point ranking (seventh of forty-one in the class of 1845), his solid military credentials in both war and peace, his performance in organizing the Washington, D.C., militia for the protection of the capital, and his work in overseeing the security for then president-elect Lincoln's inauguration. As a West Pointer, a Democrat, and a friend of General McClellan, however, Stone probably would have become a target anyway, but his perceived role in the death of Senator Baker gave the Radicals all the reason they needed to go after him, though more would come.

On December 18, Senator Sumner attacked Stone in a speech, saying that Stone "is now adding to his achievements . . . by engaging ably and actively in the work of surrendering fugitive slaves. He does this, sir, most successfully. He is victorious when the simple question is whether a fugitive slave shall be surrendered to a rebel."[35]

This was a reference to the fact that Stone had, in fact, ordered the return of two Maryland slaves who had appeared in the camp of the Twentieth Massachusetts about a month after the battle. Federal law, Maryland state law, and Lincoln's policy of placating slave states that had not seceded all required that Stone do this. But these mitigating circumstances did not matter to Sumner. Prior to Sumner's speech, however, Stone learned that the senator had been, "from his place in the Senate, writing letters to my subordinates urging them to disobey my orders."[36]

Weary of the political interference and personal attacks, Stone made the blunder of his life by writing to Sumner on December 23, accusing him of uttering "a slander and a falsehood" and calling him a "well known coward."[37] He did not directly challenge Sumner to a duel, but reading between the nineteenth-century lines, that is exactly what he did, and Sumner would have known it. It could not have helped that Stone's note was delivered to Sumner on Christmas morning.[38]

Sumner did not respond to the note but quietly began working to undermine Stone's career, even bragging about it two and a half years later in a letter to Ralph Waldo Emerson in which he took credit for getting Stone's volunteer commission as a brigadier general rescinded.[39] Though not a member of the JCCW, Sumner was extremely influential within Radical Republican circles.

Historians often name Secretary of War Edwin Stanton as Stone's chief nemesis as he was the one who eventually issued Stone's arrest order. But Stanton was merely the delivery boy acting on behalf of the JCCW and of Sumner. As Stone's friend and West Point roommate Brevet Brigadier General Horatio Gates Gibson expressed it in a memoir, Stone was done in by "the blatant vaporings of a prejudiced Senator."[40] And as one New York editorialist put it more succinctly, "Sumner was his jailor."[41]

It should be understood that it was not so much the loss of the battle that aroused the committee's ire as the return of the slaves. In addition, the Radical Republicans hated West Point. Chairman Wade even called for it to be abolished. They all believed that West Point both was unnecessary as a military academy—as, in their view, "the average American could easily make himself a master of military science in a short time"[42]—and fostered conservative principles that acted against what they felt was the proper antislavery attitude. Enamored of the citizen-soldier ideal of the "minute men" of America's War of Independence, they objected to the very idea of a professional officer corps as being elitist, antirepublican, and dangerous to the nation.

That so many West Pointers joined the Confederacy just solidified these views and led to a strong bias against West Point officers on the part of Radical Republicans in general and of the members of the JCCW in particular. The West Point connections of officers who cooperated with the committee, however, men like John Pope and Joseph Hooker, were overlooked.

The committee's initial doings, other than the sideshow investigation of General Robert Patterson for his alleged failures in connection with the battle of First Manassas, involved John C. Frémont and Charles P. Stone. This tale of two generals provides historians with a clear point-counterpoint illustration of how the committee operated as it attacked Stone while promoting the career of Frémont. As historian T. Harry Williams has written, "A justification and defense of Fremont's military record was one of the purposes back of the establishment of the Committee."[43] Writing sixty years after Williams, historian Bruce Tap concurred. When the JCCW was created, Tap wrote, "a primary reason for its formation was the administration's treatment of Fremont."[44]

Frémont, in 1856 the Republican Party's first presidential candidate, had been the darling of the Radicals since August 30 when, as commanding officer of the Department of the West, he issued an order placing Missouri under martial law and declaring the slaves of secessionists to be forfeit and free. Lincoln revoked this order as part of his effort to keep Missouri in the Union, and he especially infuriated the Radicals by relieving Frémont of command.[45] About that same time, Stone issued a general order to his division explaining that federal and state fugitive slave laws remained in effect and that soldiers must follow the law.[46] The differences between Frémont and Stone in the eyes of the committee were clear. Indeed, much of Stone's usefulness to the committee was the fact that it could treat him as a kind of anti-Frémont.

The JCCW conducted its official hearings on Ball's Bluff (though, as Tap has written, they were, in fact, "a referendum on war goals")[47] between December 27, 1861, and February 27, 1862. During that time, it called thirty-nine witnesses, only seven of whom had been present at Ball's Bluff: Stone, Lieutenant

Colonel Isaac Wistar (First California), Francis G. Young,[48] Lieutenant Church Howe (Fifteenth Massachusetts), Colonel Charles Devens (Fifteenth Massachusetts), Colonel William R. Lee (Twentieth Massachusetts), and Major Paul J. Revere (Twentieth Massachusetts, grandson of Paul Revere of Revolutionary War fame).

None of the other witnesses had been anywhere near Ball's Bluff, and several were not even in Stone's division. Two witnesses, Young and Colonel George W. B. Tompkins (Second New York State Militia), previously had been disciplined by Stone and held personal grudges against him. Moreover, nine other witnesses were members of Colonel Tompkins's regiment[49] and tended to parrot his criticisms. Stone himself testified twice during that period, on January 5 and 31, 1862 (and then again on February 27, 1863).

The questions asked about Stone's conduct of the battle were often outside of the witnesses' knowledge or expertise. For example, Major Dwight Bannister, General Frederick Lander's brigade paymaster, was asked, despite having no military experience, to evaluate General Stone's tactics and whether he thought Stone could have reinforced Baker by crossing troops at Edwards Ferry and moving them to Ball's Bluff behind the Confederates. Stone had already explained the tactical difficulties of doing this (and questioned the need) in his own testimony, but Bannister, who could not possibly have known, flatly asserted that "there was no obstacle."[50] This was what Senator Wade wanted to hear, so he accepted it along with considerable other hearsay and uninformed opinion as legitimate evidence against General Stone.

Much of the questioning focused on stories of Stone's alleged secessionist sympathies. He was accused of having had improper communications with secessionists in the Leesburg area, of having been friendly with various Confederate officers, of having protected rebel property, and of having allowed the Confederates to build earthworks unhindered.[51] Stone himself was not told of these specific accusations until the following February, after he had spent six months in prison. During his final appearance before the committee, he clearly explained his actions and refuted all the charges in detail. But it was too late. The damage had been done.

Even then, the committee, in a gratuitous act of cruelty, used Stone's third appearance as a weapon against him. Summoned to testify on February 27, 1863, Stone replied that his wife, Maria Louisa Clary Stone, lay on her deathbed and asked for a delay so that he might remain with her. The committee then sent him a "preemptory summons"[52] to appear that day, so he did. His wife died during his absence.[53]

Non–West Pointer Frémont's very different and amicable reception by the committee began with his first appearance on January 10, 1862. Given his compatible political views and the fact that committee members Ben Wade, Zachariah Chandler, and George Julian all were his close personal friends, this should not be surprising.[54] Frémont also testified on January 17 and 30. On the tenth, Fremont indicated that he would like to prepare a written statement before answering questions. Wade agreed, so actual questioning did not begin until Frémont's second appearance. At that time, some of the committee's questions dealt with the death of Brigadier General Nathaniel Lyon at the battle of Wilson's Creek, another favorite of the Radical Republicans because of his staunch antislavery views. Some of Frémont's critics had accused him of failing to send reinforcements to Lyon when he could.

Frémont cast the blame onto Lyon and blamed that officer's own poor decisions rather than any problem with reinforcements. Note that General Stone had said precisely the same things about Colonel Baker (and with greater justification). Yet the committee readily accepted that explanation from Frémont while it completely rejected it from Stone. In fact, there was blame enough for both men in the Frémont-Lyon situation, whereas the Stone-Baker question may be, and could then have been, clearly answered in Stone's favor. McClellan was correct when he placed the blame for the defeat at Ball's Bluff on Colonel Baker.

That defeat was the proximate cause of the creation of the committee. One might call it the last straw. Union forces had lost at Big Bethel, First Manassas, Wilson's Creek, and Ball's Bluff. Congress, especially the Radical Republicans, wanted to know why. The Radicals believed that the reason was excessive deference to "the Slave Power"[55] and a lack of commitment by West Point officers to the antislavery cause, an attitude they viewed as nothing short of treason.

One general effect of the committee's anti–West Point sentiments and politically motivated, near-constant investigations was to put Union army general officers on their guard. After the examples of Stone and Frémont, officers could no longer simply follow their orders and perform their duty. The committee was watching, and everyone knew it. Military success was good; political reliability was better.

The politically reliable Frémont was given command of the Mountain Department (portions of Virginia, Tennessee, and Kentucky) in early 1862 solely because of pressure from the committee. Frémont's military skills had not improved, however, and his defeat in the Shenandoah Valley by Major General Thomas "Stonewall" Jackson effectively ended his military career.[56]

The committee investigated nearly every major Union defeat and many minor ones. It was not unusual for members to travel to the site of the action and spend several days rummaging through the camps. Major Generals Fitz-John Porter and William Franklin both were concerned about these activities, Porter because of his role at Second Manassas and Franklin because of his at Fredericksburg. Porter, in fact, was court-martialed, and Franklin was blamed by the committee (albeit with good reason) for the debacle at Fredericksburg. General George Meade later wrote, "I sometimes feel very nervous about my position, [the committee is] knocking over generals at such a rate."[57]

Certainly, the JCCW did some good work in exposing several examples of bureaucratic corruption and poor management in areas such as government contracting. Arguably its most important achievement was its investigation of the Fort Pillow massacre in April 1864.

Nonetheless, the committee's different approaches to Frémont and Stone, based solely on their political views, demonstrate that it was not always an honest broker or an impartial investigative body. The members of the JCCW were determined from the beginning to push the political agenda in which they all so fervently believed. And, also from the beginning, that agenda caused problems for President Lincoln as he tried to balance different and competing political factions and conduct the war at the same time. T. Harry Williams perhaps best summed it up when he wrote, "[The Committee's] three and one-half years of existence represents the acme, in American military history, of civilian interference with the direction of military operations."[58]

General Stone, who suffered the most, and the most unjustly, from the committee's attacks later expressed his frustration, resentment, and contempt about what happened. All of those emotions came pouring out when he wrote to Benson Lossing, one of the war's earliest chroniclers: "I was called before a table full of civilians whose rest I had secured and who had none of them ever exposed a little finger for the defence of the government, to talk to them & persuade them I was loyal to the Gov't!"[59]

The Joint Committee on the Conduct of the War is an object lesson in how not to run a congressional investigation. It is well known that then-senator Harry S. Truman read the reports of the JCCW while preparing to head an investigation of irregularities in defense contracting during World War II. Having seen what Wade's committee did, Truman was determined that his committee would conduct "no white-wash or witch hunt."[60] The JCCW hearings were conducted in secret. Witnesses had to appear alone and without legal counsel. The questioners constantly led or badgered the witnesses. And the witnesses in the Stone hearings often were selected because of their hostility toward the officer who was the object of the investigation. Simply put, the railroading of General Charles Pomeroy Stone was a shameful farce. The historical record of it and other investigations provided Truman with detailed instructions on what not to do.

All of this—the creation of the JCCW, the politically motivated hearings that proceeded from it, the media furor over Generals Stone and Frémont, and the growing fears and suspicions that accompanied the process—happened because a small, accidental, militarily insignificant skirmish became a club for powerful politicians to use against the army and their own political opponents. For these reasons, as well as the fact of the military defeat, this little fight on the Potomac was an early-war turning point that became known as "that cursed Ball's Bluff."[61]

Editors' Notes

1. Henry S. Washburn, "The Vacant Chair," 1861.
2. The website of the Fifteenth Massachusetts (http://www.nextech.de/ma15mvi/) offers a slightly more complete account in a letter from Charles D. Tucker to "Friend Chas" dated November 10, 1861. Tucker writes, "Quartermaster (Church) Howe found Willie Grout's body (Lt. John William Grout, Co. D, 15 Mass) down near Chain Bridge, opposit [*sic*] Washington."
3. Gregory Coco, ed., *From Ball's Bluff to Gettysburg . . . and Beyond: The Civil War Letters of Private Roland E. Bowen, 15th Massachusetts Infantry, 1861–1864* (Gettysburg, Pa.: Thomas Publications, 1994), 32.
4. The Park Authority added the word "Battlefield" to the name in 2004: Ball's Bluff Regional Battlefield Park.
5. Washburn, "Vacant Chair."

Contributor's Notes

6. Stone to Benson Lossing, November 5, 1866, in James S. Schoff Civil War Collection, Clements Library, University of Michigan, Ann Arbor.
7. Gary Lash, *Duty Well Done: The History of Edward Baker's California Regiment* (Baltimore: Butternut and Blue, 2001), 99–101.
8. Baker could legitimately call himself "Colonel" due to his brief but creditable service in Mexico as commanding officer of the Fourth Illinois Volunteer Infantry.
9. Lash, *Duty Well Done*, 85.

10. *OR*, vol. 5, pt. 1, 347.

11. For a detailed account of the movements leading up to the battle, see James A. Morgan III, *A Little Short of Boats: The Battles of Ball's Bluff and Edwards Ferry, October 21–22, 1861* (El Dorado Hills, Calif.: Savas Beatie, 2011), 15–27.

12. Ibid., 18.

13. Ibid., 27.

14. Stone to Devens, *OR*, vol. 5, pt. 1, 299.

15. Testimony of Colonel Charles Devens before the Joint Committee on the Conduct of the War, January 27, 1862. Extracted from U.S. Congress, Joint Committee on the Conduct of the War, *Report of the Joint Committee on the Conduct of the War*, as *The Battle of Ball's Bluff* (Millwood, N.Y.: Kraus Reprint, 1977), 405 (abbreviated as *JCCW* below).

16. Testimony of Major John Mix, *JCCW*, February 14, 1862, 462.

17. Testimony of Lieutenant Church Howe, *JCCW*, January 25, 1862, 376–77.

18. Morgan, *Little Short of Boats*, 65.

19. Testimony of Howe.

20. Stone to McClellan, *OR*, vol. 51, pt. 1, 499.

21. Testimony of Colonel William R. Lee, *JCCW*, February 27, 1862, 477.

22. Morgan, *Little Short of Boats*, 91.

23. Elijah White, "Ball's Bluff Address of Col. E. V. White, 1887," Miscellany Collection, Thomas Balch Library, Leesburg, Va.

24. For a summary of the many accounts of Baker's death, see Morgan, *Little Short of Boats*, 223–31.

25. Ibid., 141.

26. Randolph Shotwell, quoted in ibid., 165. Note that the rout took place at the southern end of Ball's Bluff where it is steep and roughly thirty feet high, not sheer and a hundred feet high.

27. Stephen Sears, *Controversies and Commanders: Dispatches from the Army of the Potomac* (New York: Houghton Mifflin, 1999), 36.

28. For a full account of Young's transgressions and his role in the controversy, see Morgan, *Little Short of Boats*, 218–22.

29. *Fallen Leaves: The Civil War Letters of Major Henry Livermore Abbott*, ed. Robert Garth Scott (Kent, Ohio: Kent State University Press, 1991), 73.

30. Quoted in Lash, *Duty Well Done*, 506; "Capt. Francis G. Young's Statement," *Madison (Wis.) State Journal*, October 29, 1861; Young to Lincoln, October 21, 1861, Abraham Lincoln Papers, General Correspondence, Library of Congress, Washington, D.C.

31. Cong. Globe, 37th Cong., 2nd Sess., 6 (1862).

32. T. Harry Williams, "The Committee on the Conduct of the War: An Experiment in Civilian Control," *Journal of the American Military Institute*, Autumn 1939, 138.

33. Covode returned to Congress in 1867 and was the author of the resolution to impeach President Andrew Johnson, his former colleague on the committee.

34. Adam Goodheart, *1861: The Civil War Awakening* (New York: Alfred A. Knopf, 2011), 64.

35. Cong. Globe, 37th Cong., 2nd Sess., 130 (December 18, 1861).

36. *Boston Post*, letter to the editor from General Stone, September 28, 1867.

37. *OR*, vol. 5, pt. 1, 517.

38. *Boston Post*, Stone letter.

39. Sumner to Emerson, in *The Selected Letters of Charles Sumner*, ed. Beverly W. Palmer (Boston: Northeastern University Press, 1990), 2:68.

40. Horatio Gates Gibson, "The Trial of Charles P. Stone" (unpublished essay), p. 11, Papers of Horatio Gates Gibson, SC 2157, Wisconsin Historical Society, Madison.

41. Magazine editorial, *Old Guard*, November 1868, 878.

42. Bruce Tap, *Over Lincoln's Shoulder: The Committee on the Conduct of the War* (Lawrence: University Press of Kansas, 1998), 154; Williams, "Committee on the Conduct of the War," 145.

43. T. Harry Williams, "Fremont and the Politicians," *Journal of the American Military History Foundation*, Winter 1938, 185.

44. Tap, *Over Lincoln's Shoulder*, 85.

45. Williams, "Committee on the Conduct of the War," 140.

46. Sears, *Controversies and Commanders*, 32.

47. Tap, *Over Lincoln's Shoulder*, 56.

48. Present at the battle for a short time at most, Young was a civilian when he testified on January 16, 1862, though the JCCW transcript incorrectly refers to him as a captain. He had been court-martialed on December 12 for disobeying orders and going absent without leave. Following his conviction on these charges, he was cashiered from the army on January 2, 1862.

49. *JCCW*, introduction, list of witnesses. Tompkins himself eventually was arrested and resigned under threat of court-martial in May 1862, too late to do Stone any good.

50. Testimony of Major Dwight Bannister, *JCCW*, January 9, 1862, 288.

51. T. Harry Williams, "Investigation: 1862," *American Heritage Magazine*, December 1954, 19.

52. Gibson, "Trial of Charles P. Stone," 10.

53. Obituary of Maria Louisa Stone, *Washington Evening Star*, February 28, 1863.

54. Williams, "Fremont and the Politicians," 185.

55. Tap, *Over Lincoln's Shoulder*, 99.

56. Ibid., 100.

57. *The Life and Letters of George Gordon Meade: Major-General United States Army by George Meade (Captain and Aide-De-Camp and Brevet Lieutenant-Colonel United States Army)*, vol. 1 (New York: Charles Scribner's Sons, 1913). Quoted in reprint of Army of the Potomac Series, vol. 5 (Baltimore: Butternut and Blue, 1994), 360.

58. Williams, "Fremont and the Politicians," 185.

59. Stone to Benson Lossing, 7.

60. Tap, *Over Lincoln's Shoulder*, 2.

61. Morgan, *Little Short of Boats*, 171.

3. ❀ Shiloh

Editors' Introduction

The Tennessee River, as it flows past Pittsburg Landing, moves with the slow intentionality of a lazy summer. Its surface boils with bull's-eye ripples as fish rise up to gobble bugs from the surface. The next town north, Savannah, Tennessee—some nine miles downriver—bills itself as "The Catfish Capital of the World," and just north of the landing itself, on the edge of Shiloh National Battlefield, the famous Catfish Hotel serves up lunch and dinner daily. On the edge of the river, one can stand and listen to the sounds of the ripples of the fish.

Overlooking the bucolic riverbank, 3,892 graves rest atop the heights. Laid out in neat plots, Shiloh National Cemetery serves as the final resting place for veterans of six conflicts, including 3,584 casualties of the Civil War battle that took place there in early April 1862. That includes two Confederates, their headstones differentiated from their Federal brothers by peaked rather than round top edges.

Most of the Confederates still on the battlefield lie in mass graves. Five such burial pits have been identified, although historians know at least six others exist, their locations unknown, lost in the south Tennessee tangle of deciduous jungle. That doesn't count, either, the bodies that had been strewn and scattered through the woods by wild pigs foraging on the corpses.

"As far as the eye could reach, in every direction, lay the silent forms of those who went down before the storm of battle," an Ohio soldier, Wilbur Hinman, later wrote.[1] John T. Bell of the Second Iowa was horrified that "in places dead men lay so closely that a person could walk over two acres of ground and not step off the bodies."[2] "The battlefield was a heart sickening sight," wrote the regimental historians of the Forty-Eighth Ohio. "The dead were lying in every conceivable shape." They lamented the "horrid sights that met the gaze all around."[3]

Just a week shy of the one-year anniversary of the firing on Fort Sumter, the war had seemed relatively quiet overall. In the Eastern Theater, all eyes fixed on Major General George B. McClellan and his massive Army of the Potomac as they began their cautious advance up the Virginia Peninsula from Fort Monroe toward Richmond. Aside from the spectacular clash of ironclad battleships off

At Pittsburg Landing, a sloping roadway led up from the Tennessee River to a high bluff. The landing became a bottleneck at the height of the battle of Shiloh as fleeing survivors mingled with arriving reinforcements. *Library of Congress*

Hampton Roads on March 8, 1862, few headline-grabbing conflicts had erupted in the East since the previous fall.

In the Western Theater, though, Federal forces had not lain dormant during the winter. On February 6, 1862, the Federal brown-water navy captured Fort Henry, and on February 16, Major General Ulysses S. Grant forced the surrender of the Confederates at nearby Fort Donelson. The fall of the two forts, twelve miles apart, opened the Tennessee and Cumberland Rivers to further Federal conquest.

Nashville, situated along the Cumberland River, became immediately vulnerable. Citizens panicked, and the Confederate government and Southern press alike lamented the imminent fall of such a major Southern city. Critics began calling for the removal of the Confederate commander responsible for protecting the Tennessee capital: General Albert Sidney Johnston.

However, this was exactly the kind of calamity Johnston had fretted about for months. As the second-most senior general in the Confederacy, Johnston had been placed in command of the Western Department in September 1861, tasked with defending everything from the Allegheny Mountains to the Mississippi River. He keenly recognized the untenable nature of this position. "As my forces at neither this nor either of the other points threatened are more than sufficient to meet the force in front," he wrote to Richmond from Bowling Green, "I cannot weaken either until the object of the enemy is fully pronounced."[4] That is, rather than take the initiative, he had to wait for Federals to make the first move so he could know where to concentrate against them. Grant, who described Albert Sidney Johnston as "a man of high character and ability," nonetheless judged him "vacillating and undecided in his actions" for adhering to such a passive strategy.[5]

The quick, successive falls of Fort Henry and Fort Donelson proved the weakness of the larger Confederate strategy and endangered the rest of Johnston's forces, still trying to concentrate. "I must save this army," he declared, crossing from the north side of the Cumberland River at Nashville and moving deeper into Tennessee's interior, just two days before Federals captured the city itself. It seemed an ignoble retreat for the man once hailed as the Confederacy's top general. "It was impossible for any General to have defended the line from Columbus to Bowling Green with the forces at the command of Genl. Johnston," one of Johnston's top subordinates wrote days later, but morale in the army was still dismal.[6]

Despite the lamentation, Confederate president Jefferson Davis continued his support of Johnston and gave him greater flexibility in conducting his defense. Johnston used that new mandate to regroup scattered forces from throughout Kentucky and Tennessee, consolidating them at the vital rail center of Corinth, Mississippi. Grant, with the Tennessee River now open to him, decided to move against the rail junction—but Johnston, now boasting forty-five thousand men, decided to move against Grant first.

The result: the battle of Shiloh.

The new vigor with which Johnston moved, the new strength at his disposal, and the prestige of his reputation as the foremost officer in Confederate uniform all buoyed Confederate hope—and that hope colored what happened next. As historian Gregory A. Mertz explains in the following essay, Johnston was mortally wounded at the height of the battle, creating one of the most intriguing turning points of the war.

Had Johnston lived, would the battle have played out differently, as Lost Cause historians have contended? This idea, commonly known as the "Lost Opportunity," makes up one of the few Western Theater components of the larger Lost Cause mythology. Because of Johnston's death, they argue, Confederates did not press their attack vigorously enough at the end of the first day of battle, giving nearly defeated Federals time to regroup and take the initiative. The Confederates thus lost a major opportunity at Shiloh.

But, as Mertz asks, has Johnston's reputation been overplayed in the service of his martyrdom? Was his death at Shiloh really a turning point?

Ulysses S. Grant, writing with a victor's hindsight, certainly didn't think so. "[Johnston's] contemporaries at West Point and officers generally who came to know him personally later and who remained on our side, expected him to provide the most formidable man to meet that the Confederacy would produce," Grant wrote in his memoirs. *"I do not question the personal courage of General Johnston, or his ability. But he did not win the distinction predicted for him by many of his friends. He did prove that as a general he was overestimated."*[7]

Johnston's death perhaps overshadows Shiloh's other turning-point significance, however. "The South never smiled again after Shiloh," novelist George Washington Cable later professed.[8] *For the North, it provided a different kind of change of heart. "Up to the battle of Shiloh,"* Grant explained in his memoirs, *"I, as well as thousands of other citizens, believed that the rebellion against the Government would collapse suddenly and soon, if a decisive victory could be gained over any of its armies." After the battle, though, "I gave up all idea of saving the Union except by total conquest."*[9]

Shiloh marks a turning point, too, because it ratcheted up the scale of battle. Engagements like Bull Run, with its 60,680 participants, would no longer be the norm. Shiloh pitted 110,053 men against each other in a new level of slaughter. "The struggle had been so long, so desperate and bloody, that the survivors seemed exhausted and nerveless," William T. Sherman wrote in his memoirs; *"we appreciated the value of the victory, but realized also its great cost of life."*[10]

Ironic for a location whose name meant "place of peace."

The men who still rest there atop the bluffs, overlooking the slow-moving river, hold their peace in agreement.

Defeated Victory: Albert Sidney Johnston's Death at Shiloh

Gregory A. Mertz

An impressive Confederate monument sits on a knoll overlooking a hollow where about twenty-two hundred Federal soldiers surrendered around 5:30 p.m. on the first day of the two-day battle of Shiloh. Designer and sculptor Frederick C. Hibbard struggled to come up with a theme. "The subject was a difficult one," he explained, "for the Battle of Shiloh did not result in a Confederate victory." Hibbard concluded that the best way to memorialize the ten thousand Confederate casualties of Shiloh was to "use symbolic figures typifying the reasons for the defeat."[11]

The central figures of the monument are three women called "Defeated Victory." The woman representing the Confederacy is flanked by two women hauntingly cloaked in hooded robes, representing Death and Night. Death came to the Confederate army commander, and with Night came Federal reinforcements.

The bust of the dead Confederate army leader at Shiloh is carved into the front and center of the granite monument, just beneath the "Defeated Victory" trio. General Albert Sidney Johnston lost his life about nine hours into the battle. At the time of his death, about 2:30 p.m. on April 6, on the first day of battle, the Confederate army had achieved a measured amount of success in launching a surprise attack on the Federal army. Hubbard's theme of the monument—and a prominent interpretation of the battle of Shiloh from its earlier historiography—is that had Johnston not been killed, he would have defeated the Federal army before the massive reinforcements arrived. Those reinforcements and the decisions of Johnston's successor, this interpretation

54

Erected in 1917 by the United Daughters of the Confederacy, the Confederate monument at Shiloh was designed and sculpted by Frederick C. Hibbard. The central group, collectively known as "Defeated Victory," represents the Confederacy, Death, and Night. *Photo by Chris Mackowski*

proclaims, turned Shiloh from the Confederate success of April 6 into the Confederate defeat of April 7. Johnston's death is viewed as the turning point of the battle, and the loss of this highly regarded general may be seen as a turning point in the war as well.[12]

Historians who have attempted to address the question of whether Johnston's death was a vital blow to the Confederacy cite the limited length of service upon which to base such a critical assessment and to fully judge Johnston's talent at such a high level. While it is true that Johnston had been in command for only a short time, the battle of Shiloh is still an excellent case study to evaluate the general's capabilities. It was the most significant test that any soldier had yet been subjected to in the young Civil War. The losses at the battle exceeded the losses America had suffered in all of its wars prior to the Civil War—more than the casualties incurred in the American Revolution, the War of 1812, and the Mexican-American War combined. Shiloh was a battle unlike any that the soldiers upon that field had ever experienced, from the privates in the ranks to the highest generals.[13]

Born in Washington, Kentucky, on February 2, 1803, Albert Sidney Johnston would be called by his middle name by family and friends. A young Sidney decided to pursue the career of his father, a physician, and attended Transylvania University in Lexington, Kentucky. There he became friends with a younger fellow Kentuckian, Jefferson Davis. But his career path changed when he secured an appointment to the United States Military Academy at West Point, graduating in 1826. Davis also eventually attended West Point, forming an even deeper bond with Johnston over the two years they both studied at the academy.

Between his years at West Point and the outbreak of the Civil War, Johnston had amassed an impressive list of wide-ranging military experiences and accomplishments. Johnston held the staff position of adjutant during the Black Hawk War. After resigning from the U.S. Army to care for his ailing wife, he returned to military service after her death, this time for the Republic of Texas. When Texas president Sam Houston appointed Johnston to replace Felix Huston as the senior general in the Texan army, Huston felt that his honor had been tarnished and challenged Johnston to a duel. Though Johnston was not the querulous type, he indicated that he felt that the dignity of the republic was at stake and accepted the challenge. On February 5, 1837, Johnston was wounded in the hip during the duel, disabling him such that he could not take command of the army. Johnston was later appointed as the Texas secretary of war.

Johnston returned to the U.S. Army and was an inspector general during the Mexican War, serving Zachary Taylor with distinction at the battle of Monterrey. While close friend Jefferson Davis held the post of secretary of war in the cabinet of President Franklin Pierce, Johnston was given the distinction of being the colonel commanding the newly created Second U.S. Cavalry Regiment in 1855. Johnston led the 1857 Mormon Expedition, earning the brevet rank of brigadier general. On the eve of the Civil War, he commanded the Department of the Pacific, headquartered in San Francisco.

When Texas seceded from the Union, Johnston resigned his commission in the U.S. Army. "Texas has made me a rebel twice," Johnston remarked.[14] He began the arduous overland trip back east to offer his services to the Confederate army and became, as his biographer Charles Roland termed it, a "soldier of three republics"—the United States, the Texas Republic, and the Confederacy.[15]

On September 10, 1861, Johnston was named commander of Confederate Department No. 2, which extended from the Allegheny Mountains west to the Indian Territory (present-day Oklahoma). When Davis announced the first five full generals for service in the Confederate army, Albert Sidney Johnston was made the highest-ranking general in the field. Only Adjutant General Samuel Cooper, holding a staff position, was senior to Johnston; Johnston, meanwhile, was senior to Robert E. Lee, Joseph E. Johnston, and P. G. T. Beauregard. Sidney Johnston's high ranking reflected the high esteem he had been held in throughout the prewar U.S. Army: with the exception of the Federal general-in-chief Winfield Scott, he had been considered by most to be the premier soldier in the service.[16]

Johnston's department not only was large but also possessed any number of potential targets that incursions by the Federal army might choose as objectives. The Mississippi River was an obvious avenue of Federal advance. However, the Tennessee and Cumberland Rivers also offered excellent invasion routes and the means to flank any Confederate defenses on the all-important Mississippi. The mountainous region in eastern Tennessee was known to be a Unionist stronghold. Much of Lincoln's early war strategy was to secure areas of Union support. It was not unrealistic to anticipate a significant Federal movement into the eastern part of Kentucky and Tennessee in the vicinity of the Cumberland Gap.[17]

As long as the Federal army continued to have its forces poised to threaten all of these points, it was logical that Johnston and Davis post units in defense of each. Furthermore, politicians throughout the South heavily influenced

Davis's policy, demanding that he provide protection for all the places they represented. The resulting cordon defense consisted of small forces distributed among multiple points along the Confederate border and coastline—regardless of whether the location was vulnerable to Federal attack or occupation.

Militarily, the Confederates tried to defend the entire nation, and Johnston tried to defend his entire department. But military strategist and philosopher Frederick the Great once stated, "He who attempts to defend too much, defends nothing." That axiom was about to prove true for the Confederacy.[18]

The strategy employed in Johnston's department in the winter of 1861–62 was one of protecting a long line across southern Kentucky and northern Tennessee, with relatively small forces posted at several places—namely Columbus, Kentucky, on the Mississippi River; Fort Henry, Tennessee, on the Tennessee River; Fort Donelson, Tennessee, on the Cumberland River; Bowling Green, Kentucky, along a rail line north of Nashville; and the Cumberland Gap. Johnston's line running from the Cumberland Gap to western Arkansas was some five hundred miles in length and, when Johnston took command, was defended by fewer than forty thousand soldiers.

Johnston established headquarters at Bowling Green, near the center of his line and close to the northern bounds of his department. On September 16, less than a week after Johnston took command, he wrote to Davis, "We have not over half the armed forces that are now likely to be required for our security against disaster." Johnston's prewar experience demonstrated that he favored offensive warfare, but with the force at hand, he had to be content with trying to defend his department until such time when taking the offensive was feasible. Johnston requested reinforcements.[19]

Efforts to obtain additional troops proved futile. Instead of providing the needed reinforcements, Davis sent Johnston the Confederacy's junior full general, P. G. T. Beauregard. Davis and Beauregard had quarreled, and the general thought the president was putting him in exile. As a hero of the firing on Fort Sumter on April 12, 1861, and the man who effectively started the Civil War, as well as field commander of the victorious Confederate forces at the first large battle of the war at First Manassas or Bull Run on July 21, 1861, Beauregard felt insulted to be junior to Johnston, a general who had not yet contributed anything to the Confederate cause. Whether Davis thought that he was simply ridding himself of a problematic general or whether he believed that Beauregard would be of substantive help to his longtime friend, the president must have assumed that Johnston had the gravitas and temperament to be able to work with Beauregard.[20]

On February 4, 1862, Beauregard met with Johnston at Bowling Green, where Johnston welcomed him and took him into his confidence. Beauregard had brought with him a proposal, and Johnston welcomed hearing of it. At the time, two sizable Federal armies were poised to break the status quo of the last six months. An army under Major General Ulysses S. Grant challenged Confederate forces at Forts Henry and Donelson, while another army under Major General Don Carlos Buell confronted Bowling Green. Beauregard's plan called for a concentration of Confederate forces at Forts Henry and Donelson, which might first destroy Grant's army and then turn on Buell's forces. But when Beauregard discovered the true state of affairs in the department and the weakness of the Confederate forces, he immediately abandoned the idea and was so disgusted by his plight that he wanted to return to Virginia. Johnston convinced him to stay.[21]

Johnston's ability to work with difficult subordinates is one of the factors that marked him as a general capable of greatness. After Johnston's death, the army would spend much of its tenure under the leadership of Braxton Bragg. This period was fraught with bickering between Bragg and his corps commanders. One of the key reasons for the eventual failures of the Army of Tennessee was Bragg's inability to effectively work with his subordinates. Robert E. Lee, in contrast, had the ability to soothe things over between cantankerous subordinates, most notably Thomas J. "Stonewall" Jackson and A. P. Hill, which is one of the many reasons he was so successful with his Army of Northern Virginia.[22]

For Beauregard to step into Johnston's department with a plan for what to do without taking a moment to assess the situation was an act of arrogance that should have irritated even the most magnanimous person. Then when Beauregard wanted to leave and head back to Virginia, even the most fair-minded individual would feel it good riddance. Yet Johnston was able to put Beauregard's talents to relatively good service, though not without difficulties. Johnston would also be able to work well with the acerbic Bragg.[23]

It is very difficult to assess the relationship between Beauregard and Johnston because most of what we have to draw upon are the writings of Beauregard. He basically indicates that everything positive the Confederate army ever did was his idea, not Johnston's, and that everything negative the army ever did was something he counseled Johnston to do differently.[24]

Almost immediately after Beauregard's arrival, activity in the Western Theater of the war escalated. Grant moved against Fort Henry, and the poorly situated fort quickly fell on February 6. The next day, Johnston reluctantly ordered the evacuation of the entire Kentucky-Tennessee line. Johnston viewed the fall of Fort Henry as more than just the loss of one point—he felt the entire Confederate position had been jeopardized. However, at the same time Johnston had decided to evacuate his line, he also determined to reinforce Fort Donelson with part, but not all, of the readily available Confederate forces and gave the senior officer, Brigadier General John B. Floyd, discretion on whether to defend the fort itself.

A decision to concentrate all of his forces at Fort Donelson, as Beauregard had suggested, would have been a logical option. To carry out his plan to evacuate the entire line, including the Fort Donelson position, while unpopular and harmful to the morale of the Confederacy, might also have been a prudent call. But the partial reinforcement of Fort Donelson and not going in person to the most-threatened point of his department turned out to be, arguably, the greatest mistake Johnston ever made as a soldier.[25]

Grant moved on to Fort Donelson and found it to be a more substantial fortification than Fort Henry. On February 15, Floyd informed Johnston that Confederates at Fort Donelson had won a "victory complete and glorious," and newspapers reported the same positive account. But before dawn on February 16, Johnston's sleep was disturbed with the disastrous news that the Fort Donelson garrison had surrendered.[26]

When the Confederates fell back, they not only abandoned Kentucky but also left most of Tennessee open to Federal occupation. A delegation sent by the stunned and angered Tennessee legislature to meet with Davis called upon him to replace Johnston, "because he is no general." The department commander had indeed made mistakes, but Davis would not abandon Johnston. "If [Johnston] is not a general, we had better give up the war," proclaimed Davis, "for we have no general."[27]

Besides sustaining his confidence in Johnston, Davis made a change that would substantially aid the department commander. Many prominent soldiers, who made up an informal group collectively referred to as the "Western Concentration Bloc," felt that the Confederate heartland was of such importance that an army should be amassed there with the capability of overwhelming one of the Federal forces operating in the West. Such an army, they argued, should be comparable in size to the army the Confederates had formed earlier in the war operating in Virginia. Johnston would no longer be expected to try to defend an extended line across the entire department. He could focus his attention where he felt it was most needed and have the ability to mass a standing army that would have the strength to contest the armies the Federals had assembled and sent into Tennessee.[28]

The concentration point selected for the formation of this army—which would be named the Army of the Mississippi—was Corinth, Mississippi, an important rail junction in the northern part of the state. In addition to the troops who had pulled back from the front line of defense at Columbus, Bowling Green, and eastern Kentucky, troops from New Orleans and the Florida panhandle were rushing for Corinth. Johnston seemed to be unsure just what the respective roles should be for himself and Beauregard regarding this new army forming within his department. Johnston offered command of the army to Beauregard while retaining for himself the broader departmental control.[29]

The decision of offering army command to Beauregard is a puzzling one. One of the potential lessons to be gained from the fiasco at Fort Donelson was the need for Johnston to be at the most critical point of his department, at hand to make those decisions and adjustments himself. Yet he was willing to give Beauregard a free hand at directing the pending battle by occupying a department headquarters some distance from the field of battle. Beauregard, whose accounts of his encounters with Johnston must be read judiciously, indicated that Johnston felt that the army had lost confidence in him and that it would be in the best interest of the nation for Beauregard to lead the army.[30]

But Beauregard declined Johnston's offer to command the army—a surprisingly modest gesture from a soldier with such a huge ego and who felt slighted at being placed junior to Johnston. Johnston then assigned Beauregard as second in command, detailing him to organize the forces converging on Corinth into an army. Johnston also instructed Beauregard to draft the orders for the march and the attack upon the Federal army at Pittsburg Landing, Tennessee, twenty-two miles from Corinth.[31]

The Federal force at Pittsburg Landing, located on the Tennessee River, consisted of some forty-eight thousand troops in an army commanded by Ulysses S. Grant. The army had moved upstream, or south, on the Tennessee River from Fort Henry and had bivouacked as far as four miles out from the river landing near the Shiloh meeting house. Grant's instructions were to avoid a general engagement with the Confederates until another Federal army of twenty-four thousand under Don Carlos Buell, advancing from Nashville, 120 miles northeast of Pittsburg Landing, united with Grant. Then department head Major General Henry W. Halleck would come down from St. Louis, Missouri, and lead the combined forces against the Confederates at Corinth.

The Federal high command was of the belief that the Confederates at Corinth were there to defend the railroad junction and did not anticipate that they might be a menace to the troops at Shiloh.[32]

The Confederates were aware of Buell's approach, and Johnston was determined to take the forty-four thousand men on hand and strike Grant before the Federals could assemble all seventy-two thousand together. Though no timetable was actually given in the orders distributed to Confederate commanders, Johnston apparently wanted to attack on April 4. Inexperience in marching, confusing orders, poor roads, and bad weather all conspired to delay the Confederate advance. The battle would not be able to take place until April 6.[33]

Johnston planned to assault the Federal left flank and drive the Yankees into the swampy streams on the north and northwest edge of their bivouac. Johnston also desired that when the army formed to attack, three of the four corps that Beauregard had organized would form side by side so each corps commander would have a limited area in his front to control and would have reserves from his own corps in the rear ranks to be directed wherever the corps commander chose. On April 3, Johnston informed Davis of the alignment and his objective. But when the orders were issued, Johnston discovered that Beauregard had stacked the corps up one behind the other—a vastly inferior placement. Johnston decided, though, that it was too late to change the formations; the Confederates would have to make do with the alignment. Johnston's problems with Beauregard were only getting started.[34]

On the evening before the battle, Johnston found out that his highest-ranking officers had severe doubts about the planned attack. They argued that the Federal army had surely noticed the Confederates because of the slow march and the large amount of time consumed in the alignment of the troops. They also thought the Yankees had doubtless heard the cheering of the undisciplined Southern troops and the shots fired by the Confederate soldiers who wanted to see if, after marching in rain, their wet guns still worked. "Now they will be entrenched to the eyes," predicted Beauregard.[35]

Two months earlier, Johnston had been shocked by subordinates who confidently telegraphed him of victory at Fort Donelson, only to completely change their minds and surrender the fort just a few hours later. Now he faced another faction of subordinates who had earlier supported an attack at Shiloh, only to suddenly turn pessimistic and advocate a march back to Corinth. Johnston was evidently annoyed. The conversation was apparently short and ended "a little abruptly" by the army commander. "We shall attack them at daylight tomorrow," Johnston announced to his command team and walked away. Some indicated that Johnston declared that a retreat would cause the morale of the troops to plummet as much as if defeated.[36]

While striding away from the meeting, Johnston spoke with one of his staff officers, stating, "I would fight them if they were a million. They can present no greater front between these two creeks than we can, and the more men they crowd in there, the worse we can make it for them."[37]

Though a good working relationship with subordinates is a worthy trait, a command structure run by majority rule is doomed to fail. It has been argued that whenever a formal council of war was ever held during the Civil War, it invariably adopted the most conservative option available. Johnston was wise not to engage in a lengthy diatribe with his generals. At such a critical moment in the campaign, the strong and decisive stance of the army commander was required to keep the army focused on the important task at hand and not to divert any more attention to an alternate plan. Johnston demonstrated some important characteristics that night that would help distinguish him as someone whose value to the Confederate service would be enormous—both on the field of Shiloh as well as in battles to come.

The declaration "I would fight them if they were a million" is frequently quoted as evidence of Johnston's resolve to fight. On the surface, the statement can be considered irrational and stubborn—that Johnston, with forty-four thousand troops, would recklessly attack a million men the next morning no matter what. But putting the statement in context with the rest of what he said, and comparing it with similar comments he made that evening, provides a different meaning. Though Johnston had an imperfect map of the battlefield and an incomplete placement of troops in the Federal camps, he was aware that the Federal army rested between a pair of water courses—the Owl Creek–Snake Creek drainage to the north of the Federal army and Lick Creek to the south. The Federal army, sandwiched between the creeks, could not mass any more troops on the front line to confront the Confederate attack than the space permitted. Knowing that the Federals were still confined to that narrow space on the eve of the battle, Johnston was certain his enemy could not achieve a superior advantage on the front line.

To another member of Johnston's staff, the general expressed similar sentiments that evening. "There is Lick Creek on my right, and Owl Creek on my left. These creeks effectually protect my flanks. I have men enough to cover the front, and the more men they crowd into this small space between me and the river, the better for me and the worse for them. I think we will hammer them beyond doubt," calculated Johnston.[38]

Despite Johnston's tenacity of the night before, it did not settle the matter with his subordinates. On the morning of April 6, as a group of generals gathered, Johnston discovered that Beauregard again renewed his opposition to making the attack. The cadre of generals who would not let the matter rest may have initiated a pattern that would long plague that army. Under Bragg's tenure in particular, his subordinates, including some of the same men gathered at the Shiloh conferences, were noted not only for their squabbling but also for following orders they disagreed with in a lackluster manner or worse. While it would be an oversimplification to declare that a precedent was set at Shiloh in which it became acceptable for corps commanders to openly criticize the army commander, similar behavior in the future would affect this army like venom. Perhaps the persistent and repeated criticism from Beauregard and other corps commanders affected the role Johnston selected for himself during the battle.[39]

Soon after Beauregard rekindled his objection to proceeding with the battle plans, the first exchange of gunfire was heard. It was about 5:00 a.m. The battle of Shiloh had begun. Johnston then stated the obvious, ending the debate: "The battle has opened, gentlemen; it is too late to change our dispositions." Johnston mounted his horse, Fire-Eater, and informed his staff, "Tonight, we will water our horses in the Tennessee River."[40]

Johnston also announced that he, as army commander, was heading for the battlefront with his staff, directing the battle and making key decisions as the battle developed. Beauregard, as second in command, was to stay in the rear and direct troops to the front. Evidence suggests that this arrangement was not revealed until the very morning of the battle. Many have argued that the roles should have been reversed—that Johnston should have stayed in the rear in order to maintain overall control of the battlefield and Beauregard should have gone to the front. Critics of the arrangement observed that at the battle of First Manassas—where Beauregard's army merged with Joseph E. Johnston's army—Beauregard had already gained the experience of directing the battle at the front, while Johnston took on the rear-echelon responsibilities. At Shiloh, Beauregard would play the opposite role from that which he had proven he could do effectively.[41]

The proper place of high-ranking officers in the Civil War era has often been debated. Examples of army or corps commanders at the front being killed or wounded in action abound, supporting the belief that commanders should stay in the rear. Yet the war also contains cases of army and corps commanders appearing at the front in the thick of the heaviest combat, rallying troops and making vital decisions at moments when time was of the essence. Some of the greatest and most famous deeds of the generals held in highest regard entail instances when they stepped in to provide leadership when it was desperately needed. Stonewall Jackson rallying his broken line at Cedar Mountain and Robert E. Lee attempting to lead his men into counterattacks at the Wilderness and Spotsylvania Court House are such examples. Generals in the rear cannot react to those types of situations.

Johnston never had an opportunity to explain his reasoning, but one cannot help but wonder if the lack of confidence that his second in command had in the chance of success played a role. Beauregard's objections stemmed from the conviction that the plan hinged upon the element of surprise and his belief that the enemy was certainly aware of the Confederate presence. The initial Confederate attacks would surely demonstrate whether the Federals were ready and waiting for the Confederates and whether Beauregard's concerns had any validity. Perhaps Johnston felt that directing that first wave of battle and making sure it achieved the attention of someone completely invested in the attack was a way to guarantee that the cynicism of those generals who favored retreat would dissipate. Once Beauregard learned that the Confederates had indeed gained some element of surprise, he might effectively and even enthusiastically carry out his duties of funneling troops and supplies to the front. Should Beauregard have been positioned at the front, he would have had the opportunity to see his self-prophecy in any pocket of Federal resistance encountered. For this reason alone, Johnston's position at the front was the best place for him to be in this particular situation.

The commander of the troops occupying the bulk of Johnston's front line, Major General William J. Hardee, had not been at the evening conference, and it is not clear whether he favored a retreat. But the commander of the troops on the far right of the front line and of the entire second line, Major General Braxton Bragg, was on Beauregard's side. Bragg's troops on the far right had the vital role of turning the Federal left flank and pushing the Federal army northwestward into the swollen Owl Creek. The degree of success the Confederates achieved at Shiloh was dependent upon the ability of the Confederates to drive the left end of the Federal line away from the protection of Lick Creek and cut in behind the center of the Federal position. Since Confederate triumph hinged upon achievements of the Confederate right, the Confederate right was where Johnston should have been.

Whether Johnston went to the front to assure that key decisions would not be made by subordinates who favored retreat and may not have had their heart in the attack, or whether he wanted to make sure he was at the critical point on the field regardless of the level of faith they had in his plan, Johnston made a logical choice in making his presence at the front.

Thus the die was cast for Albert Sidney Johnston's first and only battle as an army commander.

We would not entertain the idea that Johnston's death might be considered a turning point had his successors been successful, but neither Beauregard nor Bragg nor Joseph E. Johnston nor John B. Hood led this army to consistent or even frequent victories. The general whose tenure with the army was the most substantive was Braxton Bragg, who did not display any of the key qualities that Albert Sidney Johnston possessed and displayed in the weeks leading up to and during the first nine hours of the battle of Shiloh. Whereas Johnston proved to be able to work with difficult subordinates and was able to have them positively contribute to the army, Bragg noticeably failed in that category.

The list of underlings who did not get along with Bragg was extensive. On the occasion after the battle of Murfreesboro when Bragg invited his subordinates to confirm their loyalty and support of him, division commander Major General Patrick Cleburne did just the opposite. After consultation with his brigade commanders, Cleburne wrote that "they unite with me in . . . high appreciation of your patriotism and gallantry," yet they lamented that they also had to tell Bragg, "You do not possess the confidence of the army." Bragg did not resign upon learning that his officers and men did not have faith in him, nor did he know how to win over their confidence or how to get productivity out of his disgruntled subordinates. One of Bragg's biographers, Judith L. Hallock, stated that he "lacked the tact and diplomacy necessary to meld [his] subordinates into a cohesive, cooperative unit."[42]

Even changes in high command, including bringing in generals who had served in the East, such as Lieutenant General Daniel H. Hill and Lieutenant General James Longstreet to command a corps and a wing at Chickamauga, only served to lengthen the already long list of subordinates who despised Bragg. After serving under Bragg for the first time, Longstreet made a comparison between Bragg and the Confederacy's most successful army commander, writing to President Davis that Bragg was not as active in the field as Robert E. Lee. In comparison, once the battle of Shiloh got underway, Albert Sidney Johnston would indeed be active in the field. One of the ways in which he responded when so many of his generals expressed doubt on the evening before and morning of the first day at Shiloh was to personally go to the front and take a very active, personal role in the battle.[43]

As Johnston's attack wave rolled forward, it immediately clashed with two of the five Federal divisions clustered between Shiloh Church and Pittsburg Landing. The Confederate right struck the division of Brigadier General Benjamin M. Prentiss, while the Confederate left ran headlong into the division under Brigadier General William T. Sherman. Johnston may have initially observed the attack upon Sherman, but he was soon heading for the Confederate right. Upon learning that the going had been tough to his right, Johnston ordered reinforcements in that sector and started to lead the brigade of Brigadier General Alexander P. Stewart until he decided he needed to get there more quickly and rode on ahead.[44]

The Confederate right succeeding in driving Prentiss back, and Johnston rode into the abandoned camp of the Eighteenth Wisconsin. There, Johnston encountered some of his men plundering the captured camps rather than pursuing the enemy. The general instructed them that such was not the purpose of the attack and sent the men back to the front. Johnston observed a young officer with his arms full of plunder. Johnston criticized the officer, but apparently feeling he had been too harsh, the general grabbed a tin cup from the top of a table that was within his reach from the saddle. "Let this be my share of the spoils to-day," Johnston told him.[45]

This simple episode is perhaps the best of several that demonstrated Johnston's relationship with the citizen-soldier. The officer whom Johnston had scolded was most likely a volunteer officer who had been a civilian just a few months earlier. Tens of thousands of Johnston's men were new to this harsh business of war, and it would take time and experience for them to learn their duties. An effective Civil War general understood how to deal with the citizen-soldier and appreciated the learning curve necessary before that citizen-soldier gained the proficiency of a professional soldier. Johnston had that skill.

Not every professional soldier came to this realization. At Shiloh, Braxton Bragg would send a brigade of Louisiana and Arkansas troops in repeated attacks against a Federal position aptly nicknamed the "Hornets' Nest." In Bragg's opinion, the attacks did not fail because he had sent too few troops against a strong position in a frontal attack. The attack failed, reasoned Bragg as he wrote his wife, for "a want of confidence in their leader Gibson." Colonel Randall L. Gibson was a twenty-nine-year-old, Yale-educated officer with no military experienced who bravely led his men into battle and whose men followed him—many to their death. His men hardly lacked confidence in him, yet Bragg declared Gibson "an arrant coward."[46]

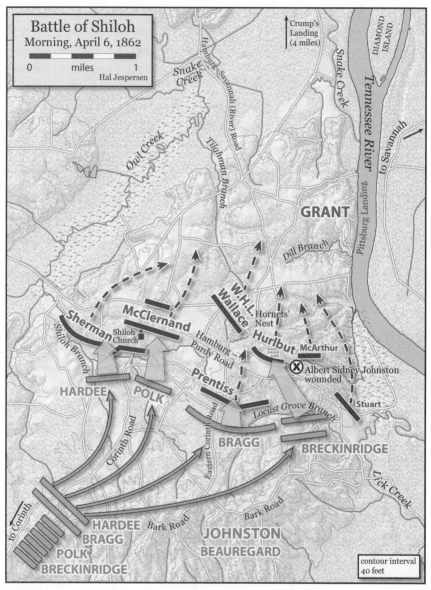

Battle of Shiloh
Morning, April 6, 1862

0   miles   1
Hal Jespersen

Crump's
Landing
(4 miles)

DIAMOND
ISLAND

Tennessee River

to Savannah

Snake Creek

Hamburg-Savannah (River) Road

Owl Creek

Tilghman Branch

Snake Creek

GRANT

Dill Branch

Pittsburg Landing

W.H.L. Wallace

Hornets' Nest

Sherman

McClernand

Shiloh Church

Shiloh Branch

Hamburg–Purdy Road

Hurlbut

McArthur

Albert Sidney Johnston wounded

HARDEE

POLK

Prentiss

Locust Grove Branch

Stuart

Corinth Road

Eastern Corinth Road

BRAGG

BRECKINRIDGE

Lick Creek

to Corinth

HARDEE
BRAGG
POLK
BRECKINRIDGE

Bark Road

Bark Road

JOHNSTON
BEAUREGARD

contour interval
40 feet

Battle of Shiloh. As the Confederate column deployed into battle, it spread out across a wide front. The Federal flanks, initially unprepared for the assault, folded, although the center of the Federal line—which later became known as the "Hornets' Nest"—held out for hours, buying time for the rest of the army to regroup in the rear. Albert Sidney Johnston, trying to break the impasse, was clipped in the leg by a stray bullet and bled to death. *Map by Hal Jespersen*

While in Prentiss's camp, Johnston made one of his most significant decisions of the battle, and one that again justified the need for his presence on the front line of his right flank. Apparently believing he had gained the Federal left flank, he redirected his troops, swinging them around to push north. At about 9:30 a.m., he began a thrust that, he reasoned, would shove Prentiss's and Sherman's men into the flooded streambed of Owl Creek. His presence at that point of the battlefield—rather than the rear—had been justified. Johnston's plan *appeared* to be working beautifully.[47]

Johnston's attack contributed to Sherman's retreat from his camps. But Sherman did not retreat in the direction Johnston had hoped. Rather than being driven into Owl Creek, Sherman's troops had been able to fall back toward the Union supply base at Pittsburg Landing.

About the same time Johnston was prying Sherman out of his position, he learned of a reconnaissance that had located the actual Federal left flank. It was much closer to the Tennessee River than the scouts who had reconnoitered prior to the battle had been able to ascertain. Once again, it was fortuitous for Johnston that he was able to learn and react to this development right away because of his place at the front. Johnston again redirected troops to this location, and by noon Confederates were attacking the true left flank of the Federal army.

The Federal troops who had been driven from their camps had been joined by other troops coming up from the rear and had taken up the most formidable position of the day. The center of the Federal line contained a slightly rutted wagon road that would come to be known as the Sunken Road. Throughout the day, Johnston had been among the troops, sending looters and stragglers back to the front, rallying the troops who had stalled, and encouraging men about to attack. As Brigadier General John S. Bowen's brigade prepared to assault, Johnston rode along his line. Utilizing the tin cup that was his share of the spoils of the day, he tapped it on the tips of the bayonets of the men as he rode by, admonishing them, "These must do the work. . . . We must use the bayonet." As the battle neared the nine-hour mark and his troops grew weary, such inspiration was an important contribution. The great generals of the Civil War recognized when situations called for personal leadership and for them to set an example or inspire the men. Johnston led the attack himself and was in the thick of the fight, pointing out to a member of his staff that the sole of his boot had been struck. The attacks succeeded, and the Federal left began to crumble.[48]

During one of those attacks, Sidney Johnston was struck in the back of his right leg. The minié ball that struck him was from a .577 Enfield rifle. Some ten thousand of those imported British rifles were received and distributed to Johnston's men shortly before the battle; Johnston may have been shot by one of his own men. Johnston may not have even realized he had been wounded because feeling in that leg had been dulled by the wound he had sustained in his hip during the duel with Felix Huston more than twenty years earlier. An aide found Johnston reeling in his saddle and helped the general reach the protection of a nearby ravine. Taking off the general's boot, they discovered it filled with blood: the minié ball had cut an artery. By 2:30 p.m., all signs of life were gone from the body of Sidney Johnston.[49]

About 3:00 p.m., Beauregard was informed that responsibility for command of the army now rested upon his shoulders. The fighting that Johnston had been directing prior to his mortal wounding, in conjunction with other simultaneous attacks by the Confederate left, had turned the flanks of the Federal position and had cut off the line of retreat of the blue-clad soldiers fighting in the Sunken Road. At about 5:30 p.m., Prentiss and some twenty-two hundred men surrendered to the Confederates. Many of the Confederates thought the battle was over.

Dealing with thousands of prisoners took time and diverted some Confederate soldiers from the continuing the fight. Ammunition was low. Troops were exhausted. Many were hungry and were aware that nearby Federal camps now in Confederate hands offered a tempting sanctuary. For most of the Confederate army, the April 6 battle came to a close with the capture of the Sunken Road.

The Federal forces that had managed to withdraw had fallen back to a position that would become known as Grant's Last Line. It was not only the last position held by the Federals on April 6 but also the last position that could be held that would also secure Federal possession of Pittsburg Landing— the Federal link to supplies, Buell's reinforcements, and the evacuation of wounded. Should Grant's Last Line fall, there was no more space and no more defensible ground between that line and Pittsburg Landing. Johnston's objective of driving the enemy into the swamps north of the Federal camps would have an excellent chance of reaching fruition if Grant's Last Line fell.

The Confederate army indeed attacked Grant's Last Line on the evening of April 6, but the attack consisted of only a fraction of the army. The terrain was some of the most challenging of the entire battlefield, the last line was bristling with cannon, and, being so close to the river, naval gunboats could rake the Confederate line as well. In the only attack on Grant's Last Line, most Confederate soldiers did not even get close enough to come under infantry fire.[50]

Beauregard suspended operations for the day. He pulled his men back to the captured Federal camps so they might try to escape the fire of the gunboats, get some shelter for the night, reorganize and resupply, and complete the victory on April 7. But the night of April 6–7 brought Federal reinforcements, and the battle of April 7 was a reverse of the battle of April 6. This time the Federals attacked. This time the Confederates fought defensively, launching counterattacks when that tactic looked promising. This time the Confederates reluctantly withdrew until the Federals had regained all that had been lost on the previous day. The second day and the battle as a whole was a Federal victory.

The Confederate monument at Shiloh would have us believe that, if Johnston had lived, he would have won the battle, which contributes to the "Lost Cause" explanation of the Civil War. The Lost Cause interpretation grew out of the need for soldiers and citizens of the former Confederacy to be able to view their defeat in the Civil War with honor. Important principles of the Lost Cause include the high integrity of its leaders, who were disappointed by subordinates, and the Confederate forces being overwhelmed by superior resources of the Federal forces. That Federal reinforcements arrived is not debatable. The Lost Cause rationalization of the battle points to the officers who wanted to retreat on the night before and morning of the battle and to Beauregard's decision to end the fighting on the evening of April 6 as examples of Johnston not receiving the proper support and dedication to his battle plan that he deserved. This aspect of the Lost Cause is questionable.

A prominent interpretation of the battle has been that, if Johnston had lived, he would have attacked Grant's Last Line with more resources and would have been successful. While it is impossible to know what Johnston would have done—much less know whether he would have been successful at it—virtually all of the recent Shiloh historians agree that any reasonable scenario for assaulting Grant's Last Line would have held little chance of succeeding. There were not enough troops, there was not enough ammunition at the front, and there was not enough daylight for the Confederates to take the position. The Confederate soldiers were too exhausted and too disorganized and the terrain too steep, too open, and subjected to too much Federal firepower for Confederates to have a reasonable chance of triumph. While some have argued that Johnston's magnetism was such that he could have inspired the men to succeed in a last attack, it is difficult to believe that inspiration alone could have had a significant impact on the battle, given the other hindrances the Confederates faced that evening.[51]

The delay in the march from Corinth to Shiloh cost Confederates the opportunity of fighting Grant for two days before Buell's second army arrived. Outside of an earlier start to the battle, it is hard to imagine a realistic scenario in which Johnston could have achieved a complete victory at Shiloh. While it is unlikely that Johnston's death affected the course of the battle, it is interesting to ponder whether his death affected the course of the war. The evidence in his brief career as a department and army commander supports that he showed characteristics and made decisions indicative of an officer with great promise.

At Shiloh, Johnston showed the following traits: He demonstrated an ability to work with obstinate subordinates. He proved that he understood the citizen-soldier, instilling the proper military bearing but showing patience as well. He showed decisiveness at the critical time when a large number of his subordinates who had previously supported his battle plan suddenly opposed it. He decided to continue with the plan because evidence suggested that the Federals were still in what Johnston considered a vulnerable position, trapped in a small area. He went to the front where he could make certain his plan would be followed (perhaps related to the opposition to his plan), where he could make decisions faster, and where he could inspire and lead soldiers at critical moments. His army—inexperienced as it was—fought some of the most impressive twelve hours of fighting that any army had fought during the entire war.

As a longtime student of the battle of Shiloh, I have seen many of the things that I had originally learned about the battle proved to be wrong. "The drummer boy of Shiloh" who was not there, the Sunken Road that was not sunken, and the stately tree under which the wounded Johnston was found that was perhaps just a sapling at the time of the battle—these are just a few of the many examples of ideas that had once captivated me but that I now find fascinating for the history of how these myths came to be "facts." I had also embraced the message depicted in the Confederate monument, that the battle of Shiloh was lost because Johnston was killed and unable to complete the victory before darkness ended the first day of the battle. I have since come to understand that it is not so. One of the early lessons of the battle was also that Johnston was a great general with the conviction to proceed with the battle despite the opposition of his generals and that his loss was a tremendous blow to the Confederacy. While I have grown to see Johnston as an officer who made some serious mistakes, the public historian in me has not been shaken from the view that Albert Sidney Johnston's death was devastating to the Confederate army and may have been one of the turning points of the Civil War. "When Sidney Johnston fell, it was the turning point of our fate," wrote friend of Johnston and Confederate president Jefferson Davis, "for we had no other to take up his work in the West."[52]

Editors' Notes

1. Wilbur F. Hinman, *The Story of the Sherman Brigade* (Ohio: Wilbur Hinman, 1897), 148.

2. John T. Bell, *Tramps and Triumphs of the Second Iowa Infantry* (Stamford, Conn.: Bethel, 2002), 20.

3. John A. Bering and Thomas Montgomery, *History of the Forty-Eighth Ohio Vet. Vol. Inf.* (Hillsboro, Ohio: Highland News, 1880), 26–27.

4. Johnston to Cooper, October 17, 1861, "Headquarters Book of Albert Sidney Johnston," quoted by Charles P. Roland, *Albert Sidney Johnston: Soldier of Three Republics* (Lexington: University Press of Kentucky, 2001), 287.

5. Ulysses S. Grant, *The Personal Memoirs of Ulysses S. Grant* (Hartford, Conn.: Charles Webster, 1885; New York: Library of America, 1990), 241.

6. Hardee to "My Dear Mrs. Shover," February 23, 1862, Hardee Papers, quoted in Roland, *Albert Sidney Johnston*, 297.

7. Grant, *Personal Memoirs*, 241–42.

8. The quote has become so widespread it is nearly apocryphal. Quoted here from James L. McDonough, *Shiloh: In Hell before Night* (Knoxville: University Press of Tennessee, 1977), 225.

9. Grant, *Personal Memoirs*, 246.

10. William T. Sherman, *Memoirs of General W. T. Sherman* (New York: Library of America, 1990), 270.

Contributor's Notes

11. Rebecca Blackwell Drake, "Frederick C. Hibbard: Master Sculptor, Part II," accessed July 14, 2016, http://battleofraymond.org/history/hibbard1.htm.

12. Albert Dillahunty, *Shiloh* (repr., Washington: Government Printing Office, 1961), 27–28.

13. Roland, *Albert Sidney Johnston*, 4, 347.

14. Ibid., 4.

15. Ibid.

16. William C. Davis, ed., *The Confederate General* (Harrisburg, Pa.: National Historical Society, 1991), 3:188–89; Roland, *Albert Sidney Johnston*, 6, 10–12, 15, 33, 55–56, 59–61, 82, 134–38, 168, 260–61; Steven E. Woodworth, ed., *The Shiloh Campaign* (Carbondale: Southern Illinois University Press, 2009), 9–10.

17. Timothy B. Smith, *Shiloh: Conquer or Perish* (Lawrence: University Press of Kansas, 2014), 2; O. Edward Cunningham, *Shiloh and the Western Campaign of 1862* (New York: Savas Beatie, 2007), 24–27.

18. Jay Luvaas, ed., *Frederick the Great on the Art of War* (New York: Da Capo Press, 1999), 120.

19. *OR*, 4:194.

20. Roland, *Albert Sidney Johnston*, 282–83; T. Harry Williams, *P. G. T. Beauregard, Napoleon in Gray* (Baton Rouge: Louisiana State University Press, 1960), 114–15.

21. Roland, *Albert Sidney Johnston*, 114–15.

22. Judith L. Hallock, *Braxton Bragg and Confederate Defeat* (Tuscaloosa: University of Alabama Press, 1991), 2:13; Lenoir Chambers, *Stonewall Jackson* (Wilmington: Broadfoot, 1988), 2:322–26.

23. Roland, *Albert Sidney Johnston*, 301, 314.

24. Ibid., 348.

25. Ibid., 290–91.

26. Ibid., 292, 298; quoted in William Preston Johnston, *The Life of Gen. Albert Sidney Johnston: Embracing His Service in the Armies of the United States, the Republic of Texas, and the Confederate States* (Austin: State House Press, 1997), 495.

27. Quoted in Roland, *Albert Sidney Johnston*, 299.

28. Ibid., 302; Cunningham, *Shiloh and the Western Campaign of 1862*, 91.

29. Roland, *Albert Sidney Johnston*, 311–12.

30. Ibid., 312; G. T. Beauregard, "The Campaign of Shiloh," in *Battles & Leaders* (Yoseloff, 1956), 1:578.

31. Beauregard, "Campaign of Shiloh," 578–81.

32. Stacy D. Allen, *Shiloh* (Columbus: Blue and Gray Enterprises, 2010), 12.

33. Ibid., 15.

34. Roland, *Albert Sidney Johnston*, 321–23; *OR*, vol. 10, pt. 2, 387.

35. Quoted in Roland, *Albert Sidney Johnston*, 323–25; Beauregard, "Campaign of Shiloh," 583–84.

36. William Preston Johnston, *The Life of Gen. Albert Sidney Johnston* (Austin: State House Press, 1997), 566–68, 570.

37. Ibid., 569–71.

38. Ibid.
39. Ibid.; William J. Cooper Jr., *Jefferson Davis, American* (New York: Alfred A. Knopf, 2000), 453.
40. Johnston, *Life of Gen. Albert Sidney Johnston*, 569; Roland, *Albert Sidney Johnston*, 326; quoted in Smith, *Shiloh*, 84.
41. Smith, *Shiloh*, 104; Roland, *Albert Sidney Johnston*, 326–27.
42. Grady McWhiney, *Braxton Bragg and Confederate Defeat* (New York: Columbia University Press, 1969), 1:378; *OR*, vol. 20, pt. 1, 684; Hallock, *Braxton Bragg*, 2:13.
43. Cooper, *Jefferson Davis*, 456.
44. Smith, *Shiloh*, 129.
45. Quoted in ibid., 129–30; Roland, *Albert Sidney Johnston*, 331–32.
46. Quoted in Smith, *Shiloh*, 67, 204–7; quoted in McWhiney, *Braxton Bragg and Confederate Defeat*, 1:237–40.
47. Smith, *Shiloh*, 130.
48. Quoted in ibid., 186–88; Roland, *Albert Sidney Johnston*, 334–36.
49. Smith, *Shiloh*, 191, 192–94; Roland, *Albert Sidney Johnston*, 336–38.
50. Smith, *Shiloh*, 220–23, 229–32.
51. Ibid., 233.
52. Davis quoted in James Arnold, *Shiloh 1862: The Death of Innocence* (Westport, Conn.: Praeger, 2004), 88; Allen, *Shiloh*, 39.

4. ❈ The Emancipation Proclamation

Editors' Introduction

More words have been written about Abraham Lincoln's writing than he ever wrote himself. Of America's literarily inclined chief executives, Lincoln stands foremost among a field that includes Thomas Jefferson, Theodore Roosevelt, and the Pulitzer-winning John F. Kennedy. Like Jefferson, Lincoln wrote soaring prose that captured American idealism and aspiration; like Roosevelt, he could appeal strongly to the common man. Lincoln was as comfortable with the poets as he was with the rustics.

Generations of schoolchildren have memorized Lincoln's Gettysburg Address, and millions of visitors to the Lincoln Memorial have stood before those words of grand eloquence made all the grander by size and granite. The address towers there opposite the equally lyrical Second Inaugural: "With malice toward none; with charity for all; with firmness in the right, as God gives us to see the right, let us strive on to finish the work we are in; to bind up the nation's wounds."[1]

Ironically, Lincoln's November 1864 letter to Lydia Bixby of Boston, expressing sympathy at the loss of her five sons, powerfully articulates the impotence of words. "I feel how weak and fruitless must be any word of mine which should attempt to beguile you from the grief of a loss so overwhelming," he wrote.[2]

While Lincoln's literary fans fawn over the beauty of his style and the clarity of his thought, his most important piece of writing actually gets little attention or love. Perhaps that is because the words of the Emancipation Proclamation—as unmistakably noble and politically shrewd as it was—appear to be among the most inelegant words Lincoln ever wrote.

Although it is frequently misconstrued as the document that freed the slaves, the Emancipation Proclamation did not, in a literal sense, free a single person. Based on Lincoln's powers as commander in chief, the proclamation freed slaves only "within any State or designated part of a State, [where] the people whereof shall then be in rebellion against the United States"—in other words, the Confederacy.[3] Just to proclaim emancipation so did not make it a reality, though. After all, who in the areas of rebellion recognized Lincoln's authority to free their

The Emancipation Proclamation, although not considered one of Abraham Lincoln's most poetic pieces of writing, was nonetheless celebrated as one of his most consequential. *Library of Congress*

slaves? Southern authorities fancied themselves an independent government; thus, Lincoln's edict was, to them, akin to applying American laws upon a foreign power. As a result, Lincoln had no way to enforce the proclamation except through military victories, and by the fall of 1862, Lincoln's armies were doing poorly on that front. Lincoln had wanted to issue the proclamation as early as midsummer, but Secretary of State William Seward argued against it without military success lest it look like an act of desperation.

The Army of the Potomac's strategic victory on the banks of Antietam Creek in mid-September 1862 finally gave Lincoln the opportunity he hoped for—although he needed to spin it just the right way. The bloodiest single day in American history, September 17, 1862, ended in a tactical draw, and although the Army of Northern Virginia slipped away from the battlefield on the night of September 18, it did so after taunting an intimidated George B. McClellan into attacking—a dare he balked at. The staggering number of casualties at Antietam along with the Federal surrender of 12,737 men at Harpers Ferry on September 15—the largest surrender of Federal troops during the war (and largest surrender of U.S. forces until Bataan in April 1942)—made the Maryland campaign hardly a smashing success for McClellan.[4] *The coup de grace came at the battle of Shepherdstown on September 19–20, where Confederates threw back a feeble Union pursuit on the banks of the Potomac River.*

Lincoln made what hay he could from it, though. "It is true, [the rebels] had greatly the advantage of position," one of his surrogates, secretary John Hay, wrote in an anonymous newspaper editorial, "but even with that, we whipped them out of every field, and they only escaped into Virginia by our kind permission."[5]

While Antietam gave Lincoln a position of perceived strength for issuing the initial Emancipation Proclamation, in the lead-up to the final proclamation, his armies failed to give him a position of strength to back it up. A messy affair in Perryville, Kentucky, in mid-October and defeats outside Vicksburg, Mississippi, and in Fredericksburg, Virginia, in early December gave the proclamation the appearance of a paper tiger. Only the slim Federal victory at Stones River at the close of the year saved the Emancipation Proclamation from looking entirely unenforceable. Lincoln had staked everything on the final proclamation, which he recognized as "the central act of my administration," so he needed supporters, opponents, and neutrals alike to believe he had the power to back up his lofty ideal.[6]

Looking at the proclamation's prose, though, one might not realize how lofty that ideal was: "I do order and declare that all persons held as slaves within said designated States, and parts of States, are, and henceforward shall be free; and that the Executive government of the United States, including the military and naval authorities thereof, will recognize and maintain the freedom of said persons."[7] *Such legalese hardly seems like it came from the same pen that gave us "four score and seven years ago" and evoked "the mystic chords of memory" and "the better angels of our nature."*[8]

However, wordsmithing is not the only secret to good writing. The most successful writers know their audience—and as Kevin Pawlak explains in the following essay, Lincoln had several tough audiences to reach: abolitionists; Unionists who were not necessarily antislavery; border states that still had slaveholding populations; foreign countries that were considering whether to intervene in the war; soldiers in both armies; the Confederacy in general; and, yes, the slaves themselves. This made for an incredibly complex context.

As a result, writes Lincoln scholar Douglas Wilson, the language of the proclamation "had to be emotionally chaste; it must avoid words and phrases that would appeal only to partisans and be landmines for others. . . . Its ultimate appeal would consist largely in its lack of linguistic or rhetorical appeal."[9]

There is a time for flourish, Lincoln knew, and a time for business. The proclamation was written in businesslike language by a president who meant business. The words themselves might not be as enduring as "of the people, by the people, for the people," but Lincoln's intent was unmistakable, and the power of that intent has endured as strongly as any speech.[10]

The Emancipation Proclamation was one of the last nails in the coffin of chattel slavery in the United States. While some could argue over the aims of the Federal war effort at the start of 1862, by the end of the year, those aims were clear—and enforceable—making the Emancipation Proclamation one of the most important turning points of the war.

"The Heavyest Blow Yet Given the Confederacy": The Emancipation Proclamation Changes the Civil War

Kevin Pawlak

George E. Stephens took his pen in hand while sitting in the camp of the U.S. Army opposite Fredericksburg, Virginia, and wrote his reflections to a Northern newspaper on the year about to close—it was December 31, 1862. He noted that watch night services were upon him. "It has always seemed like a period for moral and religious reckonings, when the errors and misdeeds of the past year are tearfully and prayerfully remembered, and a new leaf is turned over and we resolve to live better in the future," he wrote. Stephens, a black newspaper correspondent, had experienced the watch night prayer meetings, during which he asked God to bless the New Year, since his childhood. This watch night was different from previous ones, though. Indeed, when the clock struck midnight, for his fellow countrymen, a new leaf would truly turn over.[11]

"This December 31st, the watch-night of 1862, may be the watch night which shall usher in the new era of freedom," he wrote. Abraham Lincoln was about to wash away the crimes of the past eighty years of the United States with the signing of the Emancipation Proclamation, Stephens hoped.[12]

While Stephens looked forward to a bright future, he could also look back on the past few weeks and realize how dim the Federal war effort felt on New Year's Eve of 1862. The Confederate army sitting across the river from Stephens had, just weeks earlier, thrashed the Union army he followed. The news of that defeat "has produced serious depression and discouragement" among the Northern populace, wrote one New York City diarist. Both he

80

BREAKING THAT "BACKBONE."

While Henry Halleck and George McClellan tried using strategy and skill to crack the backbone of Jefferson Davis's rebellion, Edwin Stanton stands ready to take a swing with the draft. But only Lincoln, with the Emancipation Proclamation, shaped like an ax, not a mallet, seems poised to succeed. *Library of Congress*

and Stephens wondered if President Lincoln had the backbone to sign his emancipation edict amid such troublesome times.[13]

Of course, we all know that Abraham Lincoln did pen his name to the final Emancipation Proclamation on the afternoon of January 1, 1863. Despite what contemporary writers like George Stephens said—and there were others who had vastly different opinions about the proclamation—what *has* become a topic of heated discussion in the century and a half since the document's passage is the effectiveness of the Emancipation Proclamation and its worthiness of being ranked as one of the Civil War's great turning points.[14]

In fact, the Emancipation Proclamation, one of our country's most misinterpreted documents, affected the outcome of the war diplomatically and militarily and set the United States on a new course toward freedom that it had not experienced in its first eighty-seven years of existence. Lincoln's proclamation also set the bar even higher than it had been for the two warring sides, for by the end of the war, there would either be two separate nations, one with slavery and the other without, or there would be one reunited country without the institution of slavery. The people of the North and the people of the South recognized that the proclamation raised the stakes of the war, particularly for the South, which now fought for the survival of its society.

African Americans, enslaved or free, proved to be one of the war's important resources. For the Confederacy, for every black man building fortifications, driving wagons, cooking, or caring for the wounded and dying, one white man was freed up to directly fight against the invading Federal armies. Additionally, while white men went off to war, they were still supplied (theoretically) with food, clothing, and other necessities thanks to the slave labor that remained on Southern farms. At the beginning of the conflict, Southerners viewed slavery as "one of our chief sources of strength."[15] However, despite slavery's advantages for the Confederacy, a full 40 percent of the South's adult male population was not eligible for military service because of those men's status as slaves.[16]

Meanwhile, if the United States could find a way to use the slave and free black populations to their advantage, their superiority in numbers over the Confederacy would only increase. "So long as the rebels retain and employ their slaves in producing grains, &c, they can employ all the whites in the field," Union general-in-chief Henry Halleck explained to one of his generals. He continued, "Every slave withdrawn from the enemy, is equivalent to a white man put *hors de combat*."[17] These considerations, among many others, prompted President Lincoln to believe emancipation "was a military necessity, absolutely essential to the preservation of the Union." As his secretary of the navy related it years later, Lincoln believed "the slaves were undeniably an element of strength to those who had their service, and we must decide whether that element should be with us or against us."[18] Lincoln announced his intentions to the world on September 22, 1862, following the Federal army's repulse of the Confederacy's first invasion of Maryland.

In the one hundred days between Lincoln's announcement of his intention to free the slaves and the implementation of that plan on January 1, 1863, it remained unclear to many Northerners, Southerners, and Europeans—who eagerly monitored the conflict from abroad—how such a measure would change the war. Initially, it seemed that the proclamation might have a negative impact on the Union war effort as countries in Europe, particularly England and France, came perhaps closer than they ever had to taking an active role in mediating between the two sides. Additionally, shortly after Lincoln's announcement, Northerners prepared to go to the polls and vote in the midterm elections—elections that, throughout American history, inevitably paved the way for some loss of power in Congress for the ruling party.

Before news reached Europe of the Federal victory in Maryland and the announcement of the preliminary Emancipation Proclamation, England and France, the continent's two primary powers, seemed on the verge of taking part in the American conflict in some capacity. The British weighed particularly on Americans' minds as the European country that dealt with them most often. Three days after the conclusion of the Maryland campaign, but before news of that campaign's outcome made its way across the ocean, British prime minister Viscount Palmerston wrote his ambassador to the United States, Lord John Russell, that the time was close for mediation if the Federals should lose another battle to the surging Confederacy. "The iron should be struck while it is hot," Palmerston advised.[19] After the outcome of the Maryland campaign became apparent to Palmerston and the British, the prime minister still thought mediation a possibility, though that proposition stood on shakier ground following the events at the end of September. "The whole matter is full of difficulty," he wrote to Russell, "and can only be cleared up by some more decided events between the contending armies."[20]

It was not only the armies that Europeans followed, however, when it came to deciding mediation. The issue of slavery weighed heavily on their minds, and the preliminary Emancipation Proclamation sparked debates among the British people about who was in the right: the Union or the Confederacy. In 1857, the British Empire experienced a rebellion of its own in India led by people whom the citizens of England viewed as their inferiors. The British were thus gun-shy, to say the least, about having another similar rebellion in the world that might upset their government's subjects.[21] Lord Russell believed the proclamation was a call for slaves to commit "acts of plunder, of incendiarism, and of revenge."[22]

Other Europeans also believed the proclamation would not do anything. A "sham" is how one newspaper described it before going into more description, calling Lincoln's measure "the wretched makeshift of a pettifogging lawyer."[23]

Europeans were far from the only ones to accuse Lincoln of starting a race war or to claim his proclamation was an empty measure. Lincoln's declared intent even puzzled soldiers of the Union army. Captain Robert Gould Shaw, a man often associated with his role commanding a black regiment thanks to his popular depiction in the 1989 movie *Glory*, wrote his mother on September 25, 1862: "So the 'Proclamation of Emancipation' has come at last. . . . I can't see what practical good it can do now." Confederate repercussions were sure to follow, he thought, which might turn the war into one of "extermination." Shaw did not want to give the impression he thought enacting such a measure was mistaken "but that, as a war measure, the evil will overbalance the good for the present."[24]

In advance of the upcoming midterm elections, Democrats jumped on the emancipation issue to stir up votes for their party. They warned what might come from such an extreme measure. The Democratic candidate for governor of New York, Horatio Seymour, called it "a proposal for the butchery of women and children, for scenes of lust and rapine, and of arson and murder."[25] Others warned Northern white citizens that freed black slaves would take their jobs. A Democratic victory in the coming months "will be interpreted in Secessia and Europe as a vote for stopping the war," one newspaper wrote.[26]

The midterm elections of 1862 were thus the Emancipation Proclamation's first test. Despite the trend throughout American history that the ruling party—in this case, the Republicans—typically loses some degree of power in such elections, Lincoln's party and the proclamation made out quite well, as the "great, sweeping revolution of public sentiment" one diarist thought would come out of the elections never occurred.[27] Even with noteworthy Democratic gains in four states, as well as a net increase of thirty-four Democrats in the U.S. House of Representatives, Republicans retained a majority of state governorships and legislatures, gained five seats in the U.S. Senate, and still held sway over the House.[28] The elections of 1862 were far from a black eye for Lincoln and the still-ruling Republicans.

Although the proclamation's validity stood up to the American people, President Lincoln still needed teeth behind his change of policy to give the proclamation more legitimacy come New Year's Day 1863. If a Federal victory in the winter of 1862 could not be achieved somewhere, the Emancipation Proclamation might still appear as "our last shriek, on the retreat," as Secretary of State Seward warned it would become if military victories did not accompany its implementation.[29]

Winter was a poor time for nineteenth-century armies to campaign, but Lincoln and the hierarchy of the Federal army believed they had to take measures to bring the war out of the ruts it was stuck in. "The war languishes," one Northern civilian confided to his diary on November 13, 1862.[30] Though not coordinated, the Federal army launched three offensives in December. Major General Ambrose Burnside and the Army of the Potomac moved toward Richmond; elements of Major General Ulysses S. Grant's army headed to Vicksburg; and Major General William Rosecrans's army in Tennessee sought to extract the enemy from that state. Halleck told Rosecrans that Lincoln had hounded him to get "Old Rosy" to move. He did not know exactly why the president was so antsy for action but guessed that, if it did not appear the Union had made gains in Tennessee by the time of Parliament's January session, the British and French might intervene in the war along with France. "You will thus perceive that your movements have an importance beyond mere military success," Halleck wrote. "It may be . . . the very turning point in our foreign relations."[31]

Burdened with a sense of import, Rosecrans, Burnside, and Grant moved forward, and Burnside's and Grant's forces were the first to come to blows with the enemy. Both lost, Burnside at Fredericksburg and Grant's detachment under Major General William T. Sherman short of Vicksburg at Chickasaw Bayou. Rosecrans's army was the only one to meet success, driving the Confederate Army of Tennessee from its positions outside of Murfreesboro, Tennessee, between December 31, 1862, and January 2, 1863. While the two defeats, especially Fredericksburg, proved "damaging to the national cause," according to one Northerner, Rosecrans's success "inspired much confidence" in the Federal government, wrote Tennessee's military governor, Andrew Johnson.[32] Lincoln recalled the importance of Rosecrans's victory in August 1863: "You gave us a hard earned victory which, had there been a defeat instead, the nation could scarcely have lived over."[33]

That was hardly apparent on New Year's Eve 1862, though, with the fate of the Army of the Cumberland still very much up in the air at that moment. The general uncertainty of Rosecrans's situation even before battle had erupted, coupled with the defeats of Burnside and Grant, prompted Northerners to ask the question everyone wanted the answer to: would Lincoln stand by his proclamation and implement it on January 1, 1863?[34]

In Lincoln's mind, there was no reneging on the Emancipation Proclamation. "My word is out to these people, and I can't take it back," he said.[35] Besides, Lincoln viewed this as a measure that would help the North win the war both by undermining the economy of the South and because the president could now recruit black soldiers into the army. Lincoln believed the "bare sight" of fifty thousand black soldiers "on the banks of the Mississippi, would end the rebellion at once."[36] So, on New Year's Day, Abraham Lincoln, with a shaking hand, dipped his pen into the inkwell and permanently fixed his name to the Emancipation Proclamation. As if to reassure those witnessing the historic event, Lincoln spoke loud enough for all to hear: "I never, in my life, felt more certain that I was doing right, than I do in signing this paper."[37] From that moment on, the American Civil War entered a new phase.

Abraham Lincoln's Emancipation Proclamation struck at the very heart of the Confederacy and the cause that served as its cornerstone. "Without slavery the rebellion could never have existed; without slavery it could not continue," the president told Congress in his 1862 annual message.[38] The Emancipation Proclamation upped the ante for both sides in the war, but especially for the Confederacy. Lincoln tied the North to ending slavery, and thus the South was tied to that institution's perpetuation. For Northerners and Southerners, the outcome of the war was narrowed significantly. The country would come out of its great ordeal either as one nation without slavery or as two nations—one with and the other without slavery. The first day of 1863 marked a point of no return. There was no reverting to the old America.

But Lincoln's decree brought more to the table than simply ideological changes. Now, from January 1, 1863, until the war's conclusion, every forward movement into Confederate territories by Union armies moved black men and women one step closer to freedom. As Lincoln himself said, "The character of the war will be changed. It will be one of subjugation. . . . The South is to be destroyed and replaced by new propositions and ideas."[39]

While it initially seemed that the announcement of the preliminary Emancipation Proclamation might work in the favor of the Confederacy, that notion died as the calendar turned to 1863. Indeed, those clamoring to intervene on the side of the South because of Lincoln's proclamation were in the minority in Britain and the rest of Europe. Henry Adams, secretary to his father, Charles, the U.S. ambassador to Britain, wrote from London in January 1863, "The Emancipation Proclamation has done more for us here than all our former victories and all our diplomacy. It is creating an almost convulsive reaction in our favor all over this country."[40] Though Lincoln himself had his worries that the proclamation might be a foreign diplomacy nightmare for the United States, it eventually held the British out of the war. Intervention would cost too much financially, the British government reasoned. Additionally, the British had a particular penchant for freedom—they had abolished slavery throughout their empire in 1833. To turn around a mere thirty years later and aid a nation openly fighting for the enslavement of African Americans—a fact more apparent after the signing of the Emancipation Proclamation—would seem hypocritical to the world. "Personal freedom [is] still in the hearts of our people," one Englishman assured Charles Sumner. "Recognition of the South, by England, whilst it bases itself on Negro slavery, is an impossibility," he concluded.[41] England, France, and the rest of Europe sat on the sidelines for the rest of the war, the last straw having been Lincoln's transformation of the war into a clearly defined struggle between freedom and slavery.

As was the case in Europe, not everyone in America was on board with the direction Lincoln was steering the country. Union general John W. Geary applauded the president's move but feared what might come of it. He anticipated the dreadful opposition to the proclamation and worried it came at a time when the United States was "on the verge of anarchy and despotism."[42] Many Northern soldiers and civilians felt the document would be powerless to do anything. One Federal officer in the Army of the Potomac wrote that his unit received news of its execution with "universal disgust," especially the piece of it that ordered officers to ensure the proclamation was implemented anywhere the army traveled. "You may be sure we shan't see anything of the kind," the officer reassured his family back home.[43] He was resolute, to be sure, but this officer probably found himself in the minority within the Union army. While elements of the army and the nation it represented were split on the issue—which was never really healed during the war—more seemed in favor of the Emancipation Proclamation than against it for various reasons.[44]

Advances into enemy territory, increasing contact with slaves themselves, and the changing war policies of the Federal government prompted a transformation in the minds of many members of the U.S. Army beginning around the winter of 1862–63. Some, like Illinoisan Amos Hostetter, never believed in going to war to free slaves. However, on January 29, 1863, he told his sister that while neither he nor any of his comrades had grown to like the black man, "we hate his master worse and I tell you when Old Abe carries out his Proclamation he kills this Rebellion and not before. I am henceforth an Abolitionist and I intend to practice what I preach."[45] Indeed, soldiers like Hostetter realized that their wrath and finger pointing should be directed not at slaves but at the masters of slaves.

As of January 1, 1863, no matter what the reasons a Union soldier enlisted, unless he somehow directly refused to partake in the war, he was an abolitionist carrying out the policy of his government—a policy instituted to strike at the heart of the South. "The time has come, or will soon come, to march through this nest of vipers with fire and sword, to liberate every slave," one soldier told his wife even before Lincoln laid the preliminary proclamation at the country's feet. "Life seems of no value to me unless we can crush out this rebellion and restore our Government," he continued.[46] The Emancipation Proclamation dedicated the Union army to a harder prosecution of the war.

Colonel Smith D. Atkins of the Ninety-Second Illinois Infantry found himself troubled by the Emancipation Proclamation—not because of what it stood for but because it placed his conscience in a difficult situation. Prior to January 1, 1863, a master could reclaim his runaway slave who had fled into Union lines.[47] But the president's preliminary proclamation changed all of that, or at least Atkins believed it did. In the fall of 1862, while Atkins and his command served garrison duty in Kentucky, fifteen slaves ran to his camp. His superiors told Atkins to return the slaves to their owners. "Ought I to do it?" Atkins asked a friend. "I love my country, Miller," he wrote. "I have risked my life in its battles and am willing to do so again & again. I am deeply anxious to do my whole duty. But under the Presidents [*sic*] proclamation of Sept. 22d 62[,] I cannot conscientiously force my boys to become the slavehounds of Kentuckians & I am determined I will not." Atkins predicted his future, anticipating that before his friend received the letter, he would be under arrest and in the midst of a trial. He urged his friend to know that it was not for shirking from the face of the enemy "but Simply because I will not make myself & my regiment a machine to enforce the slave laws of Kentucky & return slaves to rebel masters. If I go down in disgrace it will be with a clean conscience," he concluded.[48]

Atkins and his regiment received repeated orders from various commanders to return the fugitives, but still they refused. At one point, another Federal unit threatened to fire on Atkins's men, but tempers cooled before any bloodshed occurred. All of this "for only obeying the Articles of war, the Orders of the President, and our consciences as men," a flustered Atkins told one of his state's congressmen. After all was said and done, though, Atkins proved correct in his determination to not return the runaways. To do so likely would have resulted in his dismissal from the army.[49]

General Henry Halleck and Secretary of War Edwin Stanton received reports throughout this transition period of the war that Federal officers either were telling slaves not to enter their lines or, through poor treatment, gave the slaves no other options than to return to their masters. "This is not only bad policy in itself, but it is directly opposed to the policy adopted by the government," Halleck told one of his generals. It was not the army's place to take stances on official government policy but simply to obey it and carry it out.[50] Though the policy regarding what to do with fugitive slaves in Union lines seemed fuzzy at first, by the end of 1863 it was a well-known and open Union army policy that slaves who made their way into Federal lines "are not to be driven back, but are to be protected by you," read one such order.[51] Armed with this knowledge, slaves fled to Federal forces in increasing numbers.

Ever since Lincoln penned his name to the final copy of the Emancipation Proclamation, many have viewed that document as powerless to do what it was meant to do. Because the proclamation freed slaves in territories not under the jurisdiction of the Federal government—at least according to its residents—and therefore had no power to carry out its main purpose, many have assumed that the Emancipation Proclamation was an empty measure that did little to accomplish the demise of slavery and thus of the Confederacy. As Robert Gould Shaw said days after Lincoln's September 22 announcement, "Wherever our army has been, there remain no slaves." Thus, he believed the proclamation would not change much.[52] In reality, this common misconception is far from the truth.

The preliminary Emancipation Proclamation quickened the destruction of slavery, a wavering institution by the summer of 1862 but one still far from collapsing. Days after the announcement on September 22, 1862, Federal general Grenville M. Dodge noted from Corinth, Mississippi, that slaves continued to enter his lines—"they will not even wait until [the] 1st [of] January."[53] What began as a trickle of fugitive slaves grew stronger as 1862 wore on into 1863 and beyond.

Some of the motivation for slaves to run stemmed from the Emancipation Proclamation. Lincoln used widely distributed copies of the proclamation, which lured slaves to run away with the promise of freedom, "to get the 'grapevine telegraph' clicking among slaves," as one historian put it.[54] It worked. In an expedition down the Mississippi River in November 1862, the commander of the USS *Lexington* discovered that "the slaves had heard of the President's proclamation," and no matter what the Southern white population did, they were resigned to the fact that their slaves would make it to the Yankee gunboats.[55] The superintendent of contrabands at Fort Monroe, Virginia, testified that slaves who came from as far away as North Carolina were well aware of what Lincoln had done, "and they started on the belief in it," he said.[56] By August 1863, a Union officer seeking to fill black regiments in the South noted that more fugitives seemed to arrive every single day.[57]

But just how many fugitives were these men talking about? While Civil War arithmetic is anything but a perfect science, the increasing numbers of slaves who reached Federal lines after January 1, 1863, is telling of the proclamation's effects in bringing slaves to freedom—or vice versa. In the first twenty months of the war that ended with 1862, approximately three thousand fugitives reached the Federals at Fort Monroe; by May 1863, that total swelled to approximately ten thousand.[58] John Geary wrote in August 1863 that within the past year, more than twenty-five thousand had found freedom within his lines.[59] By the end of the American Civil War, approximately one-quarter of the prewar slave population of the South found freedom and refuge within Union lines.[60]

Clearly, Lincoln's war measure touched slavery in the areas it intended to. Yet other critics point to the fact that certain areas of the Confederacy under Federal occupation were exempt from the proclamation, thus making it a hypocritical document. In reality, this too is one of the most common misinterpretations of the Emancipation Proclamation, one that often holds it back from being ranked near the top of the Civil War's turning points. Two of the areas exempted from the final draft of the Emancipation Proclamation were West Virginia and Tennessee (notably not exempted from the document were the South Carolina Sea Islands, where more than ten thousand black individuals were freed by the stroke of Lincoln's pen on the first of January despite those islands having been pacified by the Union army).[61] Lincoln exempted West Virginia because the fate of slavery in that state had already been sealed. The day before he affixed his name to the proclamation's final draft, Lincoln signed West Virginia's statehood bill, which included the Willey Amendment—a requirement for that state to gradually abolish its slaves upon admission to the Union.[62]

As for states untouched by the proclamation, such as Tennessee, Lincoln's decision only increased the pressure on them to get rid of slavery. This showed in the Volunteer State. Headquartered in Memphis, Tennessee, in the summer of 1863, Major General Stephen Hurlbut informed President Lincoln that Tennessee "is ready by overwhelming majorities to repeal the act of secession, establish a fair system of gradual emancipation, and tender herself back to the Union."[63] Emancipation had already played its hand in Tennessee, though. "Slavery is virtually dead in Tennessee, although the State is excepted from the emancipation proclamation," another Union officer noted.[64] General Sherman said the same thing four days earlier in response to calls for a state convention that might revive the institution in Tennessee—"Slavery is already dead in Tenn. . . . The question is settled."[65]

The Emancipation Proclamation successfully undermined two advantages the Confederacy hoped to gain and maintain throughout the war: foreign recognition and the benefits that slavery provided its army and society. Southerners began to realize as well that despite initial impressions, the proclamation was a profound and successful war measure. But they did not step aside and let the Yankees waltz into the South without a fight, freeing slaves and destroying

Southern society as they went. Instead, the Emancipation Proclamation only stiffened Southern resolve to gain the South's independence.

Just as Lincoln's decree defined what the North was fighting for, it had a similar effect for the Confederacy, though, in many cases, it simply confirmed what Southerners already believed. Lincoln's late proclamation "affords to our whole people the complete and crowning proof of the true nature of the designs of the party which elevated to power the present occupant of the Presidential chair at Washington," Jefferson Davis told the Confederate Congress.[66] But despite Lincoln's affirming their thoughts, many Confederates seemed unsure of the proclamation's effectiveness. Some grew concerned over what this would mean for their economy and society. "I feel much troubled in regard to Lincoln's proclamation in regard to the servants," one Warrenton, Virginia, woman admitted. "I don't expect we will have one left any where" in Virginia, she concluded.[67] Others scoffed it "as a direct bid for insurrection, as a most infamous attempt to incite flight, murder, and rapine on the part of our slave population"—thoughts that mirrored those of the British and Democrats shortly after September 22, 1862. However, one Georgia scribe thought the proclamation would be powerless to do anything, though that did not "lessen one iota the enormity of its crime."[68] Then there were those Southerners who believed the proclamation a good thing because it would provide the South with additional strength to fight for its very existence.

The strength that the South anticipated coming from the Emancipation Proclamation was both physical and ideological in nature. While one Confederate army was turned back in Maryland in late September 1862, another snaked its way into Kentucky. News had spread through that army of Lincoln's new war measure, and many Southerners anticipated that a flock of angry Kentuckians would rise up and join their army. One soldier said as much when he wrote in early 1863 that what Lincoln had done "is worth three hundred thousand soldiers to our Government at least."[69] A Louisianan in the invading rebel army hoped the proclamation would "fix the state [Kentucky] firmly on the side of the south."[70] The Confederate army then in Kentucky recognized the possibilities of this as well and sought to bring thousands of Kentuckians under its banners.

This crucial yet difficult task was assigned to Kentucky native Major General Simon Bolivar Buckner. The displaced general implored his fellow inhabitants of the Bluegrass State to join the Confederate army to prevent their homes from being "desecrated by the footsteps of the abolition oppressors."[71] Despite the boost that many in the South felt Lincoln's proclamation might give them in a border state such as Kentucky, they managed to attract only some fifteen hundred Kentuckians into their ranks.[72] It was hardly the grand reception they had anticipated. Perhaps the proclamation's exclusion of the border states from its text and the subsequent failure of the Confederates to win a victory in Kentucky kept many out of the Southern army.

Yet Southerners believed not only that the proclamation would strengthen their ranks in numbers but also that it would strengthen their prospects of winning the ever-important ideological conflict. Whichever side could sustain and withstand the astronomical losses created by every severe battle and win over the hearts and minds of its people, that side was likely to win.

When Abraham Lincoln signed the final draft of the Emancipation Proclamation into effect, the Confederacy responded by throwing in all of its chips. As Jefferson Davis saw it, the Civil War would now end in one of three scenarios: "extermination of the slaves, the exile of the whole white population from the Confederacy, or absolute and total separation of these [Confederate] States from the United States."[73] Mississippi governor Charles Clark tacked one more outcome on for good measure, something to surely rile up disheartened Southern civilians and soldiers. Subjugation to the Northern foe meant nothing less than "the elevation of the black race to a position of equality—aye, of superiority, that will make them your masters and rulers."[74] Southerners recognized that the North was willing "to pursue the affair to its extremity," which, in the eyes of the *Richmond Examiner*, turned the Civil War into a "war of extermination."[75] Even Robert E. Lee acknowledged what the proclamation meant: "success or degradation worse than death."[76] The Emancipation Proclamation clearly ratcheted up the ante for white Southerners of all ages and gender. The enslavement of the black race had been all they had ever known, something "justified by the annals of history, the laws of nature, and the will of God," one historian has said. "The defense of the Confederacy was the defense of civilization itself" for the inhabitants of the Confederacy.[77]

With their civilization and way of life seemingly facing destruction, Confederates stiffened their backbones and called for a renewed effort to defeat the enemy. "It is high time to proclaim the black flag," said General P. G. T. Beauregard—a clear indication of the severity with which the South viewed Lincoln's proclamation.[78] In his inaugural address as newly elected governor of Mississippi, Charles Clark, a former Confederate general twice wounded, called on his fellow Mississippians to fight the enemy "with renewed energy"; if they did that, "final victory will crown our banners." Clark, as mentioned above, recited what might come of the South should its citizens submit "to our hated foes." Rather than that, Governor Clark, showing steely determination few publicly exhibited in response to the changes wrought and the threat posed by the Emancipation Proclamation, implored citizens of his state to be prepared to fight to the last. Clark's statement goes far in showing the determination the Emancipation Proclamation produced in the South: "let the last of our young men die upon the field of battle, and when none are left to wield a blade or uphold our banner, then let our old men, our women, and our children, like the remnant of the heroic Pascagoulas, when their braves were slain, join hands together, march into the sea, and perish beneath its waters." In other words, he pleaded with his citizens to never give in to Northern rule. Before it came to that, he would rather see every Southern man, woman, and child die in the attempt to preserve their society.[79]

It is interesting to note that nowhere in his speech did Governor Clark call for the last slave to join in the fight for Southern civilization. Of course, for Southerners to approve of this idea would have gone completely against everything they fought for and were raised to believe. However, it was a project considered by the Confederacy and resorted to in the war's waning months in the most limited of ways. The debate raging in the Confederacy about whether to arm its slaves for its own defense opens a telling window into the importance of the Emancipation Proclamation in further tipping the numerical superiority scales in favor of the United States, a factor that served to accelerate the demise of the Confederacy and ultimately of Southern society.

Exactly one year and one day after Abraham Lincoln signed the Emancipation Proclamation, Major General Patrick Cleburne and a host of other officers of the Confederate Army of Tennessee gathered to write a memorandum to the army's high command. It began with a recounting of the bloody battles of the past three years that left the Confederacy nothing but long casualty lists and a shrinking field army while the Northern forces continually grew. Cleburne and his associates beseeched their commanders to begin to look at every possibility. If they did not, "it means the loss of all we now hold sacred"—and slaves were the first sacred item listed, especially since the addition of black men into the Union army, many of them former slaves, was one cause of the growing disparity in size between the opposing armies. Slavery was once a great resource to the South, but it was now a great weakness. The disruption of that system worried many Southerners, some of whom clamored for an end to the war at any cost. "They become dead to us, if not open enemies," the officers believed. Slaves also provided Northerners with information about the state of the enemy, both on the home front and the front lines.

Cleburne and the others proposed to begin enlisting slaves into the Confederate army. Any slave who joined would gain his freedom in return for his services. Cleburne's clique thought such a radical measure was necessary to "save our country." Furthermore, they believed doing so would "leave the enemy's negro army no motive to fight for, and will exhaust the source from which it has been recruited." The Emancipation Proclamation seemed to be gaining traction daily in the Northern states, and the sentiment "has at length ripened into an armed and bloody crusade" against the institution of slavery.[80]

By the time Cleburne made his proposal, the Emancipation Proclamation already ensured that, should the Confederacy make such a radical move, black individuals would not willingly fight for a nation now so openly tied to their enslavement. Edmund Ruffin, avowed Southern patriot, was in favor by 1865 of "furnish[ing] every means to avoid subjugation," including quitting slavery itself. This was the looming debate in Southern circles for the last year of the war. Ultimately, as Ruffin realized, no matter what official policy dictated, black males would "be more disposed to take Yankee service . . . in which they would immediately be free men."[81] As mentioned above, slaves were well aware of what Lincoln did for them and thus were easily cognizant of the fact that the Union favored them more than the South did.

It is ludicrous to say that one segment of the Union army won the Civil War. Each individual company made a contribution in bringing victory to the North in one way or another. However, it seems a fair statement that the enlistment of approximately 180,000 black soldiers into the U.S. Army, of which just over half were former slaves from Confederate states, hastened the end of the war.[82] Whereas slaves were initially used within Southern armies to free up more white men to wield a weapon on the front lines, the deteriorating status of slavery now held some Confederate forces on the home front to keep slaves out of Federal hands.[83] Despite their efforts, many black men made it into Federal service.

Black soldiers in the Union army made leaps toward victory for the Federal cause and toward applying a new hope of freedom and justice to their race. "By arming the negro we have added a powerful ally," Ulysses S. Grant wrote. "They will make good soldiers and taking them from the enemy weaken[s] him in the same proportion they strengthen us." He claimed the arming of the slaves and the Emancipation Proclamation was "the heavyest [sic] blow yet given the Confederacy."[84] One Rhode Islander noted that the use of black soldiers was a great untapped resource. Bringing them into the ranks, he said, would "press this war to a speedy conclusion."[85] Confederates themselves were not unaware of the advantages the North gained by enlisting black men. As Lieutenant General Edmund Kirby Smith bluntly put it, "Every sound male black left for the enemy becomes a soldier, whom we afterward have to fight."[86] It is in ways like this that the Emancipation Proclamation's clause allowing black men to fight in the ranks of the United States made a difference.

The Emancipation Proclamation also provided a new point in history for African Americans. For some, such as slaves in a border state like Kentucky, which was exempt from the proclamation, enlisting in the army was their path to freedom.[87] Benjamin Woodward, a surgeon in the Twenty-Second Illinois Infantry, explained to Abraham Lincoln himself how emancipation and enlistment had changed the game for a race that knew only degradation in the centuries before. A slave made his way into Union lines around Tullahoma in August 1863. There, Union soldiers began to teach him to read and write until he wrote a poem to the president. In the spring of 1864, the former slave enlisted as a soldier. "This[,] Mr Lincoln[,] is but a sample of the glorious fruits of Your 'Proclamation' of Liberty," said one Illinoisan to another.[88] At the end of the war, Abraham Lincoln predicted there would be African Americans who, "with silent tongue, and clenched teeth, and steady eye, and well-poised bayonet, . . . have helped mankind on to this great consummation," a realization that democracy could succeed despite such a tremendous and terrible war.[89]

Karl Marx ranked the Emancipation Proclamation beside the Declaration of Independence as the "most important document of American history."[90] Both from abroad and from within the United States, people recognized the proclamation's importance in ending the Civil War. In his 1865 annual report to Congress, Secretary of War Stanton—reflecting back on the past four years—listed the Union's emancipation policies as one of the causes of the rebels' demise. "The hopes of freedom, kindled by the emancipation proclamation . . . shook each day more and more the fabric built on human slavery."[91] From January 1, 1863, to the spring of 1865, the clock was ticking on the Confederacy's existence. The Emancipation Proclamation did not kill slavery in one fell swoop. Instead, it slowly bled the institution—and the Confederacy along with it—one drop at a time. While it was not Lincoln's most lavish document, the "new birth of freedom" he so eloquently described at Gettysburg would not have been possible without the transformation his Emancipation Proclamation brought to American society.

Editors' Notes

1. From Lincoln's Second Inaugural address, delivered March 4, 1865. Transcript available at https://memory.loc.gov/cgi-bin/query/r?ammem/mal:@field(DOCID+@lit(d4361300)).
2. An excellent synopsis of the story of the letter to Mrs. Bixby—and Lincoln's authorship (or not) of the letter—can be found in Michael Burlingame's "New Light on Lincoln Letter," *Journal of the Abraham Lincoln Association* 16, no. 1 (Winter 1995): 59–71.
3. Transcript of the Emancipation Proclamation available at https://www.archives.gov/exhibits/featured_documents/emancipation_proclamation/transcript.html.
4. *OR*, vol. 19, pt. 1, 549.
5. John Hay, *Lincoln's Journalist: John Hay's Anonymous Writings for the Press, 1860–1864*, ed. Michael Burlingame (Carbondale: Southern Illinois University Press, 1998), 315.
6. Henry Raymond, *The Life and Public Services of Abraham Lincoln* (New York: Derby and Miller, 1865), 764.
7. See transcript of the Emancipation Proclamation, URL in note 3 above.
8. From Lincoln's First Inaugural Address, delivered March 4, 1861. Transcript available at http://avalon.law.yale.edu/19th_century/lincoln1.asp. Transcript of the Gettysburg Address available at http://avalon.law.yale.edu/19th_century/gettyb.asp.
9. Douglas L. Wilson, *Lincoln's Sword: The Presidency and the Power of Words* (New York: Knopf, 2006), 142.
10. From the Gettysburg Address, URL in n. 8 above.

Contributor's Notes

11. George E. Stephens to "Mr. Editor," December 31, 1862, in *A Voice of Thunder: The Civil War Letters of George E. Stephens*, ed. Donald Yacovone (Urbana: University of Illinois Press, 1997), 216–20.
12. Ibid.
13. Ibid.; George Templeton Strong, *Diary of the Civil War, 1860–1865*, ed. Allan Nevins, 280–82 (New York: Macmillan, 1962).
14. Two strong examples of differing opinions on the effects and importance can be found in James McPherson, *Battle Cry of Freedom: The Civil War Era* (New York: Oxford University Press, 1988), 858, and Richard Hofstadter, "Abraham Lincoln and the Self-Made Myth," *The American Political Tradition and the Men Who Made It*, 119–74 (New York: Alfred Knopf, 1989). The

former finds the Emancipation Proclamation to be an important measure in the war, while the latter argues that it accomplished nothing.

15. Patrick Cleburne et al. to Commanders of the Army of Tennessee, January 2, 1864, *OR*, vol. 52, pt. 2, 587.

16. Stephanie McCurry, *Confederate Reckoning: Power and Politics in the Civil War South* (Cambridge, Mass.: Harvard University Press, 2010), 315.

17. Which means "out of combat" or "disabled." Henry Halleck to Ulysses S. Grant, March 31, 1863, in Ira Berlin et al., ed., *Free at Last: A Documentary History of Slavery, Freedom, and the Civil War* (New York: New Press, 1992), 101.

18. Gideon Welles, "The History of Emancipation," *Galaxy*, December 1872, 843.

19. Viscount Palmerston to John Russell, September 23, 1862, Lord Russell Papers, Public Record Office, London, England, as cited in James V. Murfin, *The Gleam of Bayonets: The Battle of Antietam and the Maryland Campaign of 1862* (New York: Thomas Yoseloff, 1965), 399–400.

20. Palmerston to Russell, October 2, 1862, Lord Russell Papers, as cited in ibid., 400–401.

21. Allen C. Guelzo, *Lincoln's Emancipation Proclamation: The End of Slavery in America* (New York: Simon and Schuster, 2004), 254.

22. Lord John Russell, "Memorandum" for Foreign Office, Great Britain, October 13, 1862, William E. Gladstone Papers, British Library, as cited in Howard Jones, *Union in Peril: The Crisis over British Intervention in the Civil War* (Chapel Hill: University of North Carolina Press, 1992), 187.

23. Charles Francis Adams, *Charles Francis Adams* (Boston: Houghton, Mifflin, 1900), 293.

24. Robert Gould Shaw to Sarah Blake Shaw, September 25, 1862, in *Blue-Eyed Child of Fortune: The Civil War Letters of Colonel Robert Gould Shaw*, ed. Russell Duncan (Athens: University of Georgia Press, 1992), 245.

25. DeAlva Stanwood Alexander, *A Political History of the State of New York*, vol. 3, *1861–1882* (New York: Henry Holt, 1909), 40.

26. *New York Tribune*, October 7, 1862, as cited in McPherson, *Crossroads of Freedom: Antietam, The Battle That Changed the Course of the Civil War* (New York: Oxford University Press), 148.

27. Strong, November 5, 1862 diary entry, *Diary*, 271.

28. *The Tribune Almanac and Political Register for 1863* (New York: Tribune Association, 1863), as cited in McPherson, *Crossroads of Freedom*, 153–54.

29. Francis B. Carpenter, *The Inner Life of Abraham Lincoln: Six Months at the White House* (Boston: Houghton, Mifflin, 1883), 22.

30. Strong, November 13, 1862 diary entry, *Diary*, 274.
31. Henry Halleck to William Rosecrans, December 5, 1862, *OR*, vol. 20, pt. 2, 123.
32. Strong, December 17, 1862 diary entry, *Diary*, 280; Andrew Johnson to Abraham Lincoln, January 11, 1863, *OR*, vol. 20, pt. 2, 317.
33. Abraham Lincoln to William S. Rosecrans, August 31, 1863, in *The Collected Works of Abraham Lincoln*, ed. Roy P. Basler (New Brunswick, N.J.: Rutgers University Press, 1953), 6:424 (hereafter cited as *CWAL*).
34. Strong, December 27, 1862 diary entry, *Diary*, 282.
35. George S. Boutwell, *Speeches and Papers Relating to the Rebellion and the Overthrow of Slavery* (Boston: Little, Brown, 1867), 362.
36. Abraham Lincoln to Andrew Johnson, March 26, 1863, in *CWAL*, 6:149–50.
37. Quoted in Frederick W. Seward, *Seward at Washington, as Senator and Secretary of State* (New York: Derby and Miller, 1891), 151. Lincoln's hand was unsteady because he had been shaking hands with visitors to the Executive Mansion for several hours before he signed the Emancipation Proclamation.
38. Abraham Lincoln 1862 Annual Message to Congress, December 1, 1862, in *CWAL*, 5:530.
39. Quoted in T. J. Barnett to Samuel L. M. Barlow, September 25, 1862, Barlow Papers, Huntington Library, San Marino, Calif., as cited in James M. McPherson, *Tried by War: Abraham Lincoln as Commander in Chief* (New York: Penguin, 2008), 132.
40. *The Letters of Henry Adams*, ed. J. C. Levenson et al., vol. 1, *1858–1868* (Cambridge, Mass.: Belknap Press, 1982), 327.
41. Richard Cobden to Charles Sumner, February 13, 1863, in *Europe Looks at the Civil War: An Anthology*, ed. Belle Becker Sideman et al. (New York: Orion Press, 1960), 221–22.
42. John Geary to Mary Geary, September 25, 1862, in *A Politician Goes to War: The Civil War Letters of John White Geary*, ed. William Alan Blair (University Park: Penn State University Press, 1995), 56.
43. Henry Livermore Abbott letter, January 10, 1863, in *Fallen Leaves: The Civil War Letters of Major Henry Livermore Abbott*, ed. Robert Garth Scott (Kent, Ohio: Kent State University Press, 1991), 161.
44. James M. McPherson, *What They Fought For: 1861–1865* (Baton Rouge: Louisiana State University Press, 1994), 64.
45. Amos Hostetter to sister and brother-in-law, January 29, 1863, Amos Hostetter Papers, Illinois State Historical Society, as cited in Chandra Manning, *What This Cruel War Was Over: Soldiers, Slavery, and the Civil War* (New York: Vintage Books, 2007), 93.

46. William P. Lyon to his wife, July 9, 1862, in Adelia C. Lyon, *Reminiscences of the Civil War: Compiled from the War Correspondence of Colonel William P. Lyon* (San Jose, Calif.: Muirson and Wright, 1907), 50–51.

47. See George E. Stephens to Robert Hamilton, October 17, 1861, in *Voice of Thunder*, 131–35.

48. S. D. Atkins to Miller, November 2, 1862, in Ira Berlin et al., eds., *Freedom: A Documentary History of Emancipation, 1861–1867*, ser. 1, vol. 1, *The Destruction of Slavery* (Cambridge: Cambridge University Press, 1985), 529.

49. Ibid., 537. Atkins's trials and tribulations are best documented in ibid., 528–38. See 537 for a case of a Union officer's dismissal for returning fugitive slaves to their masters.

50. Halleck to Grant, March 31, 1863, in Berlin et al., *Free at Last*, 102–3.

51. Ibid.; Headquarters of a Black Brigade to the Commander of a North Carolina Black Regiment, November 17, 1863, in ibid., 92–93.

52. Robert Gould Shaw to Sarah Blake Shaw, September 25, 1862, *Blue-Eyed Child*, 245.

53. Grenville M. Dodge to Nathan Dodge, September 28, 1862, Dodge Records, II, 821–22, Grenville M. Dodge Papers, Iowa State Department of History and Archives, Des Moines, as cited in Stanley P. Hirshson, *Grenville M. Dodge: Soldier, Politician, Railroad Pioneer* (Bloomington: Indiana University Press, 1967), 62.

54. James Oakes, *Freedom National: The Destruction of Slavery in the United States, 1861–1865* (New York: W. W. Norton, 2013), 344, 370.

55. U.S. Navy Department, *Official Records of the Union and Confederate Navies in the War of the Rebellion*, ser. 1, vol. 23 (Washington, D.C.: Government Printing Office, 1910), 508–9.

56. Testimony of Captain Charles B. Wilder, May 9, 1863, in Berlin et al., *Free at Last*, 109.

57. Lorenzo Thomas to Edwin Stanton, August 23, 1863, in Berlin et al., *Destruction of Slavery*, 309.

58. Ibid., 67; Wilder testimony, May 9, 1863, in Berlin et al., *Free at Last*, 107.

59. John W. Geary to Edgar Cowan, August 4, 1863, Gilder Lehrman Collection (GLC 00673), New-York Historical Society.

60. Louis S. Gerteis, *From Contraband to Freedman: Federal Policy toward Southern Blacks, 1861–1865* (Westport, Conn.: Greenwood, 1973), 193.

61. Emancipation Proclamation, in *CWAL*, 6:29; Eric Foner, *Forever Free: The Story of Emancipation and Reconstruction* (New York: Alfred A. Knopf, 2005), 50.

62. Oakes, *Freedom National*, 299; "Willey Amendment," West Virginia Division of Culture and History, 2015, accessed July 10, 2016, http://www.wvculture .org/history/statehood/willeyamendment.html.

63. Stephen Hurlbut to Abraham Lincoln, August 11, 1863, *OR*, vol. 24, pt. 3, 588.

64. Lovell Rosseau to William Whipple, January 30, 1864, ibid., vol. 32, pt. 2, 268.

65. William T. Sherman to James B. Bingham, January 26, 1864, in *Sherman's Civil War: Selected Correspondence of William T. Sherman, 1860–1865*, ed. Brooks D. Simpson and Jean V. Berlin (Chapel Hill: University of North Carolina Press, 1999), 591.

66. Jefferson Davis to the Senate and House of Representatives of the Confederate States, January 12, 1863, *OR*, ser. 4, vol. 2, 346.

67. Susan Emeline Jeffords Caldwell to Lycurgus Washington Caldwell, October 6, 1862, in *"My Heart Is So Rebellious": The Caldwell Letters, 1861–1865*, ed. J. Michael Welton et al. (Warrenton, Va.: Fauquier National Bank, 1991), 156.

68. Charles C. Jones Jr. to Rev. C. C. Jones, September 27, 1862, in *The Children of Pride: Selected Letters of the Family of the Rev. Dr. Charles Colcock Jones from the Years 1860–1868, with the Addition of Several Previously Unpublished Letters*, ed. Robert Manson Myers (New Haven, Conn.: Yale University Press, 1984), 296.

69. Henry L. Stone to his father, February 13, 1863, in Stone Papers, Kentucky Historical Society, Frankfort, as cited in McPherson, *What They Fought For*, 48.

70. E. P. Ellis to his mother, October 2, 1862, E. P. Ellis and Family Papers, Louisiana State University Libraries, Special Collections, Baton Rouge, as cited in Kenneth W. Noe, *Perryville: This Grand Havoc of Battle* (Lexington: University Press of Kentucky, 2001), 100.

71. Simon B. Buckner to the Freemen of Kentucky, September 24, 1862, *OR*, vol. 52, pt. 2, 360–61.

72. Noe, *Perryville*, 100.

73. Davis to CSA Senate and House of Representatives, January 12, 1863, *OR*, ser. 4, vol. 2, 347.

74. Charles Clark to the Citizens of Mississippi, November 16, 1863, ibid., 961.

75. Frederick S. Daniel, *The "Richmond Examiner" during the War* (New York, 1868), 60. This appeared in the September 29, 1862, edition of the newspaper.

76. Robert E. Lee to James Seddon, January 10, 1863, *OR*, 21:1086.

77. Oakes, *Freedom National*, 399–400.

78. G. T. Beauregard to W. Porcher Miles, October 13, 1862, *OR*, ser. 2, vol. 4, 916.

79. Clark to the Citizens of Mississippi, November 16, 1863, *OR*, ser. 4, vol. 2, 961; John H. Eicher and David J. Eicher, *Civil War High Commands* (Stanford, Calif.: Stanford University Press, 2001), 173. The Pascagoulas were an Indian tribe in Mississippi. According to local legend, in one battle the tribe was driven back to the shores of the Pascagoula River. Rather than be captured and enslaved, the surviving members of the tribe joined hands and waded into the river to drown themselves. See Edmond Boudreaux Jr., *Legends and Lore of the Mississippi Golden Gulf Coast* (Charleston, S.C.: History Press, 2013), 51–55.

80. Patrick Cleburne et al. to Commanders of the Army of Tennessee, January 2, 1864, *OR*, vol. 52, pt. 2, 586–92.

81. February 13, 1865, diary entry, in *The Diary of Edmund Ruffin*, ed. William Kauffman Scarborough, vol. 3, *A Dream Shattered: June, 1863–June, 1865* (Baton Rouge: Louisiana State University Press, 1989), 748–49.

82. McCurry, *Confederate Reckoning*, 319.

83. Ibid., 297.

84. Ulysses S. Grant to Abraham Lincoln, August 23, 1863, Abraham Lincoln Papers, Library of Congress, Washington, D.C.

85. J. C. Jameson to William Sprague, March 14, 1864, Sprague Special Manuscript Collection, Rare Book and Manuscript Collection, Columbia University, as cited in Guelzo, *Emancipation Proclamation*, 247.

86. E. Kirby Smith to Sterling Price, September 4, 1863, *OR*, vol. 22, pt. 2, 990.

87. Foner, *Forever Free*, 52–53.

88. Benjamin Woodward to Abraham Lincoln, April 11, 1864, Abraham Lincoln Papers, Library of Congress.

89. Abraham Lincoln to James C. Conkling, August 26, 1863, in *CWAL*, 6:410.

90. Karl Marx and Frederick Engels, *The Civil War in the United States* (New York: International Publishers, 1974), 333. This collection of articles and correspondence authored by Marx and Engels was first published in book format in 1937.

91. Edwin Stanton, November 22, 1865, Annual Report, *OR*, ser. 3, vol. 5, 533–34.

5. Chancellorsville

Editors' Introduction

During a 1923 visit to America, David Lloyd George, the recently retired lion of British politics, made a point to visit rural Caroline County, Virginia, south of the picturesque riverside city of Fredericksburg. His reason: to pay his respects at the small building where Confederate lieutenant general Thomas J. "Stonewall" Jackson died following the 1863 battle of Chancellorsville. "That old house witnessed the downfall of the Southern Confederacy," the former British prime minister said. "No doubt the history of America would have to be rewritten had 'Stonewall' Jackson lived."[1]

George, who had guided Britain through World War I, knew a thing or two about war. He appreciated the impact of individual leadership and how suddenly events can turn in a time of crisis.

His observations, sixty years after Jackson's death, echoed sentiments that many of Jackson's contemporaries had voiced. "His death was a shock alike to the South and the North," lamented Henry Kyd Douglas, the youngest officer to serve on Jackson's staff, "each [side] believing . . . that it was the first mortal wound the Southern Confederacy had received."[2]

The thirty-nine-year-old Jackson had been cut down in the prime of his life and at the height of his military career. On the morning of May 2, 1863, Jackson set off with the Second Corps of the Army of Northern Virginia on an audacious twelve-mile march that led them to infamy. The 60,000-man Confederate army had split itself into three distinct pieces in the face of a Federal force that numbered 133,000 men. Through shock and awe, Jackson and his commanding officer, General Robert E. Lee, looked to destroy their perennial nemesis, the Army of the Potomac, at the crossroads of Chancellorsville.

Lee and Jackson met at around 7:30 that morning, exchanging a few unrecorded words before Jackson's column set off into the "Wilderness" of Spotsylvania County, Virginia. Marching throughout the day, Jackson and his twenty-eight-thousand-man column wound their way to the extreme right of the Federal army. At 5:15 p.m. they pushed through the woods and hit the unsuspecting

Stonewall Jackson was accidentally wounded by his own men during the battle of Chancellorsville while doing reconnaissance along this thin path through the woods, known as the Mountain Road. The spot is just outside the visitor center at the Chancellorsville battlefield. *Photo by Chris Mackowski*

Union XI Corps, which sat on the far flank. "Stonewall Jackson had attacked us on our weakest side," wrote a member of the Eighty-Second Illinois Infantry. "They came in thick, close columns carrying a black flag as a symbol of death and destruction."[3] *In less than two hours, Jackson's men sent the entire Federal corps to flight, then drove hard for a gap in the Union center, setting in motion a wave of Confederate inertia that would carry the Army of Northern Virginia over the next two months from the Wilderness of Spotsylvania County to the banks of the Susquehanna River, outside of Harrisburg, Pennsylvania.*

Sometime after 8:30 that evening, Jackson was felled by friendly fire, knocking Lee's trusted subordinate out of the war. Complications from the wounding would lead to his death eight days later in a little white plantation office building adjacent to the rail depot at Guiney Station.

To many casual observers, buffs, and historians, the battle of Chancellorsville begins and ends with Jackson's famous flank march and his untimely wounding, as though Lee's eventual victory was preordained thanks to Jackson's bold attack. Rather than see the battle's narrative through to its end, observers instead get swept up by the Jackson mystique and the many great "what ifs" that rise from the dark, close wood like fireflies on a warm summer night: What if Jackson hadn't been wounded? What if Jackson had survived his pneumonia? What if Jackson had actually cut off the Federal army from its route of retreat at United States Ford that evening? What if Jackson had been at Gettysburg?

The questions can go on and on.

The truth of the matter is that, at the time of Jackson's wounding, the outcome of the battle of Chancellorsville was far from certain, and the loss of Jackson left his exhausted, confused, and leaderless corps dangerously separated from Lee's portion of the army, with ninety thousand Federals standing between them. All Jackson had accomplished, really, was to set the stage for the true battle of Chancellorsville, which would begin at dawn on May 3—a day that proved to be the bloodiest of the campaign and the second-bloodiest of the war. Of the 30,764 combined casualties of the battle, 21,357 were inflicted on May 3.

As Kristopher D. White points out in the following essay, the blood loss that Lee's army suffered, not just at Chancellorsville but ever since Lee's rise to command nearly a year prior, proved unsustainable. The number of casualties Lee sustained and the loss of experience in his officer corps represented irreplaceable resources. Historically, Ulysses S. Grant is credited with grinding down Confederate manpower "through attrition if by no other means," as he famously articulated in the spring of 1864, but the truth is, Lee had already started that process months earlier during the Seven Days.[4]

Yet Lee's more than thirteen thousand casualties at Chancellorsville are overshadowed by the fall of one man—Jackson—just as Chancellorsville would be overshadowed by the campaign that followed: the Confederate defeat at Gettysburg. As a result, the battle of Chancellorsville is one of the great overlooked turning points of the American Civil War.

As White points out, that turn is best understood when seen in tandem with another key moment: Lee's ascension to power following the wounding not of Stonewall Jackson but of Joseph E. Johnston at Seven Pines. Certainly Jackson's death was important, but his death—and the "what ifs" it generates—overshadows the real story at Chancellorsville: it was there that Lee won his final offensive victory of the war, which would go on for two more years.

Chancellorsville marks the high tide of the Confederacy.

The Cresting Tide: Robert E. Lee and the Road to Chancellorsville

Kristopher D. White

General Robert E. Lee rode toward the burning Chancellor Mansion. For the last three days, his vaunted Army of Northern Virginia had locked in combat with its perennial foe, the Federal Army of the Potomac. Around the Chancellorsville crossroads, the two great armies traded blows like skilled pugilists. In the end, Lee's army had the Federals on the ropes, and all that remained for Lee was landing the killing blow.

As the veteran army commander "came riding down the lines[,] . . . the sight of the old hero after such a victory was too much," recalled one Southern officer. "We had never cheered him before, but now the pride we felt in him must have vent, and of all the cheering ever heard this was the most enthusiastic. He rode by with his head uncovered, and had to keep it so as long as he passed our men."[5]

As the rebels began preparations for their final strike, word arrived that another Federal threat loomed to the east. Undaunted, Lee turned his attention to that portion of the enemy's force and stopped the Federal threat cold at the Salem Church. There and at Chancellorsville, the Confederates had managed to batter two pieces of the Federal army and corner them along the banks of the Rappahannock River. All Lee needed to do now was focus on the destruction of his enemy, one piece at a time.

Evening set in, though, forcing Lee to postpone his final strike until the following day. Problems then arose that prevented Lee from destroying either Federal wing, each of which managed to slip away to safety north of the river by May 5.

105

Before the war, Colonel Robert E. Lee was considered the most promising officer in the U.S. Army. At the outbreak of hostilities, President Lincoln offered him command of the entire army—an offer Lee refused because he did not want to fight against his native Virginia. Joining the Confederate service instead, Lee had a less-than-auspicious military career during the war's first year. One destined for great things, he was instead consigned to a desk job. *Library of Congress*

Thus, when the sun set on May 3, 1863, Robert E. Lee had reached the zenith of his eventual thirty-six-year military career. The Chancellorsville campaign, as a whole, would come to be seen as Lee's crown jewel, but every day after May 3 would be a slow and inevitable march toward his army's ultimate destruction.

During the campaign, Lee lived up to the reputation of "audacity personified."[6] In the face of an enemy that outnumbered his army more than two to one, he split his army three separate times. He allowed his most aggressive subordinate, Lieutenant General Thomas J. "Stonewall" Jackson, to launch an audacious attack on the enemy's right flank. During the majority of the battle, Lee's army fought the enemy on two fronts yet still managed to smash the Federal center and cornered its prey against the river. Throughout it all, Lee acted as a corps, wing, and army commander.

Yet, in many ways, the battle was a hollow victory representative of a highly destructive command style bound to doom the Army of Northern Virginia. For a variety of reasons, Lee was unable to land the killing blow at Chancellorsville, but the chief factor was that the rebel army lacked the manpower and command staff to finish the job.

The Chancellorsville campaign set the stage for Lee's largest invasion of the North and the most famous campaign of the entire war, the Gettysburg campaign. While Gettysburg is often viewed as the "High Water Mark of the Confederacy," the truth of the matter is that Lee's army peaked in efficiency at Chancellorsville. When Lee marched across the Potomac River, he did so with a reorganized army. This reorganization resulted, in part, from the fact that Lee felt his two infantry corps were each too large and unwieldy for one commander to handle. The other, and more pressing, reason was that Lee had been losing competent officers at an alarming pace. Over an eleven-month period, he had become one of the winningest generals in both the North and South, but his winning ways came at a tremendous cost to his army.

Lee's ascension to command was one of the Civil War's great turning points, but unlike other turning points, it was not immediately apparent. Rather than changing the course of the war in one fell swoop, Lee's ascension changed the war in the Eastern Theater over the first full year of his command. Through his leadership, the Confederates were able to push the enemy back from the gates of Richmond to the doorstep of Washington. Lee forced Abraham Lincoln to change the scope and war aims for the North, while at the same time obliging the Lincoln administration to find a leader as capable as Lee. Lee also influenced his own government's war policies, and he reinvigorated Southern morale after Federals had racked up victory after victory in early 1862.

But Lee's rise to command also had long-lasting consequences. Lee was an aggressive commander who inflicted a massive number of casualties on the enemy while absorbing an unsustainable number within his own ranks—and specifically within his officer corps. Lee would also find himself as the victim of his own success, for his victories drew the ire of the main Federal armies in the East.

There can be no doubt that Robert E. Lee made an indelible impact on the American Civil War, but his impact brought as many negatives as positives.

* * *

As improbable as the Confederate victory at Chancellorsville was, the fact that Lee commanded the principal Confederate army at all was in itself improbable. Still lauded in the South today as one of its great heroes, Lee and his reputation have surpassed reality and entered mythical status, in some circles. Historian Thomas Connelly aptly dubbed Lee "the Marble Man."[7]

Yet in the spring of 1862, Lee's was not a household name. In fact, most Southern citizens didn't even know who he was. It was only one of the most fortuitous woundings in all of military history that brought him to the fore in the American Civil War. General Joseph E. Johnston, the commander of the South's principal army in the East, was struck down in the midst of battle at Seven Pines on May 31, 1862. Felled by three wounds—a bullet to the shoulder and shell fragments in the chest and thigh—Johnston was carried on a litter from the field. "The poor fellow bore his sufferings most heroically," opined Confederate president Jefferson Davis.[8]

Davis and Lee had ridden out from Richmond earlier in the afternoon to witness the pending battle that could decide the fate of the rebel capital. Ill advised by the touchy Johnston, Lee and Davis knew little of what to expect when they arrived at the battlefront, some seven miles from the city limits. What Lee and Davis found was a commander trying his best to avoid them and figure out what was actually unfolding on the confused battlefield.

Following Johnston's fall, the first day of battle ended. Command of the field devolved to Major General Gustavus W. Smith. Pressed by Lee to renew the attack the next day, Smith buckled under the pressure of command. Unimpressed with Smith, who by all accounts had a brilliant mind but not one attuned to strategy, Davis rode back to the Confederate capital with Lee at his side. The president broke the news to him that Lee was to take command of Johnston's army.

"I know little about him," penned one South Carolina soldier on learning of Lee's promotion. "They say he is a good general, but I doubt his being better than Johnston or [James] Longstreet."[9] The truth of the matter is that, upon taking the reins of the Confederacy's principal army, Lee had been something of a failure as a Confederate officer. In fact, at fifty-five years of age, he was little known outside of regular army circles.

Lee's father, "Light Horse" Harry Lee, had been one of the great heroes of the American Revolution, but during young Robert's childhood, the family faced financial hardships. To provide opportunity for her son, Robert's mother looked to gain him a coveted appointment to the United States Military Academy at West Point. The family's reputation and Robert's excellent entrance exam scores gained him admission. Lee graduated second in the West Point class of 1829 and spent the next twenty-nine years in the U.S. Army. During his army career, Lee served as an engineer, a respected staff officer to army commander Major General Winfield Scott, and superintendent of West Point. In October 1859, he quelled John Brown's raid on Harpers Ferry.[10]

Scott thought so highly of Lee's services during the Mexican-American War that he recommended the government insure Lee's life for $5 million

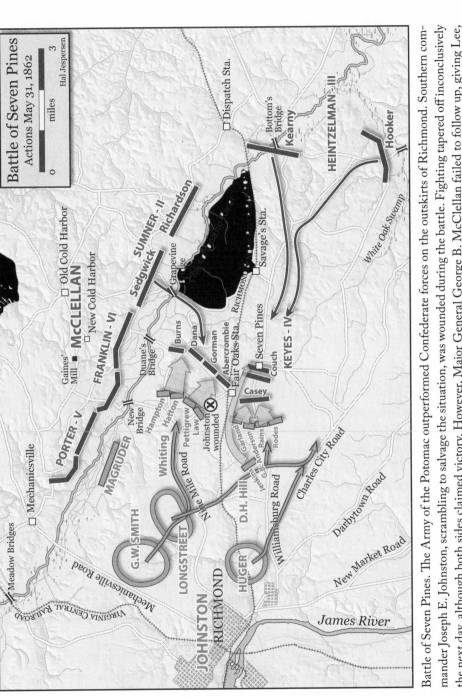

Battle of Seven Pines
Actions May 31, 1862

Hal Jespersen

0   miles   3

Meadow Bridges

Mechanicsville

VIRGINIA CENTRAL RAILROAD

Mechanicsville Road

Nine Mile Road

JOHNSTON
RICHMOND

G.W.SMITH

LONGSTREET

HUGER

D.H. Hill

Williamsburg Road

Darbytown Road

New Market Road

James River

MAGRUDER

Whiting

New Bridge

Hampton
Hatton
Pettigrew
Law

Johnston wounded ⊗

Garland
Jenkins
G.B. Anderson
Rains
Rodes

Charles City Road

PORTER - V

Old Cold Harbor

New Cold Harbor

McCLELLAN

Gaines' Mill

FRANKLIN - VI

Duane's Bridge

Burns
Dana

Gorman
Abercrombie
Fair Oaks Sta.

Casey

Couch

Seven Pines

KEYES - IV

SUMNER - II

Sedgwick

Richardson

Grapevine Bridge

RICHMOND

Savage's Sta.

Dispatch Sta.

Bottom's Bridge

Kearny

HEINTZELMAN - III

Hooker

White Oak Swamp

Battle of Seven Pines. The Army of the Potomac outperformed Confederate forces on the outskirts of Richmond. Southern commander Joseph E. Johnston, scrambling to salvage the situation, was wounded during the battle. Fighting tapered off inconclusively the next day, although both sides claimed victory. However, Major General George B. McClellan failed to follow up, giving Lee, the new Confederate commander, much-needed time to prepare. *Map by Hal Jespersen* per year. Time and again, the veteran officer wrote glowingly in after-action reports of "the gallant, indefatigable Captain Lee."[11]

At the outbreak of the Civil War, many—including Scott—believed that Lee should be the man to command the Federal army amassing around Washington to put down the rebellion. But feeling that his loyalty was to his home state of Virginia and not to the country he had served for more than a quarter century, on April 20, 1861, Lee resigned his commission and threw his hat in with the Confederacy.

Governor John Letcher appointed Lee the commander of the military and naval forces of Virginia. There was much work to be done because, in fact, the Southern Confederacy had to create a government, army, navy, and so on, all from scratch. Lee busied himself with the energy of a man half his age. "His life, since he assumed the chief command of the Virginia forces, has been a model of soldierly patience and energy and watchfulness," one observer noted.[12]

Lee's early war role was essentially that of a high-ranking staff officer. He found himself caught in the middle of a power struggle between the Commonwealth of Virginia and the newly formed Confederate government: Lee commanded Virginia's forces, but forces of the Confederate army that Lee had no control over and that did not heed his orders were pouring into the state. Eventually, the majority of the Virginia state forces, including Lee, were folded into the Confederate army.

Lee was just one of 306 West Point graduates who cast their fortunes with the Confederacy. As a prewar colonel (one of only thirteen), Lee was a natural selection for high rank, and he was made the third highest-ranking general in the Confederate army. That did not sit well with Joseph Johnston, who, in the U.S. Army, had been a brigadier general, outranking Lee.[13]

Johnston nonetheless quickly became the principal commander for the Confederacy in the East, but his reign as commander was plagued by his own ego. He began his career with a chip on his shoulder over rank, available troops, and command issues. Carrying himself with the attitude of a petulant child, Johnston wore on the nerves of Jefferson Davis. Over time, Johnston strained the initially cordial relationship between the two men. Lee, who was witness to much of Johnston's boorish behavior, quickly learned how *not* to interact with his commander in chief.

Tied to his desk job in Richmond, Lee yearned for a combat command. His opportunity came in August. The war in western Virginia was not going well for the Confederacy, so Davis sent Lee to the sector in the hope that he could turn the situation around. Lee did his best but fought to overcome green soldiers, squabbling and inept subordinates, camp disease, and Mother Nature. After a long series of setbacks, he was able to bring his small army to bear on an undersized but well-positioned Union force at the battle of Cheat Mountain. The battle was a mess from start to finish, though, and Lee was defeated in only the second battle in which he was the principal commander.[14]

Political generals—including former Virginia governor John Floyd and his staff—worked the Richmond newspapers against Lee. Some officers and men began calling him "Granny Lee" for his perceived slowness during the campaign. Unaccustomed to such tactics, Lee was blindsided. He was recalled to Richmond, his stellar reputation tarnished by the backbiting of amateurs. It was a true learning experience for the veteran officer.

Still hoping to put Lee's skills to good use, Davis transferred him to a department command where he oversaw the improvement of coastal defenses from South Carolina to the southern tip of Florida. The task in front of him was, again, nearly impossible. He had to deal with three state governors—including the haughty Joseph Brown of Georgia—and vast expanses of land, rivers, and barrier islands that had to be defended or given up to the enemy. Lee put much energy into the thankless task, accomplishing little more than improving some battery emplacements and adding to his many gray hairs. In March, Lee was again recalled to Richmond for reassignment.

Jefferson Davis knew the quality of man Robert E. Lee was. He knew that Lee could and would be a useful subordinate, if only he could find the right place for him. It seemed that Lee was better behind the desk than in the field. Thus, Davis appointed Lee to be his military adviser.

* * *

Much of what brought Davis to the decision of making Lee his principal commander revolved around the events of early 1862, which included the "insubordinate" nature of Joseph Johnston's interactions with the Confederate commander in chief.[15]

By early May 1862, Federals had won victories at Forts Henry and Donelson, Shiloh, Island Number 10, and Fort Pulaski. New Orleans had fallen, too. In Virginia, President Lincoln's principal army, the Army of the Potomac, moved from Washington to Fortress Monroe on the tip of the Virginia Peninsula that led to Richmond.[16]

Lee reached Richmond that first week of March 1862 and entered a political and military climate growing ominous, akin to a summer storm on the horizon. Lee also stepped into the developing feud between Davis and Johnston.

Since the early stages of the war, it had become abundantly clear to Davis that he had a George McClellan on his hands. Joseph Johnston allowed petty squabbles and his enormous ego to get in the way of the needs of the Southern Confederacy. His most recent prickliness arose because he felt he did not have enough men to fend off any Federal advance. His forces, which were stationed in and around Manassas, Virginia, numbered some fifty-five thousand effectives. Johnston also believed that a withdrawal from the Manassas line was a prudent choice and suggested moving some forty miles south to the more defensible Rapidan River. Vast stores of supplies, heavy artillery emplacements, rolling stock, and more were at risk should Johnston withdraw, though. Rather than taking the proper time to evacuate everything, Johnston burned much of the goods at Manassas and then made a sloppy retreat to a new line that was not properly reconnoitered. It took Johnston six full days to write to Davis to inform him of his retrograde movement.[17]

While Davis and Johnston squabbled over the next two months, Lee attempted to play intermediary. He also found himself in a unique position. While he did not have direct command over bodies of troops, almost every scrap of paper that came across Davis's desk pertaining to military operations also came across Lee's. That gave Lee the opportunity to begin planting the seeds for his ultimate impact on the war. With no real authority in Richmond and with the missives being sent from his and Davis's offices being largely ignored by Johnston, Lee focused on the exploits of a "cracked brain Gen[eral]" in the Shenandoah Valley.[18]

Thomas J. Jackson was dubbed "Stonewall" following the battle of First Manassas. Like Lee, Jackson was also a square peg who, after missteps in the late winter and early spring of 1862, teetered on the precipice of being a failure. Still, Lee saw something in him: an aggression that seemed lacking elsewhere in the Confederate high command.

Lee began communicating with Jackson, eventually funneling him much-needed troops to hold the key Shenandoah Valley. Since he could not actually order Jackson to do anything, Lee merely suggested courses of action. The perceptive Jackson took Lee's advice and ran with it. Throughout May and into June, Jackson won a series of stunning victories that tied down tens of thousands of Federal troops.

Lee and Jackson became a formidable combination, even if they were not on the field together.

* * *

As Lee and Jackson kept things interesting in the Shenandoah Valley, Joe Johnston shifted yet again, this time to the Virginia Peninsula. There, he tried to check the advance of Major General George B. McClellan's Army of the Potomac. McClellan cautiously advanced as Johnston artfully withdrew, delaying but not stopping him. Following the battle of Seven Pines, though, McClellan balked at assaulting the fortified Confederate capital head-on because he did not have the reinforcements he felt he needed.

McClellan took the news of Lee's ascension to command as a positive development. "I prefer Lee to Johnston," McClellan wrote boastfully to President Lincoln. "The former is *too* cautious & weak under grave responsibility—personally brave & energetic to a fault, he yet is wanting in moral firmness when pressed by heavy responsibility & is likely to be timid & irresolute in action."[19] In a later letter to Secretary of War Edwin Stanton, McClellan predicted, "Lee will never venture upon a bold movement on a large scale."[20]

Robert E. Lee was many things, but "timid" was not one of them. Rather than boasting of his plans to Jefferson Davis, Lee set to work on a new strategy. While Davis opted for the offensive-defensive strategy, he did not like the fact that the Confederate army on the defensive around Richmond was less than a dozen miles from the city. Lee wisely felt that "Richmond was never so safe as when its defenders were absent."[21]

Johnston's withdrawal from the Manassas region to the Rapidan line and then to Richmond had handed over large swaths of land to the Federals. While Davis was defensive-minded, he preferred that his generals fight to hold the ground the Confederacy already possessed, not timidly give it up without at least some resistance (a philosophy that had initially hamstrung Albert Sidney Johnston in the West—see Gregory A. Mertz's essay in this volume). One great advantage the South had was its vast size, although throughout early 1862 it was shrinking at a frightening pace. Federals were making inroads in the West, as well as in western Virginia (modern West Virginia), while in central and northern Virginia, only Stonewall Jackson's force held back the Federal tide. Regardless of anything else, Lee had to contend with McClellan's army on the peninsula.

Lee first set his men to work fortifying the city by digging vast lines of earthworks. Soldiers grumbled, calling him the "King of Spades" and "Granny Lee."[22] Some questioned Davis's choice of leader. Cavalryman James Ewell Brown "Jeb" Stuart, a brigadier general, felt that up to this point of the war

Lee "had disappointed me as a general."[23] The historian of Joseph Kershaw's South Carolina brigade believed that Johnston's "place could never be filled."[24] The diarist Mary Chesnut cast her eye toward Lee's brother. "I like Smith Lee better, and I like his looks, too," she wrote. "I know Smith Lee well. Can anybody say they know his brother? I doubt it. He looks so cold and quiet and grand."[25] First impressions, as everyone was about to be reminded, can sometimes be deceptive.

While the bulk of the Confederate army set to work fortifying its lines and the city, the Confederate high command worked tirelessly to come up with a cohesive plan to right the ship. Lee would not use the Fabian tactics employed by Johnston; he was not that type of commander, and the situation would not allow for it. Those tactics had slothfully brought the Army of the Potomac and the Confederate army up the peninsula to Richmond's back door. "Gen'l. Lee says there'll be no more retreating," wrote Stephen Ramseur. "The watchword of the Army must be and is 'Victory or Death.'"[26] Lee also worked to reinforce, reorganize, and officially name his army "The Army of Northern Virginia." June 2 to June 25 saw the rebirth of the Confederate army and the genesis of the new Robert E. Lee.

On June 26, Lee took to the offensive and, over the next three months, changed the perception of his leadership ability forever.

With nearly ninety thousand men, the largest army he would ever wield, Lee initiated the Seven Days Battles. From June 26 to July 1, Lee's army maneuvered and fought McClellan's time and again, forcing the Federals back from the gates of Richmond to their supply base at Harrison Landing on the James River.

The Seven Days Battles were, as James Longstreet aptly put it, "a succession of mishaps."[27] Lee and his army bumbled their way through most phases of the campaign, rather than slicing through their foe. Inaccurate maps, poor staff, and a lack of communication plagued Lee's army. By the end of the short campaign, Southern losses numbered 20,614 compared with the 15,849 sustained by McClellan's army. Still, Southern spirits were flying high. An article in the *Richmond Dispatch* declared, "No Captain that ever lived could have planned or executed a better plan."[28]

There was little truth to this statement. While Lee tried to use the element of surprise by calling on Jackson's troops to make a secret march from the valley to the peninsula and launch an attack on the Federals, Jackson failed miserably and performed quite poorly throughout the campaign. Lee also lacked a large enough command staff; he held together an unwieldy divisional command system; and he suffered from a want of communication between his subordinates. "Throughout this campaign we attacked just when and where the enemy wished us to attack," complained one of Lee's division commanders. "This was owing to our ignorance of the country and lack of reconnaissance of the successive battlefields."[29] Still, Lee prevailed because McClellan allowed Lee to fully dictate his movements rather than taking advantage of the litany of mistakes made by the Confederates.

Head-on assaults were the order of the day at Gaines' Mill (June 27) and Malvern Hill (July 1). While most students of the battle have focused on the losses of the famed Texas Brigade, Brigadier General Maxcy Gregg's South Carolina Brigade should receive its due. A recent study by historian Robert E. L. Krick places the losses of the Texans at 579 men.[30] Gregg's brigade, on the other hand, sustained 854 casualties of an estimated 2,500 engaged. This number included 36 field- and line-grade officers.[31]

At Malvern Hill, Confederate soldiers marched across an open plain, straight into the jaws of Federal artillery—the prelude to Pickett's Charge one year later. Historian Brian K. Burton aptly claims, "The first attacks had little effect besides getting a few thousand men shot."[32] Ambrose Wright's brigade carried 1,000 men into battle and lost 393 more in the course of the day.[33] Lewis Armistead's brigade, which would breach the stone wall at Gettysburg on July 3, carried some 1,500 men into action and lost 388.[34] Major General Daniel Harvey Hill thought his division numbered 6,500 men at the outset of Malvern Hill; at the end of July 1, 2,000 of those men's names lined the casualty lists.[35]

"We were lavish in blood those days," Hill lamented, referring to Lee's early campaigns, "and it was thought to be a great thing to charge a battery of artillery or an earth-work lined with infantry. 'It is magnificent, but it is not war,' was the sarcastic remark of the French general as he looked on at the British cavalry charge at Balaklava."[36] Hill went onto observe, "The attacks on Beaver Dam intrenchments, on the heights of Malvern Hill, at Gettysburg, etc. were all grand, but exactly the kind of grandeur which the south could not afford."[37]

Losses in the officer corps were appalling. An estimated 175 officers were killed and another 675 wounded; of those numbers, 110 of the fallen were field-grade officers.[38] While an army may march on its stomach, its soldiers do need officers to point them in the direction of the march and procure the rations to feed them. The total losses in Lee's army numbered 20,614—nearly 23 percent of his army.[39] Those egregious losses, especially in the officer corps, reflected a trend that was just beginning, too.

Lee's single-minded approach cost the Confederates dearly throughout the campaign, especially when it came to the concluding battle at Malvern Hill. While the most prolific writer on Lee and his army, Douglas Southall Freeman, claims that "the strategic aim of the campaign had been achieved. . . . Richmond had been relieved," Lee saw his objective otherwise.[40] Eminent Lee biographer Emory M. Thomas persuasively argues that Lee "was convinced that he must destroy the enemy if the Confederacy were to have a chance to win this war and thus Southern independence."[41] Lee lamented in his after-action report that "under ordinary circumstances, the Federal army should have been destroyed."[42] To his wife, Mary, he wrote, "Our success has not been as great or as complete as I could have desired."[43] It would seem that Lee wanted to end the war in the East in one fell swoop. Malvern Hill and the Seven Days were to have been his Gaugamela, Cannae, and Waterloo all rolled into one—though it was not to be. Unfortunately for his army, Lee would boldly roll the dice time and again in hopes of destroying the enemy. Malvern Hill was just the start.

While this was only the third military campaign where Lee served as principal commander, he showed an aggression that would cost his army in the long run.[44] The South could ill afford to absorb the number of casualties Lee was about to make his army endure. While the official Southern strategy was the offensive-defensive, Lee preferred the offensive over the defensive. In fact, Lee undertook a strategy of annihilation against his enemy over the first thirteen months of the war. On the peninsula and at Chancellorsville and Gettysburg, Lee set out not just to defeat the enemy but to totally destroy them. Even after the heavily defensive December 1862 battle at Fredericksburg, Lee wrote that "this morning they [the Federals] were all safe on the north side of the Rappahannock [River]. . . . They suffered heavily as far as the battle went but it did not go far enough to satisfy me. . . . The contest will have now to be renewed, but on what field I cannot say."[45] Lee sought that ever-elusive decisive battle where one army would utterly destroy the other.

Lee's was a confounding strategic approach at times. He managed to merge the elements of what military historians have dubbed the "Western Way of War"—the total defeat and destruction of the enemy—with a limited-war approach, yet all the while carrying forward the von Clausewitz edict that "direct annihilation of the enemy's forces must always be the dominant consideration."[46]

* * *

In the weeks that followed the Seven Days, Lee reorganized his army. He turned from the loose divisional system to a wing system, delegating James Longstreet as the right wing commander, Jackson the left wing commander, and Jeb Stuart the leader of the Southern cavalry.

However, both Jackson's successes in the valley and Lee's on the peninsula were starting to play against them. On July 2, 1862, Abraham Lincoln sent requests to Union governors for three hundred thousand new soldiers to fill the ranks.[47] By the first week of August, Federals were pressing for even more. While tens of thousands of soldiers stepped forward in those summer months, war weariness was already taking hold in the North, so response to the nation's call was slower in 1862 than it had been during the first rush of patriotism in 1861.

Looking to inject new life into his eastern armies, Lincoln called upon Major General John Pope to command the newly formed Army of Virginia. The army mainly consisted of the three armies that Jackson had bested in May and June. On top of this new Federal army, the Army of Northern Virginia also had to contend with Federal reinforcements arriving from North Carolina.

Lee put both wings of his army into motion, and by the end of August they reunited on the plains of Manassas. Jackson initiated contact on August 28 at Groveton. The next day, Pope launched a series of attacks along Jackson's line. On August 30, Longstreet crushed the Federal left flank with a sledgehammer blow.[48]

Casualties among Lee's army were again high: nearly 19 percent, between the battle of Second Manassas and the follow-up battle at Ox Hill. The losses in the officer corps were again high, too. Division commander Richard S. Ewell had his knee shattered at Groveton. The hard-fighting Isaac Trimble sustained a leg wound. Lee lost four other brigade commanders, eleven regimental commanders, and 726 line and field officers.[49] Regimental losses were also exceedingly high in some brigades. In John Bell Hood's division (formerly Whiting's), losses were staggering: William Wofford's brigade lost 573 men; George Anderson's lost 612. Confederate surgeon Harvey Black opined that "their loss is much greater than ours in numbers but not equal in worth."[50]

Lee's victories at Second Manassas and Ox Hill gave him the fuel to press his advantage across the Potomac River. The now-veteran commander felt the Federals were "weakened and demoralized."[51] The goals of the forthcoming campaign were complicated, and Lee was formulating them quickly. He hoped to draw the Marylanders into the war on the Confederate side, obtain supplies, and keep the Federals out of Virginia during harvest season. Lee also wanted to maintain the momentum the peninsula and Second Manassas campaigns had bought his army. Most important, there was the outside hope of European intervention into the war on the side of the Confederacy and the possibility of influencing the North's pending midterm elections.[52] While Lee hedged his bets on destroying the Federal army, he at least looked to prolong the war and make it so unbearable for the North that the civilian population would sue for peace through the Northern politicians.

The great flaw in drawing out the war was Lee himself. Joe Johnston had employed Fabian tactics to delay McClellan's approach on the peninsula; in doing so, he also added to the number of days of the war. In a way, it was a forerunner of the strategy that the French used in the latter stages of the First World War, dubbed by the British as "methodical battle."[53] In it, days or weeks of preparation went into the planning of a battle until everything was just right. McClellan took a similar approach to all of his campaigns. Between them, Joe Johnston and George McClellan would have prolonged the war because they were always looking for that perfect battle. Over time, the populace on both sides would most likely have tired of this. Lee, on the other hand, aggressively took the battle to the enemy, looking to make the war unbearable to Northerners by extending the casualty lists, demoralizing them through victories, and forcing the voting populace to oust the current war party. Lee's ultimate undoing was that the manpower pool of the South was considerably smaller than that of the North.[54] The Southern slave population offset part of this disparity by tending to the home front and some of the military's support tasks, but the number of actual frontline soldiers was finite. Lee could muster only a limited number of soldiers, while Lincoln had a vastly larger pool to call upon numerous times, even though the quality and quantity of these new Northern soldiers would decrease as the war dragged on. The Confederacy would have to keep the casualty lists long enough to thwart the morale of the Union troops and voter base. To do so, Lee had to risk those same losses on the battlefield.

* * *

While Confederate hopes of success in the forthcoming campaign were as high as morale, the actual likelihood of success was a long shot. "The army is not properly equipped for an invasion of an enemy's territory," Lee admitted.

"It lacks much of the material of war, is feeble in transportation, the animals being much reduced, and the men poorly provided with clothes, and in thousands of instances destitute of shoes."[55]

Civil War armies were not built for constant campaigning. Since the opening of the Seven Days, Lee's men had remained extremely active, with Jackson's wing especially making hard marches throughout the Second Manassas campaign. Coupled with all of the fighting, the Army of Northern Virginia's numbers had dipped from some ninety thousand to around forty-one thousand by the time they crossed the Potomac. Lee initiated the crossing on September 4, 1862. The broad goals he had set forth were far too lofty for his depleted army to achieve.

The Federal armies, on the other hand, had been working tag-team. The Army of the Potomac bore the brunt of the fighting on the peninsula. At Second Manassas, it was mostly the Army of Virginia, aided by only a small portion of the Army of the Potomac. After their most recent defeats, the Federals licked their wounds around Washington, where they consolidated forces and even received the first of the three hundred thousand men Lincoln had called up.

Events of the campaign unfolded quicker than Lee had anticipated. McClellan pressed the enemy harder than normal, so the Army of Northern Virginia pulled back to Sharpsburg, Maryland, near the banks of the Potomac River. There, Lee decided to give battle.

By dawn of September 17, Lee's army had dwindled to 37,351 men fit for duty.[56] The Confederate army that fought at Sharpsburg should not have fought there at all. Lee had a good understanding of the Federal strength, and he knew Lincoln's new recruits were reaching Washington as the campaign opened, yet he decided to fight.

For nearly twelve hours, the Army of Northern Virginia fought tenaciously. By the end of the day, though, losses in the army exceeded ten thousand men—or roughly 27 percent of Lee's forces.[57]

With his army below thirty thousand soldiers, exhausted from the campaign and battle, Lee stubbornly stood his ground the next day and taunted the enemy to attack. Almost any other Federal officer would have finished the job, but luckily for the Confederacy, McClellan was in the minority. Neither army attacked on September 18, and by the next day, Lee's army streamed back across the Potomac, leaving the field to the Federals, who were victors by default.

Throughout the battle, Lee had stood his ground with a river to his back, outnumbered two to one. Only the tenacity of his officers and men, the last-minute arrival of A. P. Hill's Light Division from Harpers Ferry, and the unmitigated incompetence of George McClellan allowed the Army of Virginia to live to fight another day. Lee was lucky to escape Maryland with his army intact. Edward Porter Alexander succinctly pointed out that Lee had "overdone it" at Sharpsburg: "He [Lee] gave battle unnecessarily. . . . The odds against him were so immense that utmost he could have hoped to do was what he did do—repel all assaults & finally withdraw safely across the Potomac. And he . . . only succeeded in this because McClellan kept about 20,000 men . . . *entirely out of the fight.*" Alexander closed by saying that "defeat would have meant utter destruction of his army. So he fought where he could have avoided it, & where he had nothing to make & everything to lose—which a general should not do."[58]

Some 838 officers fell as casualties, including four generals killed (one of whom was Samuel Garland, killed at South Mountain) and six others wounded.[59] Another fourteen brigade commanders were killed or wounded, and thirteen regimental commanders were killed or mortally wounded.[60] Losses in the ranks were severe. The Thirtieth Virginia Infantry lost 160 out of 236 men engaged; 320 men of the Third North Carolina fell; the First Texas sustained 186 casualties—82.3 percent of the men who entered the Miller Cornfield; and the Sixth Georgia lost a horrific 226 men out of 250 engaged.[61] The Army of Northern Virginia was essentially crippled after Sharpsburg. "The Congress must provide for reinforcing us," wrote Lee's staff officer Walter H. Taylor.[62]

Victory north of the Potomac River would have bolstered the already-soaring Southern morale, but what Lee seemed to forget was that a Federal victory north of the Potomac would steel the resolve of many Northerners while also negating all the good he and his army had done over the previous three months. Yet, Lee failed in almost every objective he had laid out to Davis prior to the campaign. Walter Taylor tried to make the best of a bad situation by saying that "the capture of H[arpers] Ferry was sufficiently important to compensate for all of the trouble experienced."[63] While important, it in no way made up for the losses in the ranks, nor for the fact that Federals could claim victory on the field north of the Potomac.

The Northern claim to victory had huge political ramifications. First, Confederate hopes of European intervention were dashed. Second, Lincoln issued the preliminary Emancipation Proclamation on September 22, shifting the Northern war aims toward ending chattel slavery in the United States. (See Kevin Pawlak's essay in this volume.)

Lee's gamble north of the Potomac River was ill conceived from the start and cost the Confederates on the military, political, and international stages. While the previous two campaigns had showed the world that the command structure of Lee, Jackson, Longstreet, and Stuart was second to none in the war thus far, their gambles on the field were far too costly to keep going in the long run.

After Sharpsburg, McClellan's impotent pursuit of the Confederates led Lincoln to remove him after the midterm elections. The lag gave Lee valuable time to again reorganize his army and receive what reinforcements he could. By December, the Confederate army contained seventy-eight thousand men— the largest number of men Lee would have with him on one field from then until the end of the war. However, Lee's ability to draw on significant pools of reinforcements to bolster his numbers would diminish as the war progressed.

Meanwhile, Lincoln's new commander, Major General Ambrose E. Burnside, set his sights on Fredericksburg, Virginia. There, for the second time in as many battles, Lee was forced to fight on the defensive. He easily beat Burnside, but the defensive victory still cost Lee some five thousand officers and men.[64] The victory was a hollow one, since Lee could not afford to strike out over the open plains and counterattack the enemy, who had more than four hundred cannon that dominated those fields.

After the victory, morale was high in the Army of Northern Virginia. "So great is my confidence in General Lee that I am willing to follow him blindfolded," Jackson said, adding, "His perceptions are as quick and unerring as his judgment is infallible."[65] Thomas Warren of the Fifteenth South Carolina thought that "General Robert E. Lee is the greatest living general."[66]

* * *

Lee waited out the winter of 1862–63 on the Rappahannock River line in and around Fredericksburg. Supply shortages forced him to spread his army over a wide area. He sent two divisions under James Longstreet to Suffolk, Virginia, to collect supplies. When the Federals opened the spring campaigning season, Lee hoped he would have time to reunite his army before engaging the enemy. In the meantime, Lee had with him one true corps commander, Jackson; his trusted cavalry leader, Stuart; and perhaps sixty thousand effectives.

On the Federal side, yet another new commander, Major General Joseph "Fightin' Joe" Hooker, had assumed the helm of the Army of the Potomac.

In late April, Hooker set his 133,000-man army in motion for what would become the Chancellorsville campaign. Lee caught wind of Hooker's plan and, leaving a portion of his army in Fredericksburg as a rear guard, turned the rest of his army west to meet the enemy. The unexpected Confederate countermove caught Hooker off guard, and its stout resistance forced him to give up the initiative. Lee had yearned to take the offensive since the Maryland campaign; now that he had that opportunity, he would not give up the initiative until he recrossed the Potomac River at the end of the Gettysburg campaign two and a half months later.

By the morning of May 3, after two days of battle, the Federal line looked like a giant U, with artillery and nearly forty-four thousand men packed in its center. Lee's army, positioned along either arm of the U, looked to renew an offensive stalled by the accidental wounding of Jackson late the previous night. "It is necessary that the glorious victory thus far achieved be prosecuted with the utmost vigor, and the enemy given no time to rally," Lee wrote to Stuart, who had taken over for the fallen Jackson. "As soon . . . as it is possible, they must be pressed, so that we can unite the two wings of the army."[67]

Limited by the terrain and enemy position, the rebels moved forward like a battering ram. Assault after assault smashed into the fortified Federal position. Brigadier General Stephen Ramseur recalled assaulting three lines of "Yankee Inf'y. with such a support [that] could not be run over without heavy loss. My list of casualties is a sad but eloquent tribute to the heroic devotion and unconquerable bravery of my glorious brigade."[68] While Ramseur's brigade "covered itself in glory," that glory came at a high cost.[69] Of the 1,400 men he carried into battle, 708 became casualties.[70]

Brigadier General Samuel McGowan's South Carolina brigade suffered heavily, too, sustaining 457 casualties, including McGowan; his second-in-command, Colonel Oliver Edwards; and his third-in-command, Colonel James Perrin. By the end of the battle, five men had commanded the brigade.[71]

James Lane's North Carolina brigade, containing the men who wounded Jackson on the evening of May 2, lost 910 men in action, including four out of the original five regimental commanders Lane carried into the battle. Two of those regiments lost two or more commanders. William Dorsey Pender's brigade also carried five regiments into action, where three of his regiments lost two or more commanders each. The dead from the state of North Carolina alone exceeded 600—the most from any southern state on the field.[72]

"I commend to the particular notice of the [War] Department the brave officers and men mentioned by their superiors for extraordinary daring and merit," Lee commented in his after-action report. "Among them will be found some who have passed, by a glorious death, beyond the reach of praise, but the memory of whose virtues and devoted patriotism will ever be cherished by their grateful countrymen."[73]

Losses on both sides on May 3 exceeded twenty-one thousand and could have been as high as twenty-two thousand. The majority of the losses were sustained between 5:00 a.m. and 10:00 a.m., when more than seventeen thousand men fell—nearly one man every second for five full hours.[74] One

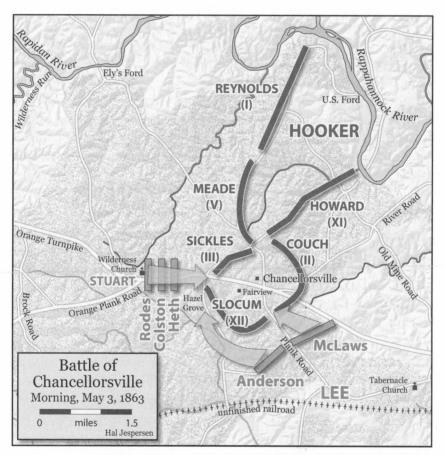

Battle of Chancellorsville. By the morning of May 3, Federal commander Joseph Hooker had withdrawn into a well-protected U, although a vulnerable salient bubbled out from the position's tip. Lee concentrated Confederate pressure against the salient, which eventually collapsed as Federal artillery began running out of ammunition. However, the morning's fight would be one of the costliest of the entire war. *Map by Hal Jespersen*

Union division commander stated, "The fire of the musketry was incessant ... almost without cessation or intermission."[75]

During the battle, Lee and Stuart managed to smash their way through the Federal salient, reunite, and force the Federal army into collapse. "Gen. Lee's victory was complete," boasted one Georgia soldier. "It was wanting in nothing."[76] An army outnumbered more than two to one, not holding the strategic or tactical initiative, outmarched and outfought the enemy and drove them back while inflicting serious losses. "When you take into consideration that the force of the enemy engaged in this fight were fresh troops, well disciplined and armed, and outnumbering three to one our force ... ," said one Georgia soldier, "you will agree with me in terming this one of the grandest victories of the war."[77]

Later historians have agreed. British military historian Colonel George Francis Robert Henderson, representing wider sentiment, described the battle of Chancellorsville "as the tactical masterpiece of the nineteenth century."[78]

There is little doubt that from the initial Confederate vantage point, Chancellorsville was a great victory—at least to most Confederates. But on May 4, it became more and more apparent that Lee would not be able to coordinate the killing blow. For the second time in six months, Lee had missed the opportunity to land the blow he so desperately yearned for. Losses in his officer corps made it impossible to fully prosecute Lee's battle plan—and thus, the Army of the Potomac was again able to escape.

"At Chancellorsville we gained another victory," Lee lamented to fellow Confederate general John Bell Hood. "Our people were wild with delight—I, on the contrary, was more depressed than after Fredericksburg; our loss was severe, and again we had gained not an inch of ground and the enemy could not be pursued."[79]

"Had I had the whole army with me," Lee believed, "General [Joe] Hooker would have been demolished."[80] This is a bold statement. Lee had inflicted some 17,304 casualties on the enemy—roughly 13 percent of the enemy's fighting force. Lee's army of 60,892 had engaged approximately 83,000 men of Hooker's army, which meant that the Federal army still had some 50,000 soldiers to field who had not yet fully engaged the enemy—an amount almost equal to Lee's effective strength at the outset of the campaign.[81]

Lee, on the other hand, had placed all of his cards on the table. Of the 60,892 Confederates who entered the campaign, 13,460 had become casualties—22 percent of the Army of Northern Virginia.[82] One comment from a Virginia artillerist tempered an apparent boast with chilling insight about those numbers: "Our losses in Officers was unparalleled, in men not so great—I regard it as by far our greatest victory."[83] Lee and Stuart had bled out the Confederate officer corps throughout the battle. The army lost five brigade commanders in the action, three division commanders, and one corps commander.[84]

While some of the officers would return to action, one did not: Jackson.[85] "The loss [of Jackson] was for several days hid from the army," wrote one Confederate staff officer, "but this could not succeed long. Thus ended the mortal career of the brightest and best jewell [*sic*] in the royal crown of the Confederacy. . . . Universal throughout the country was the gloom cast by his death."[86] Stephen Ramseur lamented, "We all mourn . . . the loss of our great and good and invincible Jackson."[87]

The fall of Jackson left an unsealable rift in the Confederate chain of command. Jackson was Lee's pit bull and, when off his leash, could tear into the enemy like no other. His single-mindedness in battle, and his inability to see a gray area in anything he did, made him an outstanding combat leader.

The fall of Jackson forced Lee to promote and reorganize his army, creating a ripple effect on Lee's command structure: reorganizing from two to three corps meant he needed two new corps commanders as well as four new division commanders. Although impossible to tell at this juncture, over time it became apparent that some of the men called upon to step into Jackson's large boots and those of other fallen leaders were not up to the task. Jackson's fall underscored a key weakness of the Southern forces: Lee lacked quality leadership to step up and take the reins.

The attrition at the lower ranks had a more immediate and longer-lasting impact on Lee's ability to wage war. The Army of Northern Virginia entered the battle with 130 regiments. Out of those 130 regiments, Lee lost sixty-four field officers.[88] Those officers were becoming harder and harder to replace. At the outset of the war, the Confederates were much better at placing impactful and quality officers in charge of units. With the best and brightest normally starting off at the upper echelons, their fall meant there were fewer worthy officers stepping into their places. This was not always the case, but by the end of the Chancellorsville campaign, this was more or less true: since Lee assumed command of the army, he had lost more than 60,000 men, which included more than three hundred field officers. One rebel thought that "[the army] is in better fighting trim than ever before."[89] That trimness, however, was more grim than he realized.

Robert E. Lee's victory at Chancellorsville marked the zenith of his career and the true high-water mark of the Confederacy. His meteoric rise that began with one turning point—his ascension to command after the wounding of Joseph Johnston—ended at the crossroads of fire, where ever after his army's fortunes would be in descent. After Chancellorsville, his army never again would win an offensive battlefield victory. The rise of Robert E. Lee represents the great turning point in the story of the Army of Northern Virginia and the war in the Eastern Theater. "From June 1, 1862, until his surrender to Grant at Appomattox Court House, Lee was the central military figure in the South," said historian J. F. C. Fuller.[90] But the truth also was that this central figure helped accelerate the downfall of his army, as well as the Southern Confederacy as a whole.

Lee's bold actions, aggressive command style, and early victories also forced the Lincoln administration to change its wartime strategy. If not for Lee's bold movements north, the Confederate capital could have fallen by mid-1862, crushing Southern morale. In the end, though, Lee's victories strengthened Southern morale by giving both the military and civilian spheres a beacon of hope just as the fortunes of war had turned against them.

Still, Lee did as much harm to his army as he did to the Federals, if not more. The Southern manpower pool was shallow and his casualty lists long. The losses Lee inflicted on his own army at the regimental, brigade, division, and corps command levels had finally become too much to bear. By the time Lee turned north toward Gettysburg, he had reorganized his army in an attempt to offset the dearth of qualified commanders. His new command team, though, would never match the unparalleled efficiency that the Army of Northern Virginia showed at Chancellorsville. While Lee may have claimed that he thought his army was invincible, "it took the battle of Gettysburg to convince General Lee that General Jackson was really dead" and the best and brightest of his vaunted army lay in shallow graves across northern Virginia.[91]

Editors' Notes

1. Quoted in Ralph Happel, *The Last Days of Jackson* (Richmond: Eastern National Park and Monument Association, 1971), 57.
2. Henry Kyd Douglas, *I Rode with Stonewall: The War Experiences of the Youngest Member of Jackson's Staff* (Chapel Hill: University of North Carolina Press, 1968), 230.
3. Unsigned letter to the *Belleviller Zeitung*, May 11, 1863, in *Yankee Dutchmen under Fire: The Civil War Letters from the 82nd Illinois Infantry*, ed. Joseph R. Reinhart (Kent, Ohio: Kent State University Press, 2013), 72.
4. *OR*, vol. 34, pt. 1, 9.

Contributor's Notes

5. *Augusta Weekly Chronicle and Sentinel*, May 20, 1863.
6. Edward Porter Alexander, *Fighting for the Confederacy: The Personal Recollections of General Edward Porter Alexander*, ed. Gary W. Gallagher (Chapel Hill: University of North Carolina Press, 1989), 91.
7. Thomas L. Connelly, *The Marble Man: Robert E. Lee and His Image in American Society* (Baton Rouge: Louisiana State University Press, 1977), 3–4, 163.
8. Jefferson Davis to Winnie Davis, June 2, 1862, Jefferson Davis Papers, Museum of the Confederacy, Richmond, Va.
9. Quoted in Jeffrey D. Wert, *A Glorious Army: Robert E. Lee's Triumph, 1862–1863* (New York: Simon and Schuster, 2011), 5.
10. Elizabeth Brown Pryor, *Reading the Man: A Portrait of Robert E. Lee through His Private Letters* (New York: Viking, 2007), 66–69, 278–81; Walter H. Taylor, *General Lee: His Campaigns in Virginia, 1861–1865* (Lincoln: University of Nebraska Press, 1994), v–xv; Steven E. Woodworth, *Davis and Lee at War* (Lawrence: University Press of Kansas, 1995), 14, 18.
11. Emory M. Thomas, *Robert E. Lee: A Biography* (New York: W. W. Norton, 1995), 140.
12. *Memphis Daily Appeal*, August 6, 1861.
13. Taylor, *General Lee*, 17, 23–24; Woodworth, *Davis and Lee at War*, 16–18.
14. Lee's first battle as principal commander came in October 1859 when he quelled John Brown's raid on Harpers Ferry.
15. Joseph T. Glatthar, *Partners in Command: The Relationships between Leaders in the Civil War* (New York: Free Press, 1994), 102–4.
16. James M. McPherson, *Ordeal by Fire: The Civil War and Reconstruction* (New York: McGraw Hill, 2001), 243–56.
17. Joseph T. Glatthar, *General Lee's Army: From Victory to Collapse* (New York: Free Press, 2008), 102.
18. James I. Robertson Jr., *Stonewall Jackson: The Man, the Soldier, the Legend* (New York: Macmillan, 1997), 362.
19. George McClellan to Abraham Lincoln, April 20, 1862, in *The Civil War Papers of George B. McClellan: Selected Correspondence, 1860–1865*, ed. Stephen W. Sears (New York: Da Capo Press, 1992), 244–45.
20. George McClellan to Edwin Stanton, April 27, 1862, ibid., 249.
21. Charles Marshall, *An Aide-de-Camp of Lee: Being the Papers of Colonel Charles Marshall Sometime Aide-de-Camp, Military Secretary and Assistant Adjutant General on the Staff of Robert E. Lee, 1862–1865*, ed. Frederick Maurice (Boston: Little, Brown, 1927), 73.

22. Richard Harwell, *Lee: An Abridgment in One Volume of the Four-Volume "R. E. Lee" by Douglas Southall Freeman* (New York: Touchstone, 1997), 189; J. Cutlery Andrews, *The South Reports the Civil War* (Pittsburgh: University of Pittsburgh Press, 1985), 114–15, 118; Thomas, *Robert E. Lee*, 231.

23. Henry B. McClellan, *I Rode with Jeb Stuart: The Life and Campaigns of Major General J. E. B. Stuart*, ed. Burke Davis (New York: Da Capo Press, 1994), 427.

24. Augustus Dickert, *History of Kershaw's Brigade* (Lexington, Ky.: Civil War Classic Library, 2013), 79.

25. Mary Chesnut, *Mary Chesnut's Civil War*, ed. C. Vann Woodward (New Haven, Conn.: Yale University Press, 1981), 116.

26. Stephen Ramseur to Dear Brother, June 5, 1862, in *The Bravest of the Brave: The Correspondence of Stephen Dodson Ramseur*, ed. George G. Kundahl (Chapel Hill: University of North Carolina Press, 2010), 96.

27. Quoted in Wert, *Glorious Army*, 56.

28. Quoted in Andrews, *South Reports the Civil War*, 194.

29. Daniel H. Hill, "Lee Attacks North of the Chickahominy," in *Battles & Leaders* (Castle Books, 1956), 2:359.

30. Robert E. L. Krick, "The Men Who Carried This Position Were Soldiers Indeed: The Decisive Charge of Whiting's Division at Gaines's Mill," in *The Richmond Campaign of 1862: The Peninsula and the Seven Days*, ed. Gary W. Gallagher (Chapel Hill: University of North Carolina Press, 2000), 205. Krick places the losses of the entirety of Brigadier General W. H. C. Whiting's brigade at 1,035. This division also included the men of Evander Law's brigade. The division totaled nearly 5,300 men as they came onto the field. Krick states, "The day's losses reached about 20 percent, a figure not as awful as the accounts make one believe" (205).

31. J. F. J. Caldwell, *The History of a Brigade of South Carolinians, Known First as Gregg's and Subsequently as McGowan's Brigade* (Philadelphia: King and Baird Printers, 1866), 78–79. Historian Stephen Sears places McGowan's losses at 815. See *To the Gates of Richmond: The Peninsula Campaign* (New York: Ticknor and Fields, 1992), 224–25. The *OR* places the brigade's total losses in the campaign at 929. See *OR*, vol. 11, pt. 2, 982.

32. Brian K. Burton, *Extraordinary Circumstances: The Seven Days Battles* (Bloomington: Indiana University Press, 2001), 337.

33. Ibid.; *OR*, vol. 11, pt. 2, 979–80.

34. Burton, *Extraordinary Circumstances*, 337.

35. Daniel H. Hill, "McClellan's Change of Base and Malvern Hill," *Battles & Leaders*, 2:395.

36. Hill is referring to the famed "Charge of the Light Brigade."

37. Hill, "Lee Attacks North of the Chickahominy," 2:352.

38. Glatthar, *General Lee's Army*, 198; Wert, *Glorious Army*, 57; *OR*, vol. 11, pt. 2, 985–91; Robert K. Krick, *Lee's Colonels: A Biographical Register of the Field Officers of the Army of Northern Virginia* (Dayton, Ohio: Morningside, 1992); Gary W. Gallagher, *Confederate War: How Popular Will, Nationalism, and Military Strategy Could Not Stave Off Defeat* (Cambridge, Mass.: Harvard University Press, 1999), 115.

39. To be exact, 22.9 percent.

40. Douglas Southall Freeman, *Manassas to Malvern Hill*, vol. 1 of *Lee's Lieutenants: A Study in Command* (New York: Scribner's, 1970), 604.

41. Thomas, *Robert E. Lee*, 243.

42. Taylor, *General Lee*, 84.

43. Robert E. Lee to Mary Lee, July 9, 1862, in *The War Time Papers of R. E. Lee*, ed. Clifford Dowdey and Louis H. Manarin (New York: Bramhall House, 1961), 230.

44. Lee's first "campaign" was the assault at John Brown's Fort at Harpers Ferry. It was more of a skirmish rather than a campaign or battle. His second campaign was in western Virginia at Cheat Mountain.

45. Robert E. Lee to Mary Lee, December 16, 1862, in *War Time Papers of R. E. Lee*, 365.

46. Carl von Clausewitz, *On War*, ed. and trans. Michael Howard and Peter Paret (Princeton, N.J.: Princeton University Press, 1989), 228.

47. McPherson, *Ordeal by Fire*, 272–73.

48. It should be noted that Pope also had assistance on the field from the Army of the Potomac's III, V, and IX Corps.

49. Wert, *Glorious Army*, 103–4; Glatthar, *General Lee's Army*, 198; *OR*, vol. 12, pts. 1 and 2.

50. Dr. Harvey Black, *A Surgeon with Stonewall Jackson: The Civil War Letters of Dr. Harvey Black*, ed. Glenn McMullen (Baltimore: Butternut and Blue, 1995), 39.

51. *OR*, vol. 19, pt. 2, 590.

52. Ibid., 590–94; Dennis Frye, *Antietam Revealed: The Battle of Antietam and the Maryland Campaign as You Have Never Seen It Before* (Collingwood, N.J.: C. W. Historicals, 2004), 5. Historian Joseph L. Harsh does not believe in the notion Lee crossed the Potomac River in hopes of influencing European intervention. He calls it a "fallacious connection." James Murfin, Dennis Frye, and Stephen Sears support the European theory. Even if it was not foremost in Lee's mind, it certainly had to be in Davis's, as John Slidell wrote from England of the status of British intervention on the eve

of the forthcoming campaign. Joseph L. Harsh, *Sounding the Shallows: A Confederate Companion for the Maryland Campaign of 1862* (Kent, Ohio: Kent State University Press, 2000), 138.

53. The French referred to the methodical battle as *bataille conduit*, which translates to "battle by guidance."

54. The South had a free population of 5,482,222 in the eleven states that made up the Southern Confederacy, whereas the North had a free population of 23,181,644, which did not include the border states or the District of Columbia.

55. *OR*, vol. 19, pt. 2, 590.

56. Harsh, *Sounding the Shallows*, 202.

57. Wert, *Glorious Army*, 141, 146–49.

58. Alexander, *Fighting for the Confederacy*, 92.

59. Glatthar, *General Lee's Army*, 198; Stephen W. Sears, *Landscape Turned Red: The Battle of Antietam* (New York: Civil War Book of the Month Club, 1983), 366–72; *OR*, vol. 19, pts. 1 and 2.

60. Glatthar, *General Lee's Army*, 198; Sears, *Landscape Turned Red*, 366–72; *OR*, vol. 19, pts. 1 and 2.

61. Frye, *Antietam Revealed*, 84, 86–87, 89.

62. Walter Taylor to Mary Lou, September 21, 1862, in *Lee's Adjutant: The Wartime Letters of Colonel Walter Herron Taylor, 1862–1865*, ed. R. Lockwood Tower (Columbia: University of South Carolina Press, 1995), 45.

63. Ibid., 44.

64. Francis Augustin O'Reilly, *The Fredericksburg Campaign: Winter War on the Rappahannock* (Baton Rouge: Louisiana State University Press, 2012), 499.

65. Robertson, *Stonewall Jackson*, 509.

66. Thomas J. Warren, 15th South Carolina, to unknown, May 10, 1863, Thomas J. Warren Papers, University of South Carolina Library, Columbia, S.C.

67. *OR*, vol. 27, pt. 2, 769.

68. General Stephen Ramseur to General Daniel Harvey Hill, May 22, 1863, in *Bravest of the Brave*, 134.

69. Stephen Ramseur to Brother, May 10, 1863, ibid., 132.

70. Ramseur to Hill, May 22, 1863, ibid., 134.

71. John Bigelow Jr., *The Campaign of Chancellorsville* (New Haven, Conn.: Yale University Press, 1910), 342, 349; Stephen W. Sears, *Chancellorsville* (New York: Mariner Books, 1998), 495; *OR*, vol. 27, pt. 2, 791, 807.

72. Wert, *Glorious Army*, 200–205.

73. *OR*, vol. 27, pt. 2, 803.

74. Wert, *Glorious Army*, 200; Sears, *Chancellorsville*, 433, 493, 501; Christian

Keller, *Chancellorsville and the Germans: Nativism, Ethnicity, and Civil War Memory* (New York: Fordham University Press, 2007), 91.

75. Alpheus Williams to Daughter, May 18, 1863, in *From the Cannon's Mouth: The Civil War Letters of General Alpheus Williams*, ed. Milo M. Quaife (Lincoln: University of Nebraska Press, 1995), 195.

76. Letter from V. A. S. P. in the *Savannah Republican*, May 19, 1863.

77. John H. Bogart to Home Folks, May 8, 1863, in William B. Styple, *Writing and Fighting from the Army of Northern Virginia: A Collection of Confederate Soldier Correspondence* (Kearny, N.J.: Belle Grove, 2003), 203.

78. Randolph H. McKim, *A Soldier's Recollections from the Diary of a Young Confederate: With an Oration on the Motives and Aims of the Soldiers of the South* (New York: Longmans, Green, 1910), 65.

79. William Jones, ed., *Southern Historical Society Papers* (Richmond, Va.: James E. Goode, 1877), 4:154.

80. Ibid.

81. Sears, *Chancellorsville*, 433, 493, 501.

82. Ibid.

83. Ham Chamberlayne to My Dear Mother, May 9, 1863, in *Ham Chamberlayne—Virginian: Letters and Papers of an Artillery Officer in the War for Southern Independence, 1861–1865*, ed. C. G. Chamberlayne (Richmond, Va.: Press of the Dietz Printing Co., 1932), 176. Ham's name was John Hampden Chamberlayne; his mother's name was Martha Burwell Chamberlayne.

84. Sears, *Chancellorsville*, 493–502.

85. It should be noted that two of the three division commanders who fell were acting division commanders taking over for wounded comrades.

86. Richard Brady Williams, ed., *Stonewall's Prussian Mapmaker: The Journals of Captain Oscar Hinrichs* (Chapel Hill: University of North Carolina Press, 2014), 78, 80.

87. Ramseur to Hill, May 22, 1863, in *Bravest of the Brave*, 135.

88. It should be noted that the losses of the officers varies from study to study. Some have placed the losses as low as fifty-seven, while others have placed the figure as high as eighty. Some officers who were wounded did not report to the hospital for their wounds; others did so after reports were filed. Thus, the reports are not always accurate, and letters and company rolls must be examined closely to find the most accurate number of losses.

89. *Savannah Republican*, May 18, 1863.

90. Quoted in Michael Korda, *Clouds of Glory: The Life and Legend of Robert E. Lee* (New York: Harper Collins, 2014), 98.

91. Douglas, *I Rode with Stonewall*, 247.

6. ❀ The Fall of Vicksburg

Editors' Introduction

In the summer of 1884, Century Magazine *contracted Ulysses S. Grant to pen four articles about his wartime service for a series that would eventually become known as "Battles & Leaders." For $500 per article—later upped to $2,000 each—Grant would write about the four most pivotal events of his Civil War career: Shiloh, Vicksburg, the Wilderness, and Appomattox.*

Shortly after he started on his project, though, Grant decided to swap out his article on Appomattox for an article on Chattanooga. "Isn't Lee's surrender of most importance to us?" an exasperated editor with the magazine asked a colleague.[1] However, Grant recognized Chattanooga's significance because it represented a new chapter in his career. Indeed, it opened a whole new book—quite literally. His two-volume Personal Memoirs of Ulysses S. Grant—*which grew from those four* Century *articles—begins with Chattanooga.*

Grant found himself in southeast Tennessee in late October 1863 because besieging Confederate forces had trapped the Federal Army of the Cumberland, commanded by Major General William S. Rosecrans. "The administration as well as the General-in-Chief was nearly frantic at the situation of affairs there," Grant wrote in his memoirs.[2] Secretary of War Edwin Stanton, serving as the personal emissary of President Lincoln, traveled west to meet Grant on October 17 and charge him with sorting the mess out. Stanton also carried orders promoting Grant to command of the newly created Military Division of Mississippi—a position and division created specifically for him. The new command combined the Departments of the Ohio, the Cumberland, and the Tennessee and covered all the territory from the Allegheny Mountains to the Mississippi River. In essence, Grant now commanded virtually all military operations in the West. His first order of business: Chattanooga.

Lincoln had had his eye on Grant for some time. As the story goes, when a jealous Henry Halleck tried to sideline Grant, Lincoln reportedly nixed the idea, saying of Grant, "I can't spare this man. He fights." While it now seems

Initially slated to be a grave marker, this white obelisk was commandeered by Federal troops for use as a monument to mark the location where Federal major general Ulysses S. Grant met with Confederate lieutenant general John C. Pemberton to discuss the surrender of Vicksburg. Over time, relic hunters chipped away at the monument, which was eventually moved to the battlefield visitor center for protection. It remains there on display. *Library of Congress*

Lincoln never uttered such an endorsement, it has nonetheless become apocryphal of Lincoln's attitude about him.[3]

In fact, Grant's most stubborn opposition came not from Confederates on the battlefield but from his former superior, General-in-Chief Henry Halleck, who did everything he could to stymie Grant's rise. Even in the wake of Grant's monumental victory at Vicksburg in July 1863, Halleck squandered Grant's momentum and dismantled his army rather than risk another Grant victory elsewhere. "The General-in-chief having decided against me," Grant wrote, "the depletion of an army, which had won a succession of great victories, commenced."[4]

But Lincoln had taken more note of Grant's victory along the river than Grant realized. "If Grant only does one thing down there," Lincoln had vowed, "I don't care much how, so long as he does it right—why, Grant is my man and I am his the rest of the war!"[5] *When Grant finally succeeded at Vicksburg, Lincoln stayed true to his word. By the fall of 1863, Grant was his go-to general. Vicksburg had sealed the deal.*

As Daniel T. Davis points out, Grant's string of victories prior to July 4, 1863, might have made him the hardest-working man in the Western Theater, but his capture of the so-called Gibraltar of the West opened the door for Grant in a way nothing else had—one that would have monumental implications on the entire course of the war. "It looks now as though Providence had directed the course of the campaign while the Army of the Tennessee executed the decree," Grant wrote in his memoirs.[6]

In a book that ran 291,000 words over an original draft of 1,231 pages, Vicksburg came at roughly the chronological midpoint of Grant's memoirs, just as it came at roughly the chronological midpoint of the war. But Vicksburg represented more than a tidy breaking point in Grant's narrative structure: it closed one volume of his career and opened the page on another.

Vicksburg: The Victory That Unleashed Ulysses S. Grant

Daniel T. Davis

The men of the Army of the Tennessee could find little comfort even in the light breeze that blew in from the west across the river. The Mississippi heat was not only pervasive but also oppressive—and combined with the humidity, it was unbearable. No matter how much water one consumed, it never seemed enough. Still, it did not keep the Union engineers from their work. As the July sun beat down and their muscles ached, they labored diligently, stopping only to wipe the sweat from their foreheads. "Every man in the investing line became an army engineer day and night," wrote one Federal soldier.[7]

All up and down the Union lines, preparations were underway for a massive assault against the Confederate works outside Vicksburg. The engineers widened the approaches and débouchés to allow the men of the infantry to move easily out of their entrenchments and toward the enemy. "The soldiers got so they bored like gophers and beavers, with a spade in one hand and a gun in the other," one said.[8] They readied planks to allow the soldiers to pass easily over ditches and stuffed bags of cotton as filler for their bridging. Major General Ulysses S. Grant had scheduled the assault for July 6, 1863.

Around ten on the morning of July 3—three days before the scheduled attack—"white flags appeared on a portion of the rebel works."[9] Shortly thereafter, Confederate major general John Bowen appeared, accompanied by an aide. Bowen carried with him a dispatch for Grant from Lieutenant General John C. Pemberton, the commander of the city's defenses. Pemberton proposed "an armistice . . . with the view to arranging terms for the

135

Grant and Pemberton met to discuss surrender terms beneath an oak tree. Today, an oak still stands on the spot. The original surrender marker has been replaced by an upturned cannon barrel. *Photo by Dan Davis*

capitulation of Vicksburg. To this end, if agreeable to you, I will appoint three commissioners, to meet a like number to be named by yourself. . . . I make this proposition to save the further effusion of blood, which must otherwise be shed to a frightful extent."[10]

Moving across the open space between the two opposing sides, Bowen was greeted by Brigadier General Andrew Jackson Smith. Bowen had been Grant's neighbor from his Missouri days, and Bowen requested a meeting with him.[11] Through Smith, Grant declined the request. Under the circumstances, he would meet only with Pemberton, not one of his subordinates. Bowen then suggested that Pemberton and Grant meet, to which Grant agreed. Grant sent Bowen back with a reply to Pemberton's letter: "Your note of this date is just received, proposing an armistice for several hours for the purpose of arranging terms of capitulation through commissioners, to be appointed, etc. The useless effusion of blood you propose stopping by this course can be ended at any time you may choose, by . . . unconditional surrender." These were words Grant had used in the past.[12]

The Vicksburg Campaign came at roughly the halfway point of the American Civil War. Coupled with the Federal victory at Gettysburg, Pennsylvania, and the successful Tullahoma campaign in middle Tennessee, the summer of 1863 was one massive turning point. But was it a turning point because of the three victories by the three principal Federal armies, or rather was it a turning point because it led to the rise of Ulysses S. Grant?

Much of the attention on that summer of 1863 focuses on the crossroads town in south-central Pennsylvania, but the reality was that Grant accomplished more at Vicksburg than the Army of the Potomac had accomplished in the previous two years of the war. By capturing the "Gibraltar of the Confederacy," Grant successfully cut the Confederacy in two. Situated on high bluffs that overlooked the Mississippi River, Vicksburg kept open the last lifeline between the eastern half of the Confederacy and the Trans-Mississippi region. The fall of the city severed that lifeline and gave the Federal navy unfettered control of the river. It was also a blow in morale to the Confederate populace. "All looks gloomy," wrote Confederate nurse Kate Cumming. "There is scarcely one bright spot to be seen."[13]

Above all, Vicksburg illustrated the capability of Grant as a commander, who was flush with "dogged persistence" and an ability to execute the war aims of the Lincoln administration.[14] While Vicksburg was not the apex of Grant's career, the Vicksburg Campaign firmly set the course for his ascension to the command of all Federal armies—the ultimate turning point for the Northern war effort.

The rise of Ulysses S. Grant began modestly. Born in Point Pleasant, Ohio, to Jesse and Hannah Grant on April 27, 1822, Ulysses had a middle-class upbringing. Appointed to the United States Military Academy at West Point, he graduated twenty-first out of thirty-nine cadets in the class of 1843. He described his time at West Point as "interminable."[15]

Grant's prewar service took him to the Mexican-American War, where he distinguished himself and showed off the equestrian skills that he was so well known for. After the war, he stayed in the army but found outpost duty dull. During this time, Grant took to the bottle, which helped shape future perceptions of him. Still, most who crossed the young officer's path thought well of him. Future Confederate general Henry Heth "found him a most genial and pleasant companion" who "never tired [of] listening to my buffalo hunts, my wolf hunts, and coursing jack rabbits."[16] Grant's close friend and confidant William T. Sherman thought, "To me he is a mystery, and I believe he is a mystery to himself."[17]

Resigning his commission from the army, Grant tried his hand at farming and bill collecting, to no avail. His father then offered him a job in his leather shop, which Ulysses accepted. When the war clouds rolled in, Grant was appointed the commander of the Twenty-First Illinois and later promoted to brigadier general.

Early in 1862, Grant led an expedition against Confederate-held Fort Henry. Along with Fort Donelson, the twin fortifications made up the cornerstone of a defensive line that guarded the entrance to northwest Tennessee. After a brief shelling by Union gunboats, Fort Henry surrendered on February 6. With the initiative firmly in hand, Grant marched his men the dozen miles overland to Fort Donelson.[18]

Confederates successfully defended their position against a naval bombardment on Valentine's Day and then launched an assault on the right flank of Grant's assembled army in the hope of breaking out. "The enemy were repelled after a closely contested battle," Grant wrote of the action. Undeterred, Grant launched a counterattack, which gained the outer Confederate works, making the position inside the fort untenable. The next morning, Confederate brigadier general Simon B. Buckner—another old friend of Grant's—sent a flag of truce through the lines for the purposes of negotiating the "terms of capitulation." "No terms except unconditional and immediate surrender can be accepted," Grant replied. Buckner surrendered the garrison on February 16.[19]

The fall of Forts Henry and Donelson gave the North its first major victory of the conflict, and Grant suddenly became a household name as the population erupted in celebration. Citizens in Cincinnati closed their shops upon hearing the news and took to the streets, setting off fireworks. Cheers exploded from the U.S. Senate when the victory was announced to them in Washington. Newspapers wrote of Grant smoking a cigar in the midst of the fighting at Donelson, and, not surprisingly, the grateful public flooded his headquarters with boxes of them. People quipped that Grant's initials, "U. S.," really stood for "unconditional surrender."[20]

Strategically, Grant had kicked open the Confederacy's western door. The Federals now had control of the Tennessee and Cumberland Rivers, giving them a line of advance into Tennessee and the northern reaches of Mississippi and Alabama. For his efforts, Grant received a promotion to major general.

Yet Grant also received what must have been puzzling pushback from his immediate superior, Major General Henry Halleck. Although the route to Nashville lay open, Halleck ordered Grant not to advance there. Recognizing the importance of the Tennessee capital, Grant pined to go, but he dared not directly disobey his superior. Instead, he found a creative way around the problem—a skill that would become one of his hallmarks. For the attack on Donelson, Halleck had sent Grant a division of reinforcements under Brigadier General William "Bull" Nelson, on loan from Major General Don Carlos Buell's Army of the Ohio. Donelson fell before Nelson arrived, so Grant diverted Nelson's men to Nashville, where they were to meet with Buell. Buell was, of course, nowhere near the city, but Nelson's presence there accomplished Grant's goal of occupying it.

Rather than appreciate Grant's ingenuity, Halleck was growing weary of his subordinate's aggressiveness.[21] By nature, Halleck was, a Union officer recalled, "sedate, deliberate, cautious." Known as "Old Brains," Halleck had built a reputation for being a brilliant military theorist—and Grant's battlefield practice threatened to jeopardize that reputation. Grant's purpose "seemed to be to strike and overcome the enemy without waiting." This unnerved the risk-averse Halleck, who, for all his brilliance, was also petty, shortsighted, and a hindrance to the prosecution of Lincoln's war effort. He tended to harbor ill feelings toward numerous officers for what he perceived as slights against him.

Ironically, Grant was among Halleck's many admirers. "I regard him as one of the great men of the age," Grant told his wife.[22] In addition, he firmly believed he sat in Halleck's good graces. "Though I say it myself I believe that I am the very last man in the Dept. Gen. Halleck would want to see taken out of it," he wrote.[23] Unbeknownst to Grant, Halleck had been plotting that very thing.

On March 1, Halleck sent Grant orders for a movement up the Tennessee River with the purpose of destroying Confederate railroad connections at

Corinth, Jackson, and Humboldt. When Halleck learned that Grant had made a daylong trip to Nashville to coordinate with Union forces under General Buell, he vented his frustration to the general-in-chief, Major General George B. McClellan. "He left his command without my authority," Halleck complained. "It is hard to censure a successful general . . . but I think he richly deserves it." McClellan instructed Halleck to arrest Grant "if the good of the service requires it." Ironically, as the two generals conspired behind his back, Grant was writing to his wife that "there are not two men in the United States who I would prefer serving under than Halleck and McClellan."[24]

Halleck promptly ordered Grant to relinquish the Tennessee expedition to another officer and return to Fort Henry. Stung and confused, Grant offered to resign. "My going to Nashville, I did not regard particularly as going beyond my district," Grant explained.[25] Halleck, spoiling for an excuse to discredit his successful subordinate, pressed the attack.

Apprised of the situation, President Lincoln interceded and directed Halleck that any wrongdoing on the part of Grant be promptly reported. With the president involved and no real charges to level at his subordinate, Halleck backed down and restored Grant to his former command.[26]

Grant rejoined his army, now encamped about Pittsburg Landing along the Tennessee River, in the middle of March. His objective lay just to the south at Corinth, Mississippi. A rail junction that connected the eastern and western Confederacy, Corinth was also the concentration point for rebel forces under General Albert Sidney Johnston. Grant planned to move on Corinth once Buell's army arrived from Nashville. Johnston, however, was not about to wait for Grant's next move. On April 6, the Confederates attacked. Although the Federals fought stubbornly throughout the day, Grant was forced to retreat to a new position along the banks of the Tennessee River. Reinforcements made it possible for him to stay on the field instead of having to retreat, and the next day Grant attacked and regained all the lost ground. By the end of the battle, which derived its name from a nearby Methodist meetinghouse known as Shiloh, Grant held the field, and the Confederates were forced to retreat back to Corinth.[27]

"Probably no single battle of the war gave rise to such wild and damaging reports," one of Grant's division commanders, Brigadier General William T. Sherman, wrote of Shiloh. "It was publicly asserted at the North that our army was taken completely by surprise; that General Grant was drunk."[28] Although completely false, such damaging accounts did not escape the eager ears of Halleck. To him, Grant had mishandled the battle. A stronger, more controlling hand was needed for the army. Four days after the fighting ended, Halleck himself stepped off a boat at Pittsburg Landing. "It soon became manifest that his mind had been prejudiced by the rumors which had gone forth to the detriment of General Grant," Sherman remembered.[29] Despite Grant's tactical victory, he was once again under the veil of Halleck's suspicions. Halleck removed Grant from his post and "promoted" him to second-in-command, effectively sidelining him. Halleck had decided that he would lead the Union drive on Corinth personally. During the campaign, Grant recalled, he was "little more than an observer. Orders were sent direct to the right wing or reserve, ignoring me, and advances were made from one line of intrenchments to another without notifying me. My position was so embarrassing in fact that I made several applications during the siege to be relieved."[30]

Corinth fell to the Federals in late May. Grant's dejection continued, as he remained a mere figurehead under Halleck. On the verge of leaving the army, Grant stayed only because Sherman reassured him that "some happy accident might restore him to favor and his true place."[31]

Sherman's words proved prophetic. In July 1862, in reward for his accomplishments—which were really mostly Grant's—Halleck was promoted to the position of general-in-chief of the army and summoned to Washington. Ranking immediately behind Halleck in seniority, Grant assumed command upon his departure.

After repulsing a Confederate offensive against Corinth that fall, Grant set his sights on the capture of a city situated along the Mississippi River: Vicksburg.[32] A major Union objective, its reduction loomed large in the eyes of the Union high command, especially those of President Lincoln. "See what a lot of land these fellows hold, of which Vicksburg is the key," he remarked while studying a map during one strategy council. "From Vicksburg . . . supplies can be distributed by rail all over the Confederacy. The war can never be brought to a close until the key is in our pocket."[33]

Likewise, its defense was also crucial for the Confederates. "Vicksburg was important," Grant wrote, ". . . because it occupied the first high ground coming close to the river below Memphis. From there a railroad runs east, connecting with other roads leading to all points of the Southern States. A railroad also started from the opposite side of the river, extending west as far as Shreveport, Louisiana. Vicksburg was the only channel . . . connecting the parts of the Confederacy divided by the Mississippi. So long as it was held by the enemy, the free navigation of the river was prevented."[34] Jefferson Davis called Vicksburg "the nail-head that held the South's two halves together."[35]

Grant's autumn efforts to capture Vicksburg failed miserably. His march overland into Mississippi was turned back by Confederate cavalry, which destroyed his supply base at Holly Springs. "The destruction of the stores . . . was an irreparable loss to Grant," a Confederate surgeon who participated in the raid recalled. "His position untenable, he fell back to . . . Memphis."[36] At the same time, a coordinated riverine expedition led by Sherman, now a major general, was repulsed above the city at Chickasaw Bluffs.[37] With winter setting in and the campaigning season coming to an end, Grant resolved to try again in the new year.[38]

Early in 1863, Grant shifted his force to Louisiana, but his fortunes did not improve. Attempts to put his army on dry ground from which to operate against Vicksburg proved to be exceedingly frustrating. An effort to construct a canal and bypass Vicksburg in March was abandoned due to the rapid rise of the Mississippi, which caused the supporting dam to give way. A subsequent naval expedition led by Rear Admiral David Porter's naval squadron along Steele's Bayou above Vicksburg also failed "from want of knowledge as to what would be required to open this route [rather] than from any impracticability in the navigation of the streams and bayous through which it was proposed to pass."[39]

It is easy to look at the string of failures and write Grant off as ineffectual, but a more suitable interpretation would be to recognize the tenacity Grant continued to show. Rather than let a failure stop him, he worked the problem and came up with yet another possible solution. It had served him following the naval repulse at Donelson, when faced with the need to occupy Nashville, after the first day of fighting at Shiloh, and even in his dealings with Halleck. "While perhaps not the Federal's most brilliant strategist or outstanding tactician," historian Wiley Sword later assessed, "Grant possessed an iron will and a courageous inner strength that enabled him to risk decisive action."[40]

Lincoln, casting a keen eye on the Mississippi, seemed patient enough to let Grant keep trying, and by mid-April, Grant decided on his next attempt: an audacious overland march through the interior of Mississippi to attack Vicksburg from the east. First, he marched his army south through Louisiana to a point below Vicksburg. Coordinating with the Union navy, Grant ordered Porter to run the Vicksburg defenses and rendezvous with him below the city. It was a risky gambit, but, under heavy Confederate fire, Porter's boats successfully ran the gauntlet. The navy then ferried the blue infantry across to the Mississippi side. Flanking the defenses at Grand Gulf, Grant landed his transports at Bruinsburg. "When this was effected I felt a degree of relief scarcely ever equaled since," Grant wrote after the war. "I was now

Grant's Attempts
at Vicksburg

0   miles   50

Hal Jespersen

1. Central Miss. Advance Nov 14–Dec 21
2. Holly Springs Dec 20
3. Chickasaw Bayou Dec 27–29
4. Arkansas Post (Fort Hindman) Jan 9–11
5. Grant's Canal Jan 24–Mar 27
6. Lake Providence Expedition Feb 3–Mar 29
7. Yazoo Pass Expedition Feb 3–Apr 10
8. Fort Pemberton Mar 11–Apr 5
9. Steele's Bayou Expedition Mar 14–27
A. Duckport Canal Mar 31–Apr 11
B. Vicksburg Campaign Mar 29–May 22
C. Grierson's Raid Apr 17–May 2
D. Siege of Vicksburg May 22–Jul 4

Grant's Attempts at Vicksburg. Between November 1862 and July 1863, Grant tried and tried again to take Vicksburg. Each time that Confederates—or Mother Nature—foiled him, he simply took another tack. He tried infantry advances, riverine expeditions, and cavalry raids, even digging a canal to simply bypass the city. Finally, at the end of March 1863, he cut loose from his supply base and marched a force through the Mississippi interior, the men living off the land as they advanced. The maneuver ended with Grant encircling Vicksburg. The ensuing siege lasted forty-five days. *Map by Hal Jespersen* in the enemy's country, with a vast river and the stronghold of Vicksburg between me and my base of supplies. But I was on dry ground on the same side of the river with the enemy. All the campaigns, labors, hardships and exposures . . . previous to this time that had been made and endured were for the accomplishment of this one object."[41]

The Federals then set off through Mississippi's interior. The first leg of the march took them to the capital at Jackson, a vital supply link for the Vicksburg garrison. Along the way, Grant fought and defeated the Confederates at Port Gibson and Raymond. After driving the enemy out of Jackson, Grant turned east, defeating his foe again at Champion's Hill and the Big Black River before he reached and surrounded Vicksburg. In an effort to take the city, Grant launched two assaults on May 19 and May 22. Both were repulsed. "The last attack only served to increase our casualties without giving any benefit whatever," Grant wrote. Rather than risk another attack, Grant decided to lay siege to the Confederates.[42]

As the siege progressed, Grant remained confident as to its outcome. "I do not look upon the fall of Vicksburg as in the least doubtful," he wrote to his father on June 15. "If, however, I could have carried the place . . . I could by this time have made a campaign that would have made the State of Mississippi almost safe for a solitary horseman to ride over. . . . The enemy have a large army in it." Although he was engaged against Pemberton, Grant was already beginning to cast his eye toward other, larger operations.[43]

It took six weeks for Grant's forces to wear the Confederates down, but by July 2, Pemberton had had enough. He later wrote it was "useless" to hope for the salvation of the city. He called a council of war at his headquarters. "After much consideration, it was advised that I address a note to General Grant . . . to arrange terms of capitulation," he remembered.[44]

With Grant's reply of unconditional surrender in hand, Pemberton acceded to a meeting with his counterpart. Around 3:00 p.m., some five hours after Bowen appeared along the Confederate line with a flag of truce, Pemberton, along with Bowen and one of Pemberton's staffers, Colonel L. M. Montgomery, met with Grant. The Federal commander was accompanied by Major Generals Edward O. C. Ord and James B. McPherson, along with General Smith.[45]

The parties met "on a hillside within a few hundred feet of the of the rebel lines." They exchanged pleasantries, and then, after a brief pause, Pemberton indicated he "understood that he [Grant] had expressed a wish to have a personal interview with me." Pemberton was unaware that Bowen had proposed the meeting, and Grant responded in the negative. Bowen then stepped in to clear up the confusion.[46]

As the conversation continued, Pemberton wished to confirm Grant's demand for an unconditional surrender. Grant replied that he had no other terms to offer. Defiantly, and as a front, Pemberton maintained that he had provisions enough to supply his garrison. In reality, cut off from the outside world, the Confederates had no hope of resupply, and it was only a matter of time before they ran out of food.

Grant paused for a moment and then suggested he and Pemberton step aside and allow the accompanying officers to discuss possible terms of surrender. Removing themselves from the conversation, "General Grant and I remained apart," Pemberton wrote, "conversing only upon topics that had no relation to the important subject that brought us together." After several minutes, the discussion culminated, and the two sides returned to their lines with a promise from Grant to submit written terms to Pemberton no later than ten o'clock that night.[47]

When Grant returned to his headquarters, he called a meeting of his division and brigade commanders. He reconsidered his terms earlier in the morning as "there would have been over thirty thousand men to transport to Cairo [Illinois], very much to the inconvenience of the army on the Mississippi." Following the conference, Grant sent new conditions to Pemberton, stating his men were to be paroled. Pemberton responded and countered with amendments. Pemberton proposed "to surrender the city and garrison under my command, by marching out with my colors and arms, stacking them in front of my lines. After which you will take possession." Officers were to "retain their side-arms and personal property, and the right and property of citizens" was "to be respected."[48]

"I can make no stipulations with regard to the treatment of citizens and their private property," Grant replied. "While I do not propose to cause them any undue annoyance or loss, I cannot . . . leave myself under any restraint by stipulations." The conditions were purely of a military nature and did not concern the residents of Vicksburg. Grant simply ignored that part of Pemberton's proposal. He wrote that if a response was not received by nine o'clock the next morning, the conditions would be considered "rejected" on the part of Pemberton and the Union troops "shall act accordingly." Pemberton decided not to push the issue and "promptly accepted these terms."[49]

On Independence Day, the "garrison . . . marched out of their works and formed line in front, stacked arms and marched back in good order." Brigadier General John "Black Jack" Logan's division then marched through the lines to occupy the city. Grant himself rode in later in the day and made his way down to the city dock to meet and congratulate Admiral Porter. "The capture of Vicksburg, with its garrison, ordnance, and ordnance stores, and the successful battles fought in reaching them, gave new spirit to the loyal people of the North," he remembered. "New hopes for the final success of the cause of the Union were inspired . . . now the Mississippi was entirely in possession of the National troops."[50]

In less than three months, Grant battled for and took Vicksburg. His men inflicted more than 9,000 battlefield casualties and captured 29,491 officers and men.[51] They also captured more than 50,000 small arms and 172 pieces of artillery—all while suffering fewer than 11,000 casualties of their own.[52] "Some even claimed that it was the most decisive campaign ever waged in American military history—and justly so," said historian Terrance Winschel.[53]

"The Father of Waters again goes unvexed to the sea," Lincoln proclaimed.[54] This gave Federals a north-south avenue of transportation for the movement of goods and supplies necessary for the continuation of the war effort. Conversely for the Confederacy, it cut their free flow of supplies from the Trans-Mississippi. The eastern and southern Confederacy was effectively severed from Arkansas, Texas, and the border state of Missouri.[55]

During the campaign, Grant had coordinated his movements over a vast amount of territory and along a major river and its surrounding swampy environs. Success depended not only on his subordinates but also on supporting naval forces. The experience of directing such a vast endeavor shifted Grant's concept of strategy. Rather than analyzing one objective, he began to see the larger scope of the war and how various pieces made up the entire whole.

With Vicksburg in hand, Grant contemplated operations for the remainder of the summer and fall. Just as he had written to his father about another campaign in Mississippi during the Vicksburg siege, he now turned his sights toward neighboring Alabama. "I suggested to the General-in-Chief the idea of a campaign against Mobile," he intimated.[56] Its capture would cut off a major seaport for the Confederacy. Coming on the heels of Vicksburg, it could potentially deal an irreparable blow to enemy fortunes in the West.

More imaginative minds, however, did not bother limiting the scope of Grant's activity to the West. By the end of July, Grant's name had begun circulating as a possible candidate to command the Army of the Potomac. This had as much to do with the administration's frustration over Major General George Gordon Meade's inability to finish off the Army of Northern Virginia after Gettysburg as it did with Grant's parallel success in Vicksburg. Either way, Grant urged Assistant Secretary of War Charles Dana to discourage the idea. "It would cause me more sadness than satisfaction to be ordered to the command of the Army of the Potomac. . . . There I would have all to learn," Grant admitted. "Besides more or less dissatisfaction would be necessarily produced by importing a General to command an army already well supplied with those who have grown up, and been promoted, with it."[57] Dana replied that "there is no probability of any change in the Army of the Potomac. . . . There is however, much dissatisfaction with the present state of things, but it takes a long time to make any movement at Hd. Qtrs."[58] His words would prove prophetic.

Meanwhile, Grant seemed content to plot against Mobile. Unfortunately, Halleck disapproved of the idea, afraid of giving his subordinate yet another opportunity to win laurels. Instead, the general-in-chief began detaching portions of Grant's army to scattered details across the Western Department. "The depletion of an army, which had won a succession of great victories, commenced," Grant wrote bitterly as his force was broken up and shuttled off.[59] Rather than moving on Mobile, Halleck envisioned a new offensive west of the Mississippi River.

To that end, in August, Grant traveled to New Orleans to coordinate operations with Major General Nathaniel Banks. Following an inspection of Banks's army, Grant's horse became unruly and then suddenly took off, out of control. Spooked by the sound of a locomotive, it reared and fell on the general. When he awakened, Grant found himself "in a hotel near by with several doctors attending me. My leg was swollen from the knee to the thigh . . . the pain was almost beyond endurance."[60] He returned to Vicksburg, confined to his bed.

Very soon the injury would be the least of Grant's concerns. Events hundreds of miles away pulled him back into the field, where he yearned to be. In the months that followed the fall of Vicksburg, Lincoln was presented with the harsh reality of the failures of two of his key subordinates. Meade's inability to follow up on his Gettysburg victory in a timely manner had allowed Robert E. Lee's army to begin campaigning in northern Virginia again. Fruitless marching punctuated by minor engagements colored the fall of 1863 for the Army of the Potomac. The despondent Meade failed to bring the wily gray fox to decisive battle. "I used to think how nice it would be to be Commander-in-Chief," Meade opined. "Now, at this moment, I would sooner go, with a division, under the heaviest musketry fire, than hold my place!"[61]

Meanwhile in the west, Major General William Rosecrans, the victor of the Tullahoma campaign, failed, too. After his victory at Stones River the previous January, Rosecrans had failed to take to the field until late June. When he did, Rosecrans outmaneuvered the Confederate Army of Tennessee but in mid-September came to grief in the choked woods of Chickamauga in northwest

Georgia. Confederates followed up by bottling up the Federals in a siege at Chattanooga, and Rosecrans's army was in danger of being captured en masse.

Confederates occupied the high ground that commanded the city and had cut off Rosecrans's line of communication along the Tennessee River to Bridgeport, Alabama. In late September, Confederate cavalry under Major General Joseph Wheeler attacked and captured a large supply train. "This loss in wagons with the roads becoming almost impassable by reason of the heavy rains and the growing weakness of the animals, lessened daily the amount of supplies brought into the town," recalled a Union officer, "so that our troops were suffering for food and were in danger of being starved out of the Chattanooga."[62] The Federal army fell into a "state of semi-siege," recalled an Ohioan.[63]

Rosecrans's predicament was not lost on Washington. Assistant Secretary of War Charles Dana, who had attached himself to the general's headquarters as an observer earlier in the fall, was sending back daily reports on the situation inside the city. "Our condition and prospects grow worse and worse," wrote Dana.[64] The idea that Rosecrans might be forced to capitulate and an entire Union army surrender was too terrible to contemplate. Further, if the enemy regained Chattanooga, they would deprive Federals of a base from which they could maneuver into Georgia and threaten the logistical center of Atlanta. Middle Tennessee would be open to a Confederate offensive. Grant wrote that losing Chattanooga "would have been a terrible disaster."[65]

To that end, Dana, however, urged that a drastic action should be taken. On September 27, he suggested that if Rosecrans were to be removed "some Western general of high rank and great prestige" should replace him—and to Dana, there was only one man capable of holding such a position: Grant.[66]

With each passing day, the dispatches from the beleaguered city grew grimmer. "At any rate, such is our present situation; our animals starved and the men with starvation before them and the enemy bound to make desperate efforts to dislodge us," Dana wrote on October 11. "I have never seen a public man possessing talent with less administrative power, less clearness and steadiness in difficulty, and greater practical incapacity than General Rosecrans." Five days later, Dana wrote, "General Rosecrans seems to be insensible to the impending danger and dawdles with trifles in a manner which can scarcely be imagined. . . . I never saw anything which seemed so lamentable and hopeless."[67]

That was enough for the administration. Lincoln agreed with Dana's assessment that Grant was the best and only officer who could handle the crisis in Tennessee. Once again, just as he had in 1862, Lincoln came to Grant's rescue. Following through on Dana's recommendation, Lincoln placed Grant in command of the newly created Military Division of Mississippi, which encompassed the Departments of the Ohio, the Cumberland, and the Tennessee. So important was the assignment that Secretary of War Edwin Stanton decided to hand-deliver the orders. Grant received orders to make for Louisville, where he was to meet "an officer of the War Department."[68] Stanton intercepted Grant on his train in Indianapolis and handed him General Orders No. 337, appointing him to the new assignment. Grant readily accepted. His first task was to proceed immediately to Chattanooga. Stanton gave him the option to keep Rosecrans on as commander of the Army of the Cumberland, but Grant decided to replace him with Major General George H. Thomas.[69]

Upon his arrival, Grant first finished Rosecrans's preparations for bolstering the army's supply line. Once that flow of supplies resumed, Grant turned his attention to breaking the Confederate grip on the city. With a series of attacks on November 23, 24, and 25, Grant systematically drove Confederates from their various perches on the heights around the city. The resultant victory opened the way for a presumed invasion of the Deep South.

In a little more than two years, Grant had become the most powerful Union officer west of the Allegheny Mountains. Significantly, during that time, Grant not only had to fight the Confederates but also his immediate superior. After the fall of Fort Donelson and again following the battle of Shiloh, Halleck had put Grant on the shelf, and after Vicksburg, Halleck had tried to strip him of his army. Every time Grant won, Halleck seemed to punish him. "So far as my experience with General Halleck went," Grant later reflected, "it was very much easier for him to refuse a favor than to grant one."[70]

In March 1864, it fell to Lincoln to give Grant the favor by permanently removing him from under Halleck's thumb. Lincoln promoted Grant to the rank of lieutenant general—the first man to hold that permanent rank since George Washington—and named him general-in-chief of all the Union forces, superseding Halleck.[71] Secretary of the Navy Gideon Welles wrote of Halleck that he "originates nothing, anticipates nothing . . . takes no responsibility, plans nothing, suggests nothing, is good for nothing."[72] Following Grant's promotion, Halleck in effect became the army's chief of staff; Lincoln would describe him at one point as "little more . . . than a first-rate clerk."[73]

On April 20, 1864, Lincoln wrote a letter to Grant that, if not an explicit acknowledgment of Grant's troubles with Halleck, certainly could be interpreted as an indirect inference to them. "I wish to express . . . my entire satisfaction with what you have done up to this time, so far as I understand it," the president wrote. "You are vigilant and self-reliant; and, pleased with this, I wish not to obtrude any constraints or restraints upon you."[74] Reading into the letter, one might see Lincoln's caveat "as I understand it" as an admission that Halleck perhaps obscured Lincoln's understanding of early war events as information made its way up the chain to the president. And as Halleck seemed to do everything in his power to restrain Grant's self-reliance, Lincoln promised just the opposite.

Perhaps it was Grant's friend the Confederate general James Longstreet who summed up Grant's rise to command best: "An officer of the Union service had worked his way during three years of severe field service from obscure position with a regiment, to command of armies, and had borne his banners in triumph through battle and siege, over the prejudice of higher officers, until President Lincoln's good judgment told him Grant was the man for the times."[75]

On March 10, 1864, Ulysses S. Grant stepped from a train car at Brandy Station, Virginia. "I was a stranger to most of the Army of the Potomac," he later wrote.[76] Meade, the commander of the army, expected to be relieved of command. Following the non-battle of Mine Run at the end of the previous November, Meade had scolded one of his subordinates, claiming, "You have ruined me."[77] Inquiries from the Joint Committee on the Conduct of the War followed, as did inner army political fighting. Now, it seemed, the final fruits of that ruination had arrived from the West.

Unlike Halleck, though, Grant had the ability to work with subordinate officers and not perceive them as threats. Though Grant decided to make his headquarters with Meade's army, Meade retained command while Grant oversaw the overarching Federal strategy to end the war; Grant also blocked the interference from Washington that had plagued Meade's army since its conception.

For his grand offensive in the spring of 1864, Grant planned to move Union armies simultaneously, from Virginia to Louisiana, in one concerted effort to defeat the Confederate armies. This was unprecedented by any previous general-in-chief; neither Winfield Scott nor George McClellan nor Henry Halleck had been able to launch such an effort.[78] "The armies in the East and West acted independently and without concert, like a balky team, no two ever pulling together," Grant later wrote. "I therefore determined, first, to use the greatest number of troops practicable against the armed force of the enemy preventing him from using the same force at different seasons against first one and then the other of our armies."[79]

Historian J. F. C. Fuller accurately stated that "a lack of grand strategy had not only prolonged the war, but encouraged the peace party in the north."[80] It fell on Grant's shoulders to start bringing a perceivable end to the war. With 1864 being an election year, there was little doubt that more setbacks, especially in the Eastern Theater, would jeopardize Lincoln's reelection bid.

Prior to Vicksburg, Grant had concerned himself only with the strategy and tactics of his own army. The consideration of a campaign across Mississippi, though—and then again against Mobile—illustrated how Grant began to appreciate the impact of operations beyond just his department of command. In the aftermath of Vicksburg, his mindset shifted to grand strategy—how each force acted in relation with one another. Fortunately, his promotion to command the Military Division of Mississippi coincided with his shifting approach to warfare, allowing him to further mature as a commander. Relieving the siege at Chattanooga required Grant to direct Thomas's army and elements of two others all at once, which he did skillfully.[81] His promotion to lieutenant general allowed him to then apply those lessons on the largest scale possible.

Grant's new perception also translated to seaborne operations. During operations against Forts Henry and Donelson, during the battle at Shiloh, and all throughout the Vicksburg Campaign, Grant had grown to understand and appreciate the value of joint operations between the army and navy. "The navy under Porter was all it could be," Grant wrote of operations on the Mississippi. "Without its assistance, the campaign could not have been successfully made." Grant's excellent working relationship with his naval counterpart proved key. "Grant and myself never indulged in long talks together," Porter recalled. "It was only necessary for him to tell me what he desired and I carried out his wishes to the best of my ability." This working relationship continued for the rest of the war. Grant encouraged greater army-navy collaboration—including the reduction of Fort Fisher outside Wilmington, North Carolina, in January 1865. His trust in Porter was so implicit that, in consultations during the war's final months with Lincoln and Sherman, Grant included Porter.[82]

Vicksburg made Grant's grand strategy possible because it made Grant-the-Grand-Strategist possible. Prior to Vicksburg's fall, he toiled under the jealous yoke of Henry Halleck yet still managed to keep succeeding in such fashion that Lincoln himself could not help but take notice. And Lincoln did, indeed, come through on his pledge of loyalty—"Grant is my man and I am his." By that time, Grant had honed his strategic skills and vision to such an extent that he was ready for the wider stage and, for him and for the nation, a new way of waging war.

On June 15, 1863, as he wrote to his father from the siege lines around Vicksburg, Grant could hardly have imagined what lay ahead for him. "The fall of Vicksburg will . . . result in the opening of the Mississippi River," he wrote. But then he added a gentle, but insightful, lamentation: "I intended more for it." He would get all he bargained for and more. In just weeks, the city would fall, unlocking the door for Grant's final, meteoric rise. Vicksburg would alter the trajectory of his military life, which in turn would alter the complexion of the war itself.

Almost as an afterthought, and as a quiet reassurance to himself, Grant closed his letter to his father with words as simple as they would be prophetic: "I did my best." Indeed, his best was yet to come.

Editors' Notes

1. *The Papers of Ulysses S. Grant*, ed. John Y. Simon, 32 vols. (Carbondale: Southern Illinois University Press, 1967–2012), 31:187.
2. *Ulysses S. Grant: Memoirs and Selected Letters; Personal Memoirs of U. S. Grant/ Selected Letters, 1839–1865*, ed. Mary D. McFeely and William S. McFeely (New York: Library of America, 1990), 260 (cited below as *Memoirs and Selected Letters*).
3. This statement, frequently attributed to Lincoln, appears to be apocryphal according to historian Brooks Simpson, who has tried unsuccessfully to track down the source. Simpson explains a little of the history of his scholarship on the topic at his blog, *Crossroads*: https://cwcrossroads.wordpress .com/2014/03/02/dont-tell-me-what-i-dont-want-to-know/.
4. Grant, *Memoirs and Selected Letters*, 259.
5. Quoted in Brooks D. Simpson, *Ulysses S. Grant: Triumph over Adversity, 1822–1865* (New York: Houghton Mifflin, 2000), 215.
6. Grant, *Memoirs and Selected Letters*, 257.

Contributor's Notes

7. Unidentified source, miscellaneous files (XV Corps), Vicksburg National Military Park, Miss.
8. Quoted in Terrance J. Winschel, *Triumph and Defeat: The Vicksburg Campaign* (New York: Savas Beatie, 2004), 131.
9. Ulysses S. Grant, "The Vicksburg Campaign," in *Battles & Leaders* (Castle Books, 1956), 3:530.
10. Ibid.
11. Ibid.

12. Ulysses S. Grant, *The Personal Memoirs of Ulysses S. Grant*, 2 vols. (Hartford, Conn.: Charles Webster, 1885), 1:555–58 (cited below as *Personal Memoirs*).

13. Richard Barksdale Harwell, ed., *Kate: The Journal of a Confederate Nurse* (Baton Rouge: Louisiana State University Press, 1998), 115.

14. Jean Edward Smith, *Grant* (New York: Simon and Schuster, 2001), 117–18; Bruce Catton, *Terrible Swift Sword* (New York: Doubleday, 1963), 29.

15. Ulysses S. Grant to Julia Dent Grant, July 13, 1851, in *Papers of Ulysses S. Grant*, 1:219.

16. *The Memoirs of Henry Heth*, ed. James L. Morrison (Westport, Conn.: Greenwood Press, 1974), 111.

17. Quoted in Jeffrey Wert, *The Sword of Lincoln: The Army of the Potomac* (New York: Simon and Schuster, 2005), 326.

18. Manning Ferguson Force, *From Fort Henry to Corinth* (Wilmington, N.C.: Broadfoot, 1989), 24, 27–28, 30–31.

19. *OR*, vol. 7, pt. 1, 159–61.

20. Bruce Catton, *Grant Moves South* (Boston: Little, Brown, 1960), 179–81; Jean Edward Smith, *Grant* (New York: Simon and Schuster, 2001), 165–66.

21. Force, *From Fort Henry to Corinth*, 64–65, 9.

22. Grant to Julia Dent Grant, March 1, 1862, in *Papers of Ulysses S. Grant*, 4:306. Grant repeated the assertion in an April 30 letter to Julia, as well, reprinted in *Memoirs and Selected Letters*, 1006.

23. Grant to Julia Dent Grant, March 23, 1862, reprinted in *Memoirs and Selected Letters*, 992.

24. Grant to Julia Dent Grant, March 1, 1862, in *Papers of Ulysses S. Grant*, 4:306. Grant repeated the assertion in a March 23 letter to Julia, as well, reprinted in *Memoirs and Selected Letters*, 992.

25. Grant to Henry Halleck, March 24, 1862, in *Memoirs and Selected Letters*, 991.

26. Ibid.; Force, *From Fort Henry to Corinth*, 92–96.

27. Grant, *Personal Memoirs*, 1:330–33, 335–36, 338–39, 345, 349–50, 354.

28. William T. Sherman, *Memoirs of General W. T. Sherman* (New York: Literary Classics of the United States, 1990), 1:265.

29. Ibid., 270.

30. Ibid.; Grant, *Personal Memoirs*, 1:377. Ironically, when Grant traveled with the Army of the Potomac in the spring of 1864, his immediate subordinate, Major General George Gordon Meade, would feel much the same way under Grant that Grant felt in the spring of 1862 under Halleck.

31. Sherman, *Memoirs*, 276.

32. Grant, *Personal Memoirs*, 1:392–93, 419–20.

33. David Dixon Porter, *Incidents and Anecdotes of the Civil War* (New York: D. Appleton, 1885), 95–96.

34. Ibid.; Grant, *Personal Memoirs*, 1:422.

35. Steven E. Woodworth. *Jefferson Davis and His Generals: The Failure of Confederate Command in the West* (Lawrence: University Press of Kansas, 1990), 221.

36. Emily Van Dorn Miller, *A Soldier's Honor with Reminiscences of Major-General Earl Van Dorn by His Comrades* (New York: Abbey Press, 1902), 236.

37. The battle of Chickasaw Bluffs is also known as the battle of Chickasaw Bayou.

38. S. H. Lockett, "The Defense of Vicksburg," in *Battles & Leaders*, 3:484–85.

39. Ibid.; *OR*, vol. 24, pt. 1, 44–46.

40. Wiley Sword, *Mountains Touched with Fire: Chattanooga Besieged, 1863* (New York: St. Martin's, 1995), 152.

41. Ibid.; *OR*, vol. 24, pt. 1, 46–48; Grant, *Personal Memoirs*, 1:480–81.

42. *OR*, vol. 24, pt. 1, 48–56; Grant, *Personal Memoirs*, 1:531.

43. *Letters of Ulysses S. Grant to His Father and His Youngest Sister, 1857–7*, ed. Jesse Grant Cramer (New York: G. P. Putnam's Sons, 1912), 99.

44. John C. Pemberton, "The Terms of Surrender," in *Battles & Leaders*, 3:543.

45. Ibid., 543–44; Grant, *Personal Memoirs*, 1:558.

46. Grant, *Personal Memoirs*, 1:558–59.

47. Ibid.; Pemberton, "Terms of Surrender," 544; Grant, *Personal Memoirs*, 1:558–59.

48. Grant, *Personal Memoirs*, 1:559–62.

49. Ibid., 562.

50. Ibid., 564, 571.

51. Winschel, *Triumph and Defeat*, 185.

52. Ibid.

53. Ibid.; Edward H. Bonekemper, *Grant and Lee: Victorious American and Vanquished Virginian* (Westport, Conn.: Regnery History, 2012), 456.

54. Henry Steele Commager, ed., *The Blue and Gray: The Story of the Civil War as Told by the Participants*, 2 vols. (Indianapolis: Bobbs-Merrill, 1950), 2:677.

55. Grant, *Personal Memoirs*, 1:571.

56. Ibid., 578.

57. *Papers of Ulysses S. Grant*, 9:146.

58. Ibid., 148.

59. Grant, *Personal Memoirs*, 1:579.

60. Ibid., 581.

61. Quoted in Theodor Lyman, *Meade's Headquarters, 1863–1865: Letters of*

Colonel Theodore Lyman from the Wilderness to Appomattox, ed. George Russell Agassiz (Boston: Massachusetts Historical Society, 1922), 36.

62. Quoted in Henry Cist, *The Army of the Cumberland* (New York: Charles Scribner and Sons, 1909), 230, 231, 233.

63. Charles T. Clark, *Opdycke Tigers, 125th O.V.I.: A History of the Regiment and of the Campaigns and Battles of the Army of the Cumberland* (Columbus: Spahr and Glenn, 1895), 137.

64. *OR*, vol. 30, pt. 1, 221.

65. Dana's correspondence can be found in *OR*, vol. 30, pt. 1; Grant, *Personal Memoirs*, 2:24.

66. *OR*, vol. 30, pt. 1, 202.

67. Ibid., 215, 218–19.

68. Grant, *Personal Memoirs*, 2:17.

69. *OR*, vol. 30, pt. 4, 404; Grant, *Personal Memoirs*, 1:583, 2:18–20.

70. Grant, *Personal Memoirs*, 1:571.

71. Ibid., 2:85–86.

72. Gideon Welles, *The Diary of Gideon Welles: Secretary of the Navy under Lincoln and Johnson*, 2 vols. (Big Byte Books, 2014), Kindle version without page numbers, vol. 1, chap. 10.

73. Grant, *Personal Memoirs*, 1:579, 2:85, 114; Michael Burlingame and John R. Turner Ettlinger, eds., *Inside Lincoln's White House: The Complete Civil War Diary of John Hay* (Carbondale: Southern Illinois University Press, 1998), 191–92.

74. Abraham Lincoln to Ulysses S. Grant, April 20, 1864, in *Lincoln: Speeches and Writings, 1859–1865* (New York: Library of America, 1989), 591.

75. James Longstreet, *From Manassas to Appomattox: Memoirs of the Civil War in America* (1896; New York: Mallard Press, 1991), 543.

76. Grant, *Personal Memoirs*, 2:117.

77. William B. Styple, ed., *Generals in Bronze: Interviewing the Commanders of the Civil War* (Kearny, N.J.: Belle Grove, 2005), 97.

78. *OR*, vol. 36, 12–14.

79. Ibid., 12.

80. J. F. C. Fuller, *Grant and Lee: A Study in Personality and Generalship* (Bloomington: Indiana University Press, 1982), 207.

81. Edwin C. Bearss, *The Vicksburg Campaign* (Dayton: Morningside Press, 1985), 1314.

82. Grant, *Personal Memoirs*, 1:574, 2:387–88; Horace Porter, *Campaigning with Grant* (New York: Century, 1897), 126, 261.

7. ❀ No Turning Back

Editors' Introduction

These days, the Wilderness of Virginia is not so wild anymore. Once, a second-growth forest carpeted more than seventy square miles of Spotsylvania and Orange Counties. "Here were stunted trees, such as scraggy oaks, bushy firs, cedars, and junipers, all entangled with a thick, almost impenetrable undergrowth, and criss-crossed with an abundance of wild vines," a Federal officer once noted.[1]

Here, May 5–7, 1864, General Robert E. Lee's Army of Northern Virginia clashed with Major General George Gordon Meade's Army of the Potomac in one of the most infamous battles of the Civil War. "All circumstances seemed to combine to make the scene one of unutterable horror," a Union officer recalled.[2] Dense vegetation severely restricted visibility and made maneuvering impossible. Forest fires raged. Wounded men burned alive. Federals sustained more than eighteen thousand casualties and Confederates more than eleven thousand. "The great, dark woods are filled with dead and wounded from both sides," a Mainer wrote. "Blue and Gray sink side-by-side in its gloomy thickets and slimy pools."[3]

Now, more than fifteen thousand people make their home in the Wilderness—most of them neatly tucked away behind screens of trees that preserve the illusion of wildness. The modern invasion of the Wilderness began in earnest in 1967 with the establishment of Lake of the Woods, a gated community on the western edge of the former battlefield. With a 550-acre lake, plus a 35-acre "fishing lake," a golf course, and an equestrian center, the community now houses more than seven thousand people.

East of Lake of the Woods, between the two roads that had once brought Confederates to the battlefield, a similar but smaller development sprang up in 1970. Named Lake Wilderness, it consists of nearly 870 homes that house nearly 3,000 people. Then came Fawn Lake, established in 1988 by a group of developers that included former Washington Redskins coach Joe Gibbs. With a 288-acre lake and a golf course designed by Arnold Palmer, Fawn Lake set a new standard for living in the wild. Approximately 2,450 people occupy 825 homes, with plans for a total of 1,396 homes when fully developed.[4]

The Brock Road–Plank Road intersection, at the heart of the Wilderness battlefield, can look quiet today, but several nearby gated communities mean thousands of cars pass through it daily. When Ulysses S. Grant found himself at this crossroads in May 1864, he decided on an uncharted, unprecedented route forward. *Photo by Chris Mackowski*

Woven through and around these three gated communities, the Wilderness National Battlefield—part of Fredericksburg and Spotsylvania National Military Park—preserves the key areas of the battle. A small exhibit shelter—built by the National Park Service in the early 1960s for the centennial and now staffed seasonally—sits next to busy State Route 20, the main east-west road through this part of Virginia.[5] Along a slightly wobblier but roughly parallel route to the south, Plank Road funnels commuters to their gated bedroom communities tucked away in the woods. The same roads that brought the armies into the Wilderness in 1864 help ensure its lack of wildness today.

Between those parallel roads, a scattering of wayside markers and a handful of monuments mark the battlefield, which otherwise remained largely undeveloped and uninterpreted well into the twenty-first century. Historically, the park's interpretive staff instead focused much of its attention on the battlefield's more famous counterparts in Fredericksburg and Chancellorsville, where the allure of Robert E. Lee and Stonewall Jackson held sway over popular—and interpretive—imagination.

Development pressure on the Wilderness battlefield received national attention in 2009 when retail giant Walmart proposed a new store on an unprotected edge of the battlefield. After nearly five years of furious controversy, Walmart won the right to build its store—and then surprised everyone by moving its location a few miles farther west and donating the original fifty-acre plot to preservation. "This is a wonderful legacy gift from Wal-Mart that comes during the mid-point of the Sesquicentennial of the Civil War," said Kathleen S. Kilpatrick, director of Virginia's Department of Historic Resources. Governor Bob McDonnell said he was "delighted" by the "generous and voluntary gift."[6]

Efforts in recent years have focused on improved visitor interactions at Ellwood, a historic home on the Wilderness battlefield that once belonged to the James Horace Lacy family and that served, during the battle, as the headquarters for the Union V Corps. Today, it is the hub of activity for a vibrant battlefield friends group and a collection of exhibits.

The southern sector of the Wilderness remains largely overlooked, though, except for the thousands of cars that pass through, each pausing at the four-way stop at the intersection of Brock and Plank Roads. Once upon a time, in May 1864, it was the most important crossroads in America; now, modern traffic smothers the spot.

But that is the spot—there in the Wilderness, at the Brock Road–Plank Road intersection, on May 7, 1864—that Ulysses S. Grant inexorably changed the course of the Civil War.

As Ryan Longfellow explains in the following essay, Grant did something no other Union commander had done before: rather than withdraw from the field following a rough handling in battle, Grant chose to maintain contact with the enemy. "There will be no turning back," he quipped to a reporter.[7] His decision to march around Lee's right flank and renew the battle on better ground shifted strategy from a traditional war of annihilation—the attempt to bring on a major decisive battle—to one of attrition. The North had the numbers, and Grant intended to use them. In doing so, he would wear the Confederates down until they had no choice but to surrender. "That man will fight us every day and every hour till the end of the war," predicted Confederate lieutenant general James Longstreet, who had been a prewar friend of Grant's.[8]

Since the battle of Gettysburg the preceding July, the two armies had seesawed in an indecisive fall campaign, punctuated by moderate-sized clashes at Bristoe Station, Rappahannock Station, Kelly's Ford, and Mine Run. Lee's army, bled out first by Chancellorsville and then Gettysburg, had been too weakened for aggressive offensives, and Meade's leadership, scrutinized by the armchair generals in Washington, was too conservative because of the political climate. "Lee is unquestionably bullying you," General-in-Chief Henry Halleck wired to Meade, oblivious to the irony that he was bullying Meade far more than Lee was.[9]

Stalemate became the status quo. By the time the two armies settled into winter quarters in a line along the Rapidan River, they sat just thirty miles to the west of where they had spent the previous winter, essentially right back where they had started the year. Meade, writing home that December following the failed Mine Run expedition, hardly sounded like a man riding a wave of momentum. He "acknowledged the movement was a failure," admitting he was "yet on the anxious bench" about his fate.[10] For days, the victor of Gettysburg fretted that he would be relieved because of his subsequent lack of success.

This "forgotten fall" casts Gettysburg in an entirely different light: popularly considered the turning point of the war, Gettysburg instead becomes the single bright spot in an otherwise fruitless year for the Army of the Potomac.

The stalemate on Meade's front—coupled with the success that Ulysses S. Grant found in Chattanooga—set the stage for Lincoln to once more go to his go-to general. "I see General Grant's assuming command and announcing that his headquarters will be with the Army of the Potomac, is in the public journals, and by to-morrow will be known in Richmond," Meade wrote to his wife in mid-March. "Of course this will notify the rebels where to look for active operations, and they will prepare accordingly."[11]

And indeed Lee did. As soon as Grant directed Meade to begin the spring campaign, Lee hit him as the Army of the Potomac marched through the Wilderness. Lee entered the battle with some 66,000 men, Meade and Grant with some 119,000. As the campaign wore on, Grant could replace far more men than Lee could—and Lee certainly forced him to.

Still, it did not stop Grant. As Longfellow shows, the road through the Wilderness would lead all the way to Appomattox.

"Oh, I Am Heartily Tired of Hearing about What Lee Is Going to Do": Ulysses S. Grant in the Wilderness

Ryan Longfellow

Major General Ulysses S. Grant's victories at Forts Henry and Donelson, Shiloh, and Vicksburg, in 1862 and 1863, vaulted him to the national forefront and center of the U.S. war effort. After his latest triumph at Chattanooga, Tennessee, President Abraham Lincoln elevated Grant to the rank of lieutenant general, the first since George Washington. With his new rank, Grant assumed the post of general-in-chief and responsibility for the overall 1864 Union offensive. Grant faced a litany of obstacles, including heightened attention from both Northerners and Southerners, increased political pressure resulting from the approaching presidential election, and the imminent confrontation with the Confederacy's most successful general. The decision to remain in Virginia fixated the nation's attention on the first meeting of Grant and Robert E. Lee. The encounter occurred in the tangled undergrowth of the Wilderness, located in Orange and Spotsylvania Counties of Virginia. After two days of combat and nearly twenty-nine thousand casualties, the battle proved inconclusive. However, Grant's decision to advance in the aftermath of the battle marked the Wilderness as the beginning of the end for the Army of Northern Virginia. The movement south toward Spotsylvania Court House proved to be a critical step toward U.S. victory and secured Grant's reputation as the Union's finest general.

Grant's promotion to lieutenant general in March 1864 made him the toast of Washington. Newspapers hailed him as the savior of the Union and the central figure in the conflict. The *New York Tribune* declared, "We have

Exhausted by more than two days of brutal fighting, Federal soldiers nonetheless cheered wildly for Grant when he ordered them out of the Wilderness—not in retreat but on toward Richmond. *Library of Congress*

found our hero!"[12] The *New York Herald* wrote that Grant inspired "the public confidence to a reasonable anticipation of quick work and great results."[13] While less enthusiastic, Union officers who encountered Grant came away with a cautiously optimistic impression of the general. Repeatedly, Army of the Potomac soldiers referenced Grant's look of determination. Army of the Potomac staff officer Lieutenant Colonel Theodore Lyman, who first saw Grant at Willard's Hotel in mid-March, noted, "His face has three expressions: deep thought; extreme determination; and great simplicity and calmness."[14] Upon Grant's arrival to the Army of the Potomac, Lyman recorded, "He habitually wears an expression as if he had determined to drive his head through a brick wall, and was about to do it. I have much confidence in him."[15] Grant's determination was apparent when he reviewed the principal eastern army in April. Colonel Robert McAllister informed his daughter, "Grant is not a very fine-looking General, but he has the appearance of a man of determination."[16] Despite the optimism, doubt remained, which even Grant perceived. In his memoirs he remembered, "It was not an uncommon thing for my staff-officers to hear from Eastern officers, 'Well, Grant has never met Bobby Lee yet'"[17]—a statement echoed in the Confederacy.

Rebel soldiers and civilians had similarly taken note of Grant and his new position. Most Confederates remained confident of success and mocked the North's fawning over Grant. Writing of the enthusiastic welcoming of the general in Washington, D.C., the *Richmond Daily Dispatch* observed, "The new Napoleon of the North is having a very fine time just now. Like all the other Napoleons, his Elba is not far ahead of him."[18] Southern diarist Catherine Edmondston sarcastically mocked the arrival of Grant, writing, "This is the seventh *Hero* that the Yankees have found! I suppose they 'think there is luck in odd numbers.' Poor 'little Napoleon,' unfortunate 'fighting Joe,' Burnside the Christian, Pope the despiser of his 'rear,' McDowell, Meade—where are you all now?"[19] Walter Taylor, a Confederate staff officer, wrote to his future wife, Bettie Saunders, about Grant, "I do not think he is to be feared. He has been much overrated and in my opinion owes more of his reputation to Genl Pemberton's bad management than to his own sagacity & ability."[20] To most Southerners, and many Northerners, Grant had yet to ascend to the elite pantheon of American generals. In order to do so, his accomplishments needed to be achieved against a worthy adversary: Robert Edward Lee, commander of the Confederacy's most effective fighting force, the Army of Northern Virginia.

In addition to confronting the Confederacy's most revered commander and accomplished combat force, Grant also needed to take into account the intricacies of Washington's political scene. As Grant arrived in the U.S. capital, the state of civil-military relations was contentious. Major General George Meade had just been called in front of the Joint Committee on the Conduct of the War to explain his actions in the Gettysburg campaign, a campaign in which Meade was the victor. Meade saw the congressional inquiry as a "conspiracy to have me removed."[21] A week later Meade elaborated that his "enemies consist of certain politicians who wished me removed to restore Hooker."[22] The political pressures directed at Meade forced the new lieutenant general to alter his plans. After Grant received his new commission, he initially envisioned a return to the West to conduct the Northern war effort. However, as Grant noted in his memoirs, "when I got to Washington and saw the situation it was plain that here was the point for the commanding general to be. No one else could, probably, resist the pressure that would be brought to bear upon him to desist from his own plans and pursue others."[23]

The impending presidential election amplified the ever-present political attention directed toward the Army of the Potomac. While historians disagree over the possible repercussions of a Democratic Party victory, both Northerners and Southerners were well aware of the importance of the approaching fall event. The *New York Herald* acknowledged, "The grand military campaign upon which General Grant is about to enter will be decisive against the rebellion, or . . . it will bring disgrace and financial and political confusion upon the government and the loyal States."[24] The *Atlantic Monthly* opined, "The election will have much effect on the operations of the war, and those operations in their turn will have no light effect on the election."[25] At a political speech in Georgia, Confederate congressman Benjamin H. Hill focused his constituents' attention on the political contest. Hill asserted, "The presidential election in the United States, in 1864, then, is the event which must determine the issue of peace or war, and with it, the destinies of both countries."[26] The national media also targeted Grant directly: "In a word, we consider the military situation now in the hands of General Grant, and that in his new position he is placed, not only on the high road to the crowning successes of the war, but to the crowning reward of the next Presidency."[27] The increased expectations for the Army of the Potomac, combined with the magnified political pressure, led Grant to accept the advice of his good friend William T. Sherman, "For God's sake and for your country's sake, come out of Washington."[28]

In order to distance himself and the Army of the Potomac from Washington politicos, Grant chose to make his headquarters in the field alongside George Meade's. Grant intended to be hands-off with the day-to-day operations of the Army of the Potomac and wrote after the war, "I tried to make General Meade's position as nearly as possible what it would have been if I had been in Washington or any other place away from his command."[29] Meade realized quicker than Grant that that would not be possible and immediately wrote to his wife, "You may look now for the Army of the Potomac putting laurels on the brows of another rather than your husband."[30]

Regardless of who received the accolades, Grant's presence with the army portended hard fighting for the Army of the Potomac. Porter Farley, an officer in the Union V Corps, recalled after the war "that this time it was to face an ordeal more serious than any we had passed through before. The presence of General Grant at army headquarters did much to strengthen this feeling. . . . Wherever he had been his presence implied hard fighting. We felt now the army was advancing to a death grapple."[31] Hard fighting to destroy the rebellion was exactly what Grant intended. He directed Meade, "Lee's army will be your objective point. Wherever he goes, there you will go also."[32]

The Rapidan River divided the two opposing forces. North of the river Grant fielded 119,063 U.S. soldiers, split into two large forces. Meade commanded the recently reorganized Army of the Potomac, which now consisted of three infantry and one cavalry corps, all headed by major generals: Winfield Hancock led the II Corps, Gouverneur Warren commanded the V Corps, and John Sedgwick directed the VI Corps. Recently arrived Philip Sheridan headed the Cavalry Corps. Along with artillerymen, escorts, and the provost guard, the Army of the Potomac tallied 99,813 soldiers.[33] Grant's second force in central Virginia, 19,250 men from Major General Ambrose Burnside's IX Corps, augmented Meade's army.[34] Burnside outranked Meade and could not be easily incorporated into the Army of the Potomac, which resulted in an awkward Federal command structure.

Lee's army numbered significantly less, yet for the first time since August 1863, he had all three of his infantry corps at his disposal. James Longstreet, who recently had returned from his Western Theater odyssey, commanded the Confederate I Corps, Richard Ewell led the II Corps, and A. P. Hill directed the III Corps. The effervescent Major General J. E. B. Stuart led the Confederate cavalry. Along with artillery and other attachments, the Army of Northern Virginia mustered 66,140, a little more than half of what it confronted.[35]

Grant laid out two options for striking Lee: "to cross the Rapidann [*sic*] above or below him."[36] In the first, the Army of the Potomac would move westward around Lee's flank. This option presented the best terrain for maneuvering but created logistical difficulties. The second option, a move eastward around Lee's right flank, took the Union back into the gloom of the Wilderness, where twice before Northern hopes were dashed at Chancellorsville and at Mine Run. While the general-in-chief may have intended to treat Meade as if he was in Washington, his proximity gave him the opportunity for increased oversight and mutual planning. Grant informed Meade, "These advantages and objections I will talk with you more fully than I can write them."[37] Due to supply concerns, the pair decided to hazard the Wilderness.

The foreboding and inhospitable nature of the Wilderness nullified Grant's numbers by strangling his maneuverability, which in turn radically reduced the Army of the Potomac's chances of success against Lee. "The Wilderness, which was certainly all that its name implies," noted a Federal captain, "was covered with a thick mass of trees and underbrush."[38] Sartell Prentice, a soldier who served in the Twelfth U.S. Infantry, described the terrain after the war. He wrote, "The jungle through which we now had to struggle was almost impassable. The undergrowth was rank and heavy; the trees, averaging three to five inches in diameter, and reaching up from twenty-five to forty feet, grew abundantly,—in places so thickly that a man must turn sideways to pass

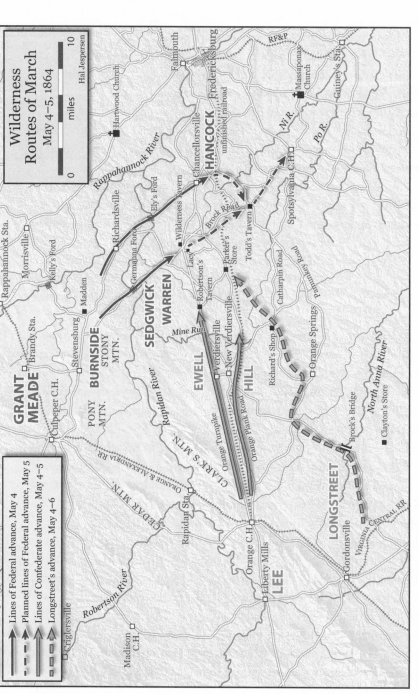

Wilderness
Routes of March
May 4–5, 1864

Hal Jespersen

miles

0   10

Lines of Federal advance, May 4

Planned lines of Federal advance, May 5

Lines of Confederate advance, May 4–5

Longstreet's advance, May 4–6

Wilderness Routes of March. Federals entered the Wilderness from their winter camps around Culpeper and Brandy Station, moving southeast toward Spotsylvania Court House where the ground opened up. However, Robert E. Lee sent the Army of Northern Virginia forward to hit the Federals in the flank while they were still in the Wilderness. The second-growth forest helped negate the superior Federal numbers and make it difficult to deploy cavalry and artillery. *Map by Hal Jespersen* between them."[39] The tangled vegetation made it difficult for Union troops to maneuver, as another Federal soldier noted: "Maneuvering was out of the questions; the troops could only receive direction by point of the compass and were soon hidden from the sight of the commander, as no officer could see ten files on either side of him."[40] Frank Walker, a staff officer of Winfield Hancock's, aptly concluded, "The region was beyond bad . . . viewed as a battle-ground, [it] was simply infernal."[41]

The Army of the Potomac started toward the Rapidan River just after midnight on May 4. By starting at night, Meade hoped to steal several hours on Robert E. Lee and get into and out of the Wilderness before Lee could respond. The opening march went well. Lieutenant Colonel Horace Porter, one of Grant's staff officers, recalled the general saying, "Well, the movement so far has been as satisfactory as could be desired. We have succeeded in seizing the fords and crossing the river without loss or delay. . . . We shall probably soon get some indication as to what he [Lee] intends to do."[42] Grant was correct; the opening moves of the Army of the Potomac went well, yet Grant remained unsure of how Lee would react. He telegraphed Henry Halleck, "Forty Eight hours now will demonstrate whether the enemy intends giving battle this side of Richmond."[43] Lee fully intended to give battle north of Richmond, preferably as soon as possible.

The Federal high command based its timetable for Lee's response on his reaction to the Union's advance during the Mine Run campaign. Lee, however, acted more decisively in 1864. In his history of the campaign, Army of the Potomac chief of staff Andrew Atkinson Humphreys recalled, "It will be observed that General Lee moved more promptly toward the Army of the Potomac than he had done in the preceding November."[44] Despite the urgency of starting the army during the night, the Federal high command stopped the advance early on the afternoon of May 4 in order for the wagon train to close up. That decision from Meade, combined with a quicker than expected reaction from Lee, placed the two forces on a path for collision in the Wilderness.

On the morning of May 5, the two armies encountered each other along the Orange Turnpike. George Meade immediately reported on the opening skirmish, "The enemy have appeared in force on the Orange pike, and are now reported forming line of battle in front of Griffin's division, Fifth Corps. I have directed General Warren to attack them at once with his whole force."[45] Grant's reply illustrated his eagerness to bring Lee to battle. He responded, "If any opportunity presents [it]self for pitching into a part of Lee's Army do so without giving time for [di]sposition."[46]

Grant planned to wait for the arrival of Burnside at Germanna Ford before joining Meade; however, impatience got the best of him and he left the ford early. Grant met up with Meade around ten in the morning and proposed that they locate their headquarters together. The pair selected a small knoll, which "was high enough to afford a view for some little distance, but the outlook was limited in all directions by the almost impenetrable forest."[47] From the top of the knoll Grant and Meade discussed the situation as they waited for Warren to begin his attack. The generals wanted to maintain the initiative and ordered George Getty's division of the VI Corps to the intersection of the Brock and Orange Plank Roads. Orders were also sent to Hancock to quicken his pace. After the commands were issued, "General Grant lighted a cigar, sat down on the stump of a tree, took out his penknife, and began to whittle a stick."[48]

Increased rifle fire interrupted Grant's tranquility. Getty's division reached the intersection of the Brock and Plank Roads just in time to prevent the key crossroads from falling into rebel hands. With a reduced division and no support in the immediate area, Getty could not protect the intersection and launch an attack. Instead, he ordered his men to prepare defensive works and await the arrival of Hancock's corps. Grant's plan to seize the initiative along the Orange Plank Road had to wait. It was now left to Warren's soldiers to take the fight to the Confederate army.

During the seven o'clock hour, Meade had ordered Warren to strike Ewell's force. Unfortunately for Warren, his march on May 4 left his corps scattered throughout the Wilderness, and by noon no attack had occurred. Warren and V Corps division commander Charles Griffin hesitated to attack until they had support. Just before one in the afternoon, James Wadsworth's division of the same corps made tenuous contact with Griffin. By then patience had evaporated at Union headquarters. As a staff officer recalled, "It was afterwards a common report in the army that Warren had just had unpleasant things said to him by General Meade."[49] Despite no support on his right and protest from his commanders, Warren ordered his divisions forward, and the Union offensive got under way. The charge momentarily achieved success, before the Wilderness thwarted the Federals' effort. Attacking through Saunders Field, Griffin's division outpaced Wadsworth's on its left. Griffin's men broke the Confederate line, but a lack of support on both flanks allowed rebel infantrymen to launch a successful counterattack. The tangled thicket disorganized Wadsworth's men, and freshly arrived Southern troops drove them back in confusion. By three in the afternoon, the Union offensive along the Orange Turnpike faltered.

For Union success on May 5, Grant and Meade once again directed their focus toward the Orange Plank Road. Orders to launch an attack flowed for most of the day toward that sector of the battlefield. Union leadership believed that Hancock's corps was close at hand and sent several orders for Getty's division to cooperate with the II Corps in an attack. Due to the narrow roads and dense woods of the Wilderness, Hancock's troops remained unready at three in afternoon when a direct order arrived from headquarters "to attack at once without waiting for the Second Corps."[50] Getty, who prided himself on following the orders of a superior, immediately attacked Henry Heth's division of A. P. Hill's corps. Had Getty waited for Hancock's two divisions, the Union army would have achieved a significant numerical advantage. Instead, units attacked as they arrived, and while Federal thrusts damaged the Confederate troops, they could not destroy them. The pressure from the general-in-chief prevented concerted efforts.

After the fighting concluded on May 5, the Federal leadership gathered to plan their attack for May 6. Since Burnside's independent IX Corps had arrived on the battlefield, Grant played a decisive role in creating the tactical plan for the morning assault. According to Washington Roebling, a staff officer for General Warren, "Two options presented themselves—either go and join Wadsworth by day light, or else obtain possession of the heights at Tuning's [Chewning's] and fall upon the enemy's rear by that route; if successful in carrying the heights the latter plan promised the results. . . . Gen. Grant therefore decided that the 9th Corps should go to Tuning's [Chewning's]."[51] Grant wanted to destroy the Army of Northern Virginia and put his faith in Burnside to promptly attack the rear of A. P. Hill's corps.

Army of the Potomac corps commanders did not think that Burnside would be ready for action at four-thirty in the morning and wanted to delay an hour and a half. Lyman noted in his journal, "They suggested that Burnside would not be up until that time."[52] Meade's chief of engineers, Major James C. Duane, declared, "He won't be up—I know him well!"[53] Meade diplomatically requested the attack be delayed citing an array of reasons, including the dense woods, tired troops, and necessity of daylight to align the units. Grant refused the requested start time but did compromise. His military secretary responded, "I am directed by the lieutenant-general commanding to say that you may change the hour of the attack to 5 o'clock, as he is afraid of that if delayed until 6 o'clock the enemy will take the initiative, which he desires specially to avoid."[54] Grant's fear was well founded.

The delayed start allowed Lee to embarrass Union plans on the Orange Turnpike sector of the battlefield. At 4:45 a.m., Richard Ewell's Confederates lunged toward the Union lines. John Sedgwick joked that "Ewell's watch must be fifteen minutes ahead of his."[55] The fighting swayed back and forth in a no-man's-land without either force being able to budge the other. News that the VI Corps could not drive the Confederates from their defenses forced Warren to delay his attack. Despite Meade's prodding, Warren refused to attack. After a failed assault by Sedgwick, the northern part of the battlefield quieted with nothing to show for the Union efforts.

Along the Orange Plank Road, the Union offensive went much better. Benefiting from an unprepared Confederate defense, the Union army smashed through the Confederate lines and routed much of the Confederate III Corps. Hancock reported, "We have driven the enemy from their position . . . taking quite a number of prisoners."[56] Theodore Lyman wrote to Meade, "General Hancock went in punctually and is driving the enemy handsomely."[57] Hancock exclaimed to Lyman, "Tell Gen. Meade we are driving them most beautifully."[58] Meade's staff officer could only counter with bad news; the IX Corps was not yet in position but "would attack as soon as possible."[59] Hancock retorted, "I knew it! Just what I expected! If he could attack now, we could smash A. P. Hill all to pieces!"[60] Despite Hancock's early morning success, the density of the Wilderness forced him "to halt and restore the contact between his commands."[61]

As the Union offensive slowed, Lee's last and most reliable corps arrived on the battlefield. With his army put in crisis by Grant's hammering blow, Lee personally attempted to lead James Longstreet's men in a counterattack. Soldiers from Texas and Arkansas demanded that Lee go to the rear and promised to drive the Federal soldiers back. Once the Confederate counterattack stabilized their line, the two forces settled into a slugging match. Finally, around ten in the morning, the fighting died down and the two armies repositioned themselves for the next phase of the battle.

Union leadership focused on regaining the initiative. Meade's chief of staff directed Sedgwick and Warren to dig in "and report at once what number of men you will have disposable for an attack upon Hancock's right."[62] General Grant's staff also tried to speed Burnside along. Grant mistakenly believed that the delayed start provided Burnside ample time to position the IX Corps to participate in the morning assault. However, the IX Corps moved insufferably slowly. Lyman noted of Burnside, "He had a genius of slowness."[63] As noon approached, the majority of Burnside's corps still groped through the dense thicket. Grant's chief of staff, John Rawlins, directed Burnside to "push in with all vigor as to drive the enemy. . . . Hancock has been expecting you for the last three hours."[64]

Before Union preparations were complete, rebel commanders seized the initiative. Around eleven in the morning, four Confederate brigades crashed into the left flank of the Union army and sent the Federal soldiers reeling back toward the Brock Road. Hancock in a postwar conversation with James Longstreet stated, "You rolled me up like a wet blanket, and it was some hours before I could reorganize for battle."[65] However, rebel momentum stalled after Longstreet's own soldiers left him severely wounded.

In those hours gifted to the Union army by Confederate infantry, the Federal high command focused on creating a defensive line along Brock Road and preparing for an evening assault. Grant informed Burnside, "General Hancock is directed to make an attack at 6 o'clock this evening. Be prepared to aid him in it."[66] Hancock did not think an attack prudent and wrote to Meade, "The present partially disorganized condition of this command renders it extremely difficult to obtain a sufficiently reliable body to make a really powerful attack."[67] It mattered little, as the Confederates preempted Grant's plans.

Once the Army of Northern Virginia regrouped, Lee ordered his right flank forward. Rebel units crashed into the intersection. Engulfed in flames, Union regiments wavered and broke, yet a shift in winds, and Union counter-attacks, chased the Southern soldiers away. Hancock noted, "The attack and repulse was of the handsomest kind."[68] Confederate artillerist E. P. Alexander declared, "The attack ought *never, never* to be made. . . . It was wasting good soldiers whom we could not spare."[69] Whether or not the attack had a chance of success, it forced the Federal high command to cancel the evening attack. Porter noted, "It felt like the day's strife had ended, unless Lee should risk another attack."[70]

As the fighting died down on the southern part of the battlefield, it roared back to life north of the Orange Turnpike. The previous night Ewell had adroitly repositioned his soldiers, which resulted in the Confederate II Corps overlapping the Army of the Potomac's right flank. Throughout the course of the day, Confederate brigadier general John Gordon campaigned to launch a flank attack against the exposed Union right. Finally, around dusk, the rebels crashed into the end of the Union line. Gordon, leading three Confederate brigades, slammed into two tired and fought-out Federal brigades commanded by Alexander Shaler and Truman Seymour, both of whom were at Sedgwick's headquarters. Shaler and Seymour rushed to rejoin their units. As they did, Confederate soldiers swarmed in and captured both generals.

Shaler and Seymour's brigades lost heavily; however, Gordon did not possess the necessary troops to significantly damage the Army of the Potomac, and the Wilderness choked the life out of the limited Confederate offensive. This did not prevent a stream of panicked couriers from heading toward Grant and Meade's headquarters. Union officers, whom Theodore Lyman described "as quite out of their heads," made extravagant claims about Gordon's attack and the collapse of the VI Corps.[71] Couriers reported rumors "that probably both Sedgwick and [Brigadier General Horatio G.] Wright were captured,"[72] while others "reported that Sedgwick's whole line has given way."[73] According to Lyman, Grant "seemed more disturbed than Meade" by the reports. If he was disturbed, it only showed for a moment. Grant issued precautionary orders to one of Burnside's division commanders and then settled "on a stool in front of his tent, lighted a fresh cigar, and continued to receive further advices from the right."[74]

While seated outside of his tent, Grant's calmness gave way to agitation. A fretful general appeared and cautioned, "General Grant, this is a crisis that cannot be looked upon too seriously. I know Lee's methods well by past experiences; he will throw his whole army between us and the Rapidan, and cut us off completely from our communications."[75] The Union officer's reverence for Robert E. Lee's abilities was more than Grant could tolerate, and he uncharacteristically lashed out at the officer, "Oh, I am heartily tired of hearing about what Lee is going to do. Some of you always seem to think he is suddenly going to turn a double somersault and land in our rear and on both of our flanks at the same time. Go back to your command, and try to think what we are going to do ourselves, instead of what Lee is going to do."[76] The officer departed, and Grant returned to his customary composed demeanor.

As the fighting sputtered out on the night of May 6, the active battle of the Wilderness came to an end. Two days in the tangled woodland proved costly to both armies. The Federal forces lost 17,666 men killed, wounded, and missing.[77] The Army of Northern Virginia lost considerably fewer at 11,033.[78] Proportionately, both armies suffered similarly. The Union army lost roughly 14.8 percent of its men, while the Confederate army lost 16.7 percent of its soldiers. Despite the substantial casualties, the results were indecisive; both armies were in roughly the same positions as when the battle started. Grant admitted to Henry Halleck, "At present we can claim no victory over the enemy, neither have they gained a single advantage."[79] Lieutenant Colonel Adam Badeau recalled that Grant "would indeed have desired a more complete success, and did not assume to call this a victory."[80] Political importance attached to the opening engagement required Grant to quickly evaluate his first contact with Lee and make adjustments moving forward.

The fighting on May 5 and 6 taught Grant two lessons. First, he had not faced an opponent like Robert E. Lee. Grant acknowledged during the battle that "Joe Johnston would have retreated after two such days of punishment."[81] Lee, on the other hand, remained on the battlefield. Second, Grant concluded that he needed to take a more hands-on approach with the Army of the Potomac. Grant had remained fairly aloof, especially for a general who felt apprehensive only when he gave "an order for an important movement of troops in the presence of the enemy."[82] Grant had attempted to remain hands-off during the battle, but that would change in the aftermath. Now, Grant not only set objectives for the army but also informed Meade how he wanted them accomplished. Grant's orders for May 7 demonstrated that he had mastered the lessons of the previous days.

Grant rose early on Saturday, May 7. The crisis and the agitation of the previous night had passed, and the general-in-chief's stoic demeanor had returned. Worried about rumors that the Union army might withdraw, cavalry division commander James Wilson stopped by Grant's headquarters. According to Lieutenant Morris Schaff, a V Corps staff officer, Wilson approached Grant with "an anxious face."[83] Wilson's concern was justifiable. The Army of the Potomac had a history of inaction and retreat after it confronted Robert E. Lee. Following the battle of Antietam, it took the Union army more than a month to cross the Potomac River, despite the river being a mere five miles from the battlefield. During the Fredericksburg campaign, the army fought its way across the Rappahannock River on December 11, only to return to the north side of the river five days later. From start to finish, the spring 1863 Chancellorsville campaign lasted ten days, and the fall campaign of Mine Run lasted a little more than a week. Grant, who sensed Wilson's anxiety, declared, "It's alright, Wilson; the Army of the Potomac will go forward to-night."[84]

Grant's exchange with Wilson in the early morning hours of May 7 was not the first time he discussed the possibility of moving south. While talking to several of his staff officers during the evening of May 6, Grant stated, "If he falls back and intrenches, my notion is to move promptly toward the left. This will, in all probability, compel him to try and throw himself between us and Richmond, and in such a movement I hope to be able to attack him in a more open country, and outside of his breastworks."[85] Badeau noted of Grant, "To retreat did not suggest itself to his mind. His only thought was to renew the fight where he could secure for himself the advantage of the ground."[86] At six thirty in the morning, Grant instructed Meade to "make all preparations during the day for a night march, to take position at Spotsylvania Court-House."[87]

Just after dark, the Union troops withdrew from the main line. Many soldiers initially thought the Army of the Potomac's night march indicated a retreat. A Massachusetts infantryman remembered, "Most of us thought it was another Chancellorsville, and that the next day we should recross the river."[88] A Union artilleryman then stationed in reserve recalled that "Grant's military standing with the enlisted men this day hung on the direction we turned at the Chancellorsville House. If to the left, he was to be rated with Meade and Hooker and Burnside and Pope—the generals who preceded him. At the Chancellorsville House we turned to the right. Instantly all of us heard a sigh of relief."[89] For the first time, the Army of the Potomac engaged Robert E. Lee and, at the conclusion of the battle, did not retreat. It did not sit still. It did not meekly follow behind. Instead, for the first time, the Army of the Potomac advanced after fighting the vaunted Army of Northern Virginia. As the headquarters cavalcade turned south on the Brock Road, Union troops exploded with enthusiasm. "Soldiers weary and sleepy," Horace Porter recalled, "rushed forward to the roadside" and unleashed "wild cheers [that] echoed through the forest, and glad shouts of triumph rent the air. . . . The demonstration was the emphatic verdict pronounced by the troops upon his first battle in the East."[90] Grant recalled in his memoirs, "The greatest enthusiasm was manifested by Hancock's men as we passed by. No doubt it was inspired by the fact that the movement was south."[91]

Federal soldiers in the ranks were not the only ones to applaud Grant's decision to advance. In Washington, President Lincoln anxiously awaited news. Secretary of the Navy Gideon Welles noted in his diary, "The President came into my room about 1 p.m. and told me he had slept none last night."[92] Finally, a newspaperman ended Lincoln's suspense. *New York Tribune* correspondent Henry Wing, who had started the campaign with the army and had spoken with Grant, obtained an audience with the president. After making his way across northern Virginia, Wing delivered his message: "General Grant told me to tell you, from him, that, whatever happens, there is to be no turning back."[93] Lincoln was ecstatic. Wing described Lincoln's reaction as "a great soul glowing with a newly kindled hope."[94] Over the next few days the president radiated glee and left those around him with a sense of his confidence in the general-in-chief. Lincoln's personal secretary John Hay recorded in his diary, "The President thinks highly of what G[rant] has done. He was talking about it to-day with me, and said:—'How near we have been to this thing before, and failed! I believe if any other General had been at the head of that army, it would have now been on this side of the Rapidan. It is the dogged pertinacity of G[rant] that wins.'"[95]

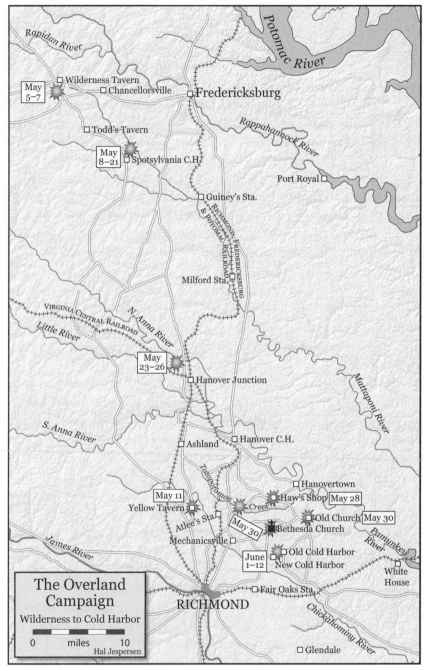

The Overland Campaign. From the Wilderness, Federals moved to Spotsylvania Court House (May 8–21), the North Anna River (May 23–26), Totopotomoy Creek (May 28–30), and around Cold Harbor (June 1–12). While Lee's defensive warfare continued to stymie Grant, Grant continued to outflank Lee's entrenched positions and move closer to Richmond. Eventually, Grant would jump the James River to strike at Petersburg; Lee would again counter, and the war would settle into a nine-month siege. *Map by Hal Jespersen*

Newspapers hailed Grant's first meeting with Lee as a Federal success. The headlines of the Washington, D.C., newspaper the *National Republican* announced, "Glorious News: Grant Victorious, Lee's Army in Full Retreat, Grant in Pursuit."[96] The front page of the *New York Daily Tribune* claimed "Victory for the Union" and declared that "Gen. Grant is master of the field." The paper continued, "There is no longer any doubt. Gen. Grant has won a great victory."[97] The forward movement of the Army of the Potomac merited the enthusiasm displayed in the press, even if the claims were exaggerated.

Declarations of victory were premature, as the road to Appomattox still needed to pass through Spotsylvania, Cold Harbor, and Petersburg. Yet the fighting in the Wilderness left an indelible mark on the course of the American Civil War. Theodore Lyman noted, "The result of this great Battle of the Wilderness was a drawn fight, but strategically it was a success, because Lee marched out to stop our advance on Richmond, which, at this point, he did not succeed in doing."[98] Grant's continued drive toward the Confederate capital transformed the state of military affairs in Virginia. Prior to the Wilderness, the Army of the Potomac crossed the Rappahannock and Rapidan Rivers for the battles of Fredericksburg, Chancellorsville, and Mine Run. In the aftermath of each contest, the Federal army quickly withdrew across the river, Grant did not. Rebel artillerist E. P. Alexander observed, "Both Burnside and Hooker had given up their campaigns, & recrossed the river after less severe & bloody repulses than Grant had received in the Wilderness."[99] Grant ended the cycle of attack and withdraw that had characterized the Army of the Potomac's efforts in Virginia.

After two days of bloody combat, Grant faced a choice: to turn back and prolong the war, threaten Lincoln's reelection, and damage his reputation, or to advance and bring the conflict one step closer to its conclusion. Even Grant recognized his decision to advance as a pivotal turning point in the course of the American Civil War. Adam Badeau wrote, "He [Grant] felt that one step was taken towards the end. Lee was not destroyed, it was true, but his army was weakened materially and morally."[100] In his memoirs, Grant recalled the importance of the movement south on the Union soldiers: "It indicated to them that they passed through the 'beginning of the end' in the battle just fought."[101] Grant intended to see the campaign through to the end, as his friend James Longstreet had noted before the campaign began: "That man will fight us every hour of every day until this war is over."[102] Although Union victory remained eleven months away, Ulysses S. Grant's decision to move forward, out of the Wilderness, brought the United States one step closer to peace. As a Federal private noted, "It [Grant's army] has obtained a grip upon the throat of the Confederacy, a grip that will not be relaxed until treason gasps and dies."[103]

Editors' Notes

1. Oliver Otis Howard, "Jackson's Attack upon the Eleventh Corps," *Century Illustrated Monthly Magazine*, May 1886–October 1886 (New York: Century Company, 1886), 763.

2. Horace Porter, *Campaigning with Grant* (New York: Mallard Press, 1991), 73.

3. John Haley, *The Rebel Yell and the Yankee Hurrah* (Camden, Maine: Down East Books, 1985), 152.

4. Joane Canny e-mail interview, March 12, 2016. Canny is a realtor with the Fawn Lake Real Estate Company.

5. A brief history of the establishment of the Wilderness exhibit shelter can be found in FSNMP's administrative history, "At the Crossroads of Preservation and Development: A History of Fredericksburg and Spotsylvania Military Park" by Joan Zenzen (produced internally by FSNMP, 2011), pg. 164. Although the shelter was constructed as part of the park service's "Mission 66" initiatives, the report does not indicate the exact year the shelter opened. It does mention the opening of another of the park's shelters, in late 1962, and says that by 1965, the park was keeping visitation statistics, suggesting an opening date of 1963 or 1964, prior to the 100th anniversary of the battle.

6. Civil War Trust press release, November 8, 2013, http://www.civilwar.org /aboutus/news/news-releases/2013-news/governor-mcdonnell-announces -1.html.

7. Quoted in Louis M. Starr, *Bohemian Brigade: Civil War Newsmen in Action* (New York: Knopf, 1954), 246.

8. Quoted in Porter, *Campaigning with Grant*, 46.

9. Henry Halleck to George Meade, October 18, 1863, *OR*, vol. 29, pt. 2, 346.

10. George Gordon Meade, *The Life and Letters of George Gordon Meade, Major-General United States Army* (New York: Charles Scribner's Sons, 1913), 2:160.

11. Ibid., 181.

Contributor's Notes

12. Hamlin Garland, *Ulysses S. Grant: His Life and Character* (New York: Doubleday and McClure, 1898), 261.

13. *New York Herald*, March 18, 1864.

14. Theodore Lyman, *Meade's Army: The Private Notebooks of Lt. Col. Theodore Lyman*, ed. David W. Lowe (Kent, Ohio: Kent State University Press, 2007), 80.

15. Ibid., 81.

16. Robert McAllister to Henrietta, April 24, 1864, in *The Civil War Letters of General Robert McAllister*, ed. James I. Robertson (Baton Rouge: Louisiana State University Press, 1998), 408.

17. Ulysses S. Grant, *The Personal Memoirs of Ulysses S. Grant* (Hartford, Conn.: Charles Webster, 1885; New York: Library of America, 1990), 514.

18. *Richmond Daily Dispatch*, March 18, 1864.

19. Catherine Ann Devereux Edmondston, April 18, 1864, *"Journal of a Secesh Lady": The Diary of Catherine Ann Devereux Edmondston, 1860–1866*, ed. Beth Gilbert Crabtree and Hames W. Patton (Raleigh: North Carolina Division of Archives and History, 1999), 547–48. Emphasis in original.

20. Walter Taylor to Bettie Saunders, March 20, 1864, in *Lee's Adjutant: The Wartime Letters of Colonel Walter Herron Taylor, 1862–1865*, ed. R. Lockwood Tower (Columbia: University of South Carolina Press, 1995), 139.

21. Meade to Wife, March 8, 1864, Headquarters Army of the Potomac, in *Life and Letters of George Gordon Meade*, 176.

22. Ibid., March 15, 1864, 179.

23. Grant, *Personal Memoirs*, 404.

24. *New York Herald*, March 23, 1864.

25. C. C. Hazewell, "The Presidential Election," *Atlantic Monthly*, May 1864, 631.

26. Quoted in Larry E. Nelson, *Bullets, Ballots, and Rhetoric: Confederate Policy for the United States President Contest of 1864* (Tuscaloosa: University of Alabama Press, 1980), 14.

27. *New York Herald*, March 18, 1864.

28. William T. Sherman to U. S. Grant, March 10, 1864, in *Memoirs of William T. Sherman* (New York: Appleton, 1875; reprint, New York: Da Capo, 1984), 400.

29. Grant, *Personal Memoirs*, 405.

30. Meade to Wife, March 15, 1864, 178.

31. Porter Farley, "Reminiscences of the 140th Regiment of New York Volunteer Infantry," in *Rochester in the Civil War*, ed. Blake McKelvey (Rochester: Rochester Historical Society, 1944), 235.

32. Ulysses S. Grant to George Meade, April 9, 1864, in *The Papers of Ulysses S. Grant*, ed. John Y. Simon (Carbondale: Southern Illinois University Press, 1982), 10:274.

33. *OR*, vol. 33, pt. 1, 1036. The commanding general and staff, engineer attachments, and signal corps were not listed in the "present and equipped for duty" chart. When those soldiers were added to the "present for duty" returns, the Army of the Potomac totaled 99,813.

34. *OR*, vol. 33, pt. 1, 1045. A total of 19,250 soldiers are listed as present for duty. The aggregate strength of the IX Corps tallied 21,357.

35. Alfred C. Young III, *Lee's Army in the Overland Campaign: A Numerical Study* (Baton Rouge: Louisiana State University, 2013), 232.

36. Grant to Meade, April 9, 1864, 10:274.

37. Ibid.

38. Henry Cribben, *The Military Memoirs of Captain Henry Cribben of the 140th New York Volunteers*, ed. J. Clayton Youker (private printing, 1911), 46.

39. Sartell Prentice, "The Opening Hours in the Wilderness in 1864," in *Military Essays and Recollections: Papers Read before the Commandery of the State of Illinois, Military Order of the Loyal Legion of the United States* (Chicago: A. C. McClurg, 1894), 2:114.

40. Robert Monteith, "Battle of the Wilderness and the Death of General Wadsworth," in *War Papers: Read before the Commandery of the State of Wisconsin, Military Order of the Loyal Legion of the United States* (Milwaukee: Burdick, Armitage, and Allen, 1891), 1:411.

41. Francis A. Walker, *General Hancock* (New York: D. Appleton, 1895), 160.

42. Horace Porter, *Campaigning with Grant* (Lincoln: University of Nebraska, 2000), 43.

43. Grant to Halleck, May 4, 1864, in *Papers of Ulysses S. Grant*, 10:397.

44. Andrew A. Humphreys, *The Virginia Campaign of 1864 and 1865* (New York, 1883; reprint, New York: Da Capo, 1995), 22.

45. *OR*, vol. 36, pt. 2, 403.

46. Grant to Meade, May 5, 1864, in *Papers of Ulysses S. Grant*, 10:399.

47. Porter, *Campaigning with Grant*, 49. In 2001 the Central Virginia Battlefield Trust purchased the knoll where Grant and Meade located their headquarters. Today it is the first tour stop on the National Park Service driving tour of the Wilderness battlefield.

48. Ibid., 50.

49. William Swan, "The Battle of the Wilderness," in *The Wilderness Campaign: May–June 1864, Papers of the Military Historical Society of Massachusetts* (Boston: Military Historical Society of Massachusetts, 1905), 4:129.

50. *OR*, vol. 36, pt. 1, 677.

51. Washington A. Roebling's report, May 5, 1864, Gouverneur Kemble Warren Collections, New York State Library, Albany.

52. Lyman, *Meade's Army*, 135.
53. Quoted in Morris Schaff, *The Battle of the Wilderness* (Boston: Houghton Mifflin, 1910), 225.
54. *OR*, vol. 36, pt. 2, 405.
55. Quoted in Charles A. Page, *Letters of a War Correspondent* (Boston: L. C. Page, 1899), 52.
56. *OR*, vol. 36, pt. 2, 439.
57. Ibid.
58. Lyman, *Meade's Army*, 136.
59. Ibid.
60. Ibid.
61. Porter, *Campaigning with Grant*, 58.
62. *OR*, vol. 36, pt. 2, 452.
63. Lyman, *Meade's Army*, 136.
64. *OR*, vol. 36, pt. 2, 461.
65. James Longstreet, *From Manassas to Appomattox: Memoirs of the Civil War in America* (Philadelphia: J. B. Lippincott, 1896), 568.
66. *OR*, vol. 36, pt. 2, 462.
67. Ibid., 445.
68. Ibid., 446.
69. Edward Porter Alexander, *Fighting for the Confederacy: The Personal Recollections of General Edward Porter Alexander*, ed. Gary W. Gallagher (Chapel Hill: University of North Carolina Press, 1989), 363. Emphasis in original.
70. Porter, *Campaigning with Grant*, 68.
71. Lyman, *Meade's Army*, 140.
72. Humphreys, *Virginia Campaign*, 51n.
73. *OR*, vol. 36, pt. 2, 438.
74. Porter, *Campaigning with Grant*, 69.
75. Ibid., 69–70.
76. Ibid., 70.
77. *OR*, vol. 36, pt. 1, 133.
78. Young, *Lee's Army in the Overland Campaign*, 235.
79. *OR*, vol. 36, pt. 2, 480.
80. Adam Badeau, *The Military History of Ulysses S. Grant: From April, 1861 to April, 1865* (New York: D Appleton, 1882), 2:131–32.
81. Lyman, *Meade's Army*, 141.
82. Porter, *Campaigning with Grant*, 63.
83. Schaff, *Battle of the Wilderness*, 328.

84. Quoted in James Harrison Wilson, *Under the Old Flag: Recollections of Military Operations in the War for the Union, the Spanish War, the Boxer Rebellion, Etc.* (New York: D. Appleton, 1912), 1:389.

85. Quoted in Porter, *Campaigning with Grant*, 65–66.

86. Badeau, *Military History of Ulysses S. Grant*, 2:131.

87. *OR*, vol. 36, pt. 2, 481.

88. John G. B. Adams, *Reminiscences of the Nineteenth Massachusetts Regiment* (Boston: Wright and Potter, 1899), 88.

89. Frank Wilkeson, *Recollections of a Private Soldier in the Army of the Potomac* (New York: G. P. Putnam, 1887), 80.

90. Porter, *Campaigning with Grant*, 79.

91. Grant, *Personal Memoirs*, 461.

92. Gideon Welles, May 7, 1864, *Diary of Gideon Welles: Secretary of the Navy under Lincoln and Johnson*, 2 vols. (Boston: Houghton Mifflin, 1911), 2:25.

93. Henry Wing, *When Lincoln Kissed Me: A Story of the Wilderness Campaign* (New York: Eaton and Mains, 1913), 38.

94. Ibid.

95. John Hay, May 9, 1864, in *Letters of John Hay: And Abstracts from Diary* (Washington, 1908), 1:191.

96. *National Republican* (Washington, D.C.), May 9, 1864.

97. *New York Daily Tribune*, May 10, 1864.

98. Theodore Lyman, May 17, 1864, Headquarters Army of the Potomac, *Meade's Headquarters, 1863–1865: Letters of Colonel Theodore Lyman from the Wilderness to Appomattox*, ed. George R. Agassiz (Boston: Atlantic Monthly Press, 1922), 98.

99. Alexander, *Fighting for the Confederacy*, 365.

100. Badeau, *Military History of Ulysses S. Grant*, 2:132.

101. Grant, *Personal Memoirs*, 461.

102. Quoted in Porter, *Campaigning with Grant*, 47.

103. Theodore Gerrish, *Army Life: A Private's Reminiscences of the Civil War* (Portland, Maine: Hoyt, Fogg, and Donham, 1882), 172.

8. ❈ Hood Takes Command of the Army of Tennessee

Editors' Introduction

For Jefferson Davis and General Joseph E. Johnston, the spring of 1864 might have felt like déjà vu. As in the spring of 1862, Johnston faced a superior Union foe, and, as in that same year, he waged a long, retreating defense, waiting for an opportunity to strike the enemy. All the while, as in 1862, Davis sent a chattering string of messages that Johnston largely ignored.

In 1862, the opponent had been George B. McClellan on the Virginia Peninsula. Now, in 1864, Johnston faced William T. Sherman, whose 110,000-man army group—consisting of the Army of the Cumberland, Army of the Tennessee, and Army of the Ohio—pushed inexorably out of Chattanooga, Tennessee, toward the vital rail and supply center at Atlanta, Georgia. Johnston mustered some 53,800 Confederates to oppose them. "Our army that takes the offensive should be our strongest in relation to its enemy," he counseled, hoping to leverage more reinforcements and more supplies.[1] "If we are ready to fight him on our own ground, we shall have a very plain course, with every chance of success," he later added—without including details for any actual plan.[2]

Davis, a thousand miles away in Richmond, must have felt maddened as he watched a replay of the peninsula unfold through the mountain passes of northwest Georgia. It did not help that the two men bitterly disliked each other—a feud that traced its origins to the very beginning of the war when Davis named his original list of general officers, where Johnston ranked fourth. The three men ahead of him on the list, Johnston felt, were less qualified than he.

The bitterness ran deep and public. "The President detests Joe Johnston for all the trouble he has given him, and General Joe returns the compliment with compound interest," South Carolinian Mary Chesnut noted in her diary. "His hatred of Jeff Davis amounts to a religion."[3]

Davis nonetheless backed Johnston in the field until Johnston's wounding at the battle of Seven Pines on May 31, 1862. By the time Johnston recovered to assume field command, Lee had reversed Confederate fortunes in Virginia

John Bell Hood's presence in the Western Theater was somewhat of a fluke to begin with. Wounded at the battle of Chickamauga in September 1863, he convalesced in Richmond while the rest of his troops—part of James Longstreet's I Corps—went first to Knoxville and then, eventually, back to the Army of Northern Virginia. When the spring campaign in the West opened, a paucity of capable officers and Hood's friendship with Confederate Jefferson Davis—cultivated during Hood's convalescence—ensured Hood a promotion to corps command in the western army. *Photo by Chris Mackowski*

over the course of the following summer. Davis had no intention of returning Johnston to command there. However, Davis could not ignore the value of a well-respected veteran commander like Johnston, either.

Because Johnston was a full general, few posts existed commensurate with his rank. Davis solved the problem in the same way countless other government bureaucrats have solved similar personnel issues: he promoted Johnston and transferred him out of Virginia. On November 24, Johnston took command of the Confederacy's Department of the West.

The post was largely administrative. However, by May 13, 1863, Johnston found himself in the field in Jackson, Mississippi, charged with the relief of embattled Vicksburg commander General John C. Pemberton. "It is a matter of great anxiety to me to add this little force to your army," Johnston told Pemberton, preferring to avoid direct conflict with the Federals.[4] Instead, he counseled evacuation. "Vicksburg is of no value, and cannot be held," he contended. "If, therefore, you are invested in Vicksburg, you must ultimately surrender. Under such circumstances, instead of losing both the troops and the place, we must, if possible, save the troops."[5] Ordered by Jefferson Davis to hold the city, Pemberton disobeyed Johnston and endured a siege nearly eight weeks long. After Vicksburg's fall, Davis blamed the debacle on a "want of provisions inside [the city] and a general outside who would not fight"—a clear finger pointed at Johnston.[6]

The fall of Chattanooga in mid-November 1863 again cast the spotlight on Johnston. General Braxton Bragg, the polarizing commander of the Army of Tennessee—whose greatest skill as a general was his ability to snatch defeat from the jaws of victory—lost his grip on the vital rail center. The debacle rivaled the fall of Vicksburg, and Davis could no longer sustain Bragg, his longtime crony. At Bragg's request, Davis relieved him—then transferred and promoted him in much the same fashion as he had done with Johnston in 1862.

With Bragg's removal, Davis had no one to take his place other than his longtime thorn, Johnston. On December 27, 1863, Johnston found himself in Dalton, Georgia, in command of the Army of Tennessee. "He was the very picture of a general," recalled Sam Watkins in his memoir Co. Aytch. "He restored the soldier's pride; he brought the manhood back to the private's bosom. . . . He was loved, respected, admired; yea, almost worshipped by his troops. I do not believe there was a soldier in his army but would gladly have died for him."[7]

The Army of Tennessee had an ill-starred history, fighting well in all its engagements yet failing to achieve victory time and time again due to bad leadership (much like the Federal Army of the Potomac in the Eastern Theater). Only at Chickamauga in September 1863—in what became the war's second-bloodiest battle—did the army score a major victory. Bragg failed to fully exploit that victory, however, ultimately losing everything he gained when Federals broke out of Chattanooga.

On a map, the amount of real estate the army had given up consisted of thousands of square miles—from the northernmost point of its advance to Perryville, Kentucky, in the fall of 1862 all the way back to northwest Georgia in the spring of 1864. But the army had still mounted credible resistance to the Federals, and with the fall election coming in the North, war weariness was the South's greatest weapon. The Confederacy needed only to lengthen the already long Northern casualty list and hang on until November, when the ballot box could change everything. "For my own part, I think that Johnston's tactics were right," Ulysses S. Grant assessed in his memoirs. "Anything that could have prolonged the war a year beyond the time that it did finally close, would probably have exhausted the North to such an extent that they might then have abandoned the whole context and agreed to a separation."[8]

Thus, Johnston did not necessarily have to win—he just had to not lose. That defensive-minded style, one of the great lessons George Washington took out of the Valley Forge winter of 1777–78, might have been exactly what the Confederacy needed in the spring and summer of 1864. "Johnston acted wisely," Grant later attested: "he husbanded his men and saved as much of his territory as he could, without fighting decisive battles to which all might be lost."[9]

Grant and William T. Sherman both had a healthy respect for Johnston. "General Grant told me that he was about the only general on that side whom he feared," Sherman admitted.[10] Johnston, for his part, saw such postwar compliments as vindication of his strategy. "The testimony of an enemy in one's favor is certainly worth more than that of a friend, as he who receives a blow can better estimate the dexterity of the striker than any spectator," he wrote.[11]

By then, Johnston's blows fell as part of the postwar war of words, not during the final phases of the Atlanta campaign. As Stephen Davis (no relation to Jefferson Davis) explains in the following essay, the Confederate president fired Johnston on September 20 and, in his stead, promoted John Bell Hood to command the Army of Tennessee.

"Sherman and I were rejoiced when we heard of the change," Grant admitted. "Hood was unquestionably a brave, gallant soldier and not destitute of ability, but unfortunately, his policy was to fight the enemy wherever he saw him, without thinking much of the consequences of defeat."[12]

Those consequences proved to be dire for the Confederate war effort in the West, making Davis's decision to replace Johnston with Hood one of the most controversial turning points of the war.

"Far Better in the Present Emergency": John Bell Hood Replaces Joseph E. Johnston

Stephen Davis

Relieving an army commander in the middle of a war is a huge decision for a commander in chief. Understandably it is very rarely done, and only after the executive's grave and prolonged consideration. President Abraham Lincoln relieved Major General George B. McClellan after Antietam, primarily for failing to reap the fruits of his strategic victory. Following his defeat at Second Manassas, Major General John Pope was transferred to fight the Sioux in Minnesota. Major Generals Ambrose E. Burnside and Joseph Hooker were removed after losing big battles at Fredericksburg and Chancellorsville. But none of these actions by Lincoln materially affected the Army of the Potomac, which slogged on into 1864–65 under Major General George G. Meade and Lieutenant General Ulysses S. Grant to eventual victory at Appomattox.

In the west, Major General Don Carlos Buell was relieved for giving up middle Tennessee to General Braxton Bragg and then for failing to pursue him after Perryville. One might argue that replacing Buell with Major General William S. Rosecrans led to the Union defeat at Chickamauga a year later, but drawing such a line of cause and effect is very tortuous indeed. Besides, Rosecrans fought at least a drawn battle at Murfreesboro in late December 1862 and managed to maneuver Bragg out of middle Tennessee six months later. After Rosecrans was sacked following Chickamauga, Major General George H. Thomas replaced him and would lead the Army of the Cumberland until its end.[13]

On the Confederate side, President Davis, who had wanted to remove General P. G. T. Beauregard, seized the opportunity after the latter took an

186

unannounced medical leave from command. The decision led in turn to the appointment of Bragg, whose record as commander of the Army of Tennessee was notoriously mixed. In late 1863 Bragg was relieved at his own request after the army's rout at Missionary Ridge. General Joseph E. Johnston took over the army and rebuilt it to a strong fighting force in the spring of 1864. But as we know, after retreating from Dalton to Atlanta in the first two months of Major General William T. Sherman's Georgia campaign, Johnston was relieved of command by the Confederate government on July 18. Lieutenant General John B. Hood, corps commander in the army, was promoted and given leadership of the army.[14]

What Johnston might have done had he remained in command—whether, for instance, he could have held onto Atlanta or defeated Sherman in a big pitched battle—is an intriguing subject for speculation, but it is not my interest in this chapter. Rather, I wish to point out that Jefferson Davis's relief of neither Beauregard nor Bragg led to a major Confederate disaster, which here I define as the ruination or destruction of a major Southern field army. A reversal of that magnitude occurred only once during the war, when the Army of Tennessee essentially dissolved after Hood's defeat at Nashville in December 1864. Hood failed to prevent Sherman's capture of Atlanta in September 1864, an event that James M. McPherson has termed "the final decisive turning point toward Union victory," contributing to Lincoln's presidential reelection. After Atlanta, Hood led his army into Tennessee, fighting the bloody battle at Franklin, suffering a humiliating rout from the battlefield at Nashville, and retreating back into Mississippi during bitter winter weather.[15]

Within short order, the Army of Tennessee, the largest in the entire Confederacy under Johnston, essentially ceased to exist when Hood asked to be relieved of command in January 1865. All historians agree on this. "The Army of Tennessee suffered so severely in the Nashville campaign that it no longer was an effective fighting force," writes Herman Hattaway in his biography of Stephen D. Lee, one of Hood's corps commanders. After its retreat from Nashville, "the Army of Tennessee," in James Lee McDonough's words, "had essentially ceased to exist." With only about fifteen thousand men at Tupelo, most of whom were "barefooted and naked," according to one officer, Wiley Sword judges that Hood's army was "on the verge of collapse." "The disaster at Nashville had . . . destroyed it as a viable combat force," writes the historian of the Nineteenth Tennessee (which lost a third of its strength, captured at Nashville); "the Army of Tennessee was finished." Worse, the army's demise had occurred in just six months under Hood's command. Actually, Stanley

Joe Johnston had given up a significant amount of real estate in northwest Georgia in the spring of 1864. With their back to the city of Atlanta, Confederates had no more room to maneuver and were forced to dig in, inviting a siege of the Deep South's most important city. *Library of Congress*

Horn counts only six *weeks*; from the time his troops crossed the Tennessee River to their arrival back in Tupelo, Hood "had all but wrecked his army."[16]

It is not hard to argue that the virtual death of an army renders Jefferson Davis's decision to remove Johnston and replace him with Hood as a "turning point" of the war, the kind of pivotal event being considered in this book. My contribution to it will be to recount how and why President Davis and his advisers made the decision they did.

Sometimes it is worthwhile to approach an issue from a different angle. In this case, the question to be raised is not why Davis relieved Johnston in the summer of 1864 but why he placed him in command of the Army of Tennessee in the first place. In mid-February 1865, when members of Congress were calling upon the president to bring Johnston out of retirement and give him a field command in the Carolinas, Davis penned a long document

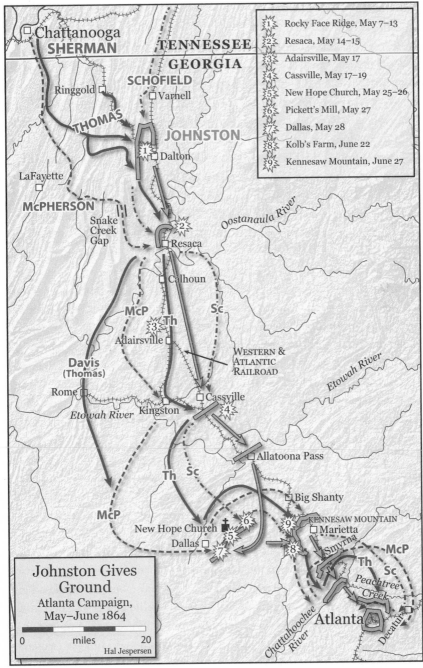

1	Rocky Face Ridge, May 7–13	
2	Resaca, May 14–15	
3	Adairsville, May 17	
4	Cassville, May 17–19	
5	New Hope Church, May 25–26	
6	Pickett's Mill, May 27	
7	Dallas, May 28	
8	Kolb's Farm, June 22	
9	Kennesaw Mountain, June 27	

Chattanooga
SHERMAN
TENNESSEE
GEORGIA
SCHOFIELD
Ringgold
Varnell
THOMAS
JOHNSTON
Dalton
LaFayette
McPHERSON
Snake Creek Gap
Resaca
Oostanaula River
Calhoun
McP
Th
Sc
Adairsville
WESTERN & ATLANTIC RAILROAD
Davis (Thomas)
Rome
Etowah River
Kingston
Cassville
Etowah River
Allatoona Pass
Th
Sc
Big Shanty
McP
New Hope Church
Dallas
KENNESAW MOUNTAIN
Marietta
Smyrna
McP
Th
Sc
Peachtree Creek
Atlanta
Chattahoochee River
Decatur

Johnston Gives Ground
Atlanta Campaign,
May–June 1864

0   miles   20
Hal Jespersen

Johnston Gives Ground. Johnston tried to resist William T. Sherman by taking up defensive positions that would force Sherman to make costly assaults. Instead, Sherman continually looked for ways to outflank Johnston and pry him out of his positions. Several fights between opposing forces did erupt over the course of the maneuvers, but Sherman inexorably backed Johnston across northwest Georgia to the Chattahoochee River. *Map by Hal Jespersen* detailing all the reasons that he would not do so. He went all through the war, cataloging more than a dozen and a half of Johnston's "defects which unfit him for the conduct of a campaign." The president was meticulous in detailing them. In the spring of 1861 Johnston had withdrawn from Harpers Ferry when it was unnecessary to do so. He initially resisted Davis's plan for reinforcing Beauregard at Manassas. He had resisted offensive operations unless reinforced. In his retreat from Centreville he had left behind large amounts of valuable supplies and goods. Withdrawing up the peninsula, he had crossed the Chickahominy without notifying the administration. He had remained inert before Richmond while McClellan drew up and prepared a siege. He had mismanaged the battle at Seven Pines. And all of this was in the first year of the war. Put in command of troops in Mississippi in the spring of 1863, Johnston had done nothing to help Lieutenant General John C. Pemberton at Vicksburg. "It should be added, " Davis wrote, "that neither in this nor in his previous command had it been possible for me to obtain from General Johnston any communications of his plans or purposes beyond vague statements of an intention to counteract the enemy as their plans might be developed." Six months later, after Bragg's departure and when Lieutenant General William J. Hardee, ranking corps leader in the Army of Tennessee, declined the command, Davis gave it to Johnston against his better judgment. As it turned out, Davis never sent to the Confederate Congress his memorandum critical of Johnston; it continues to be called the "unsent message."[17]

While the president of the Confederate States was accumulating a list of criticisms of Joe Johnston's generalship, he was taking favorable note of another officer's. John Bell Hood of Kentucky had risen in rank from lieutenant to major general in Lee's army in barely a year and a half. His reputation as combat leader soared after Gaines' Mill, Second Manassas, and Sharpsburg. Hood had received a crippling arm wound at Gettysburg and had lost a leg at Chickamauga, but after his amputation he determined to return to field service. During the winter of 1863–64, Hood spent several months convalescing in Richmond. There he was lionized by the capital's elite circles and befriended by Davis himself. When General Johnston called for a corps commander for his army at Dalton, Georgia, the government promoted Hood to lieutenant general and sent him there.[18]

Hood got a warm reception by Johnston, and the two generals developed a close relationship, often riding and dining together. But a rift soon emerged. In early 1864 the administration wanted Johnston to seize the initiative and launch a campaign into Tennessee before the enemy could launch its own toward Atlanta. Davis and Bragg, by that time the president's military adviser, peppered Johnston with cajoling letters throughout the winter. Johnston objected for what must be judged as good reasons: the enemy, by now under command of Sherman based at Chattanooga, outnumbered him; the country into which he would advance was barren of subsistence; the army had shortages of horses and wagons to carry supplies. Johnston won out when Sherman launched his forward movement in early May.[19]

Hood chose to enter this epistolary altercation when he broke the chain of command and wrote President Davis, General Bragg, and Secretary of War James A. Seddon five letters during March and April, all favoring the kind of offensive movement he knew the government wanted. It is uncertain whether Davis, before Hood left the capital, encouraged the newly promoted lieutenant general to keep him apprised of the situation in Georgia. Regardless, with such statements to Bragg as "You know how anxious I have been to advance" and "You know I am fond of large engagements and hope you will not forget me," Hood was clearly seeking to position himself favorably in the eyes of his superiors. Moreover, to an administration already suspicious of Johnston, Hood was further undermining the reputation of his commanding officer.[20]

When the campaign began in early May, Johnston repeated the behavior President Davis had seen two years before in Virginia. He fell back before Sherman's advance, giving up one defensive position after another. Once, at Cassville on May 19, he planned an attacking battle, but the tactical situation changed abruptly that morning and Hood, known for his boldness on the battlefield, ended up calling off the engagement. After that, Johnston won only defensive victories at New Hope Church, Pickett's Mill, and Kennesaw Mountain. These delayed the enemy's steady advance on Atlanta but did not stop it, much less reverse it. Sherman's tactical master plan was to use his superior numbers to keep Johnston busy on the front lines while sending columns around his flank. The process worked. From Dalton to Atlanta the Confederates gave up nine separate positions over a seventy-mile stretch of north Georgia.[21]

With each of Johnston's retreats, Jefferson Davis became not just concerned and worried; irritation, even anger, can be read in his telegrams to the army commander. After Johnston sent word of his retreat from Resaca, Davis on May 18 wired back, "Read with disappointment." The administration was sending fifteen to twenty thousand reinforcements to the Army of Tennessee: Lieutenant General Leonidas Polk's Army of Mississippi would become a third infantry corps; other troops came from Mobile and other coastal garrisons. Davis hoped that these reinforcements "will enable you to achieve important results."22

The hoped-for important results did not materialize, and tongues in Richmond started wagging. Robert G. H. Kean, head of the Bureau of War, entered in his diary on May 22 that Secretary Seddon was "greatly dissatisfied." "He told me this morning," Kean wrote, "that General Johnston's theory of war seemed to be never to fight unless strong enough certainly to overwhelm your enemy, and under all circumstances merely to contrive to elude him." This kind of talk in Confederate officialdom weakened Johnston's already shaky reputation.23

Hood certainly did his commanding officer no favor when he sent his aide, Colonel Henry Brewster, to Richmond to tell the president personally how bad things were in Georgia. We have no record of Brewster's conversation with Davis, only this diary entry from Mary Boykin Chesnut a few days later, after she talked with Colonel Brewster: "He said Joe Johnston was kept from fighting at Dalton by no plan—by no strategy." "What is the matter with him?" she wrote. "Overcautious."24

Braxton Bragg proved he was no friend of Johnston, either. On June 4 he addressed a memorandum to the president. "The condition of affairs in Georgia is daily becoming more serious," he began. Bragg enumerated the seven corps known to be presently with Sherman or soon to join him. "Should all these forces concentrate on the Army of Tennessee," he warned, "we may well apprehend disaster." The only possible solution would be if somehow the enemy could be defeated before effecting its concentration of strength.25

Bragg was at least civil enough to send Johnston a copy of his memo. Army headquarters, then near Marietta, Georgia, received it on June 9. Johnston was apparently unfazed, as he did not respond to Bragg's assertions. When he wired the president's adviser on the eleventh, it was only to report no change in the situation.26

In truth, Johnston seemed not to care that he was being disparaged in Richmond. A few days before the campaign even began, Brigadier General William W. Mackall, Johnston's chief of staff, wrote his wife that he had learned from an officer recently in the capital that the president was speaking ill of his army commander. On June 8, just before Bragg's memo arrived, one of Johnston's aides, Lieutenant Richard Manning, wrote home, "I understand that in consequence of the General not having provoked a *General Engagement* . . . the *enemy* at Richmond . . . are busy criticizing—blaming—abusing & undermining." "What does our General think of all this?" Manning added. "He thinks little of it."27

Meanwhile the president kept up with the reports from Georgia and hoped for the best. "Unless Genl Johnston strikes before the enemy has brought up all the reinforcements reported to be moving," Davis confided to General Lee on June 9, "his chances will be greatly diminished for the success which seemed attainable before he retreated." Nevertheless, Davis believed that success "still seems to be practicable."[28]

In this assessment, it must be said that Jefferson Davis was dreaming. Not only was Johnston not seeking to strike a blow at Sherman, but he also evinced no confidence that he could even stop the Union general. After he had been maneuvered out of yet another defensive position, he lamented to Bragg, "I can find no mode of preventing this." After his defensive victory at Kennesaw Mountain on June 27, arguably the best day of his campaign, he rued, "I have been unable so far to stop the enemy's progress."[29]

Johnston's only idea was to call for help from outside of his department. "I repeat the suggestion," he wrote Bragg, "that the cavalry in Alabama be put in the enemy's rear." "Repeat" is the correct word, for Johnston had indeed been hitting the administration with the idea that cavalry be ordered to raid into north Georgia, cut the Western & Atlantic Railroad feeding Sherman's forces, and maybe compel them to retreat out of hunger. "Cavalry on the rear of Sherman, this side of the Tennessee," he telegraphed Bragg on June 3, "would do him much harm at present." To Lieutenant General Stephen D. Lee, commanding forces in Alabama, he suggested that at least a cavalry brigade be sent against the railroad south of Chattanooga. "It may produce great results. That line is thinly guarded and Sherman's supplies deficient."[30]

Hood has been criticized for going around Johnston's back with his letters to Richmond, but he was scarcely the only general in the Army of Tennessee conducting this private correspondence. On June 22 no less than General Hardee addressed a letter to Jefferson Davis. His assessment of affairs was very negative. "I don't see under present circumstances when a collision is likely to occur. The enemy wont attack us in our entrenchments, and we are not disposed to attack him in his," he wrote. Then he added, "So if the present system continues we may find ourselves at Atlanta before a serious battle is fought."[31]

On June 24, Johnston's friend Senator Louis T. Wigfall of Texas was passing through Georgia on his way home. The senator bluntly told the general that the administration was considering relieving him of command. Asked about his plans, Johnston could only reiterate his hope for a cavalry raid against Sherman's communications. A month and a half into the campaign,

Joe Johnston still had no hope of repelling or defeating Sherman with the army at his disposal.[32]

Worse, he refused to employ his own forces to do what he was asking the government to do: send cavalry against Sherman's supply line. On July 1 Major General Joseph Wheeler, commander of cavalry in the Army of Tennessee, wrote General Bragg—yet another Confederate general to do so—that he had "nearly every day for the last three months" asked Johnston for permission to raid into the enemy's rear. And every time Johnston had refused, claiming "that my presence is necessary upon the flanks." All the more galling, Wheeler was being criticized in the press, "the papers abusing me for not being in Sherman's rear."[33]

With his calls for a cavalry raid, Johnston had a number of political figures on his side. One of them was the governor of Georgia, Joseph E. Brown, who shared the general's opinion that the Confederacy's two greatest cavalry raiders, Major General Nathan B. Forrest and Brigadier General John H. Morgan, should be dispatched to cut Sherman's lines of communication. "Could not Forrest or Morgan, or both, do more now for our cause in Sherman's rear than anywhere else?" Brown telegraphed President Davis on June 28. The next day Davis wired back that he could not spare Forrest from his assignments in north Mississippi.[34]

Brown sought support for his position from Georgia's senior senator, Benjamin H. Hill. Hill was a friend of the administration—sometimes called one of the president's "pets"—so Brown believed that Davis would listen to him. The governor asked Hill to meet with Johnston, hear his argument for sending Forrest or Morgan into the enemy's rear, and write the president advocating the move. Hill offered to do better than that: he would meet with the general and carry his message personally to Davis in Richmond.

The senator met Johnston on July 1 at his headquarters in Marietta. They had a wide-ranging conversation, with Hill asking how long he thought he could hold his lines north of the Chattahoochee. (Years later Hill remembered that Johnston "did not answer this question with directness": "He said I could make the calculation" based on the fact that it had taken Sherman a month to cover the few miles from New Hope Church to Marietta.) But the nub was the cavalry raid. Johnston explained why he could not send Wheeler and so emphasized his argument that Hill confirmed it three times before he left: "And I understand you to say, General Johnston, that Sherman cannot be defeated except by the proposed attack in his rear, and that this work must be done by Forrest or Morgan or by some such force?" Johnston said yes.[35]

Before Senator Hill could deliver this message to the president, things moved fast at the front. Sherman flanked Johnston out of his Kennesaw line; the army retreated during the night of July 2–3 to a new position five or six miles to the south. That line held all of forty-eight hours against another Federal thrust around the Confederate left. During the night of July 4–5, Johnston's troops occupied fortifications with their very backs against the Chattahoochee.

Johnston informed Richmond of this on the fifth. "In consequence of the enemy's advance toward the river below our left we this morning took this position, which is slightly intrenched," the general wrote from "near Chattahoochee bridge." Beyond mentioning the wounding of a brigadier and that cavalry was guarding river crossings downstream, that was all the news Johnston offered. It was enough to agitate the president, though. "The announcement that your army has fallen back to the Chattahoochee renders me more apprehensive for the future," Davis replied, with considerable understatement. He reminded Johnston that other areas had been stripped of troops to strengthen his army and that much rested upon it. Yet Johnston refused to accept responsibility for his fate and that of the campaign. He informed the president he had learned that up to sixteen thousand cavalry were in Mississippi and Alabama. He asked if just a quarter of this mounted force might not be sent against the enemy's railroad in north Georgia, "thus compelling Sherman to withdraw."[36]

It was clear that the president could get nothing done with Johnston over the telegraph. On July 9 he instructed General Bragg to travel to Atlanta as fast as he could "and confer with General Johnston in relation to military affairs there."[37]

The "military affairs there" were deteriorating more quickly than Davis could have foretold. With his army backed up against the Chattahoochee, Johnston knew that it was only a matter of time before he would have to give up the last river barrier to Sherman's advance on Atlanta. He expected the enemy to move downstream and attempt a crossing beyond his left—throughout the campaign, almost all of Sherman's maneuvers had been against that flank of the Confederate line. But here Sherman changed things up and sent cavalry and infantry columns beyond Johnston's right. On July 8 Federals got across the Chattahoochee upstream of the Southerners' position. More did so on the ninth. Johnston ordered his troops across the river that night.[38]

On July 10, the army commander's telegram to Richmond was quite succinct: "On the night of the 8th the enemy crossed at Isham's, or Cavalry

Ford; intrenched. In consequence we crossed at and below the railroad, and are now about two miles from the river, guarding the crossings." Aside from the manifest falsity of how his troops could be guarding the river when they had withdrawn two miles south of it, Johnston's dispatch to his superiors bore the more grievous fault of brevity. In his famous "unsent message" of February 1865, Davis blamed Johnston for his chronic lack of communication. "No information was sent to me which tended to dispel the apprehension then generally expressed," he complained, "that Atlanta also was to be abandoned."[39]

July 10 was also the day that Davis received a visitor from Georgia: Ben Hill. After arriving in Richmond and checking into a hotel, the senator made his way quickly to the executive mansion. There the president and war secretary listened to Hill's argument that he believed Johnston could hold Sherman north of the Chattahoochee if Forrest or Morgan were sent onto the enemy's supply lines. Davis answered that neither could help Johnston; Forrest was facing enemy advances in Mississippi, and Morgan's command had been so thoroughly defeated a month before that it was out of action. Hill got the point. He really got it when Davis asked him how long Johnston claimed he could hold the enemy north of the river. Hill suggested at least a month. The president then drew forth the telegram just received, informing the astonished senator that Johnston's army had already crossed the Chattahoochee.[40]

At some point Seddon told Hill that he wanted to see Johnston relieved of command, but the president was opposed. Indeed, Davis still held out hope that Johnston could somehow save Atlanta or defeat Sherman. But the general in Georgia was undermining his own position. On the eleventh Johnston telegraphed Richmond his recommendation, without offering any reason, that the enemy prisoners of war being held at Andersonville (which was 110 miles south of Atlanta) be moved elsewhere. More than any previous message, this one seemed to indicate that Johnston was going to abandon Atlanta. It therefore convinced the president that Johnston would have to be relieved of command. But who would replace him? Davis hinted at his thinking in a telegram sent on July 12 to his trusted adviser, General Lee: "General Johnston has failed, and there are strong indications that he will abandon Atlanta. He urges that prisoners should be removed immediately from Andersonville. It seems necessary to relieve him at once. Who should succeed him? What think you of Hood for the position?" Lee's reply was anything but reassuring. "It is a bad time to release the commander of an army situated as that of Tenne [ssee]." "We may lose Atlanta and the army too," he added. Then, as to Davis's last question, Lee replied, "Hood is a bold fighter. I am doubtful as to other qualities necessary." That night, in a longer letter, Lee offered Davis more of his thoughts. Changing army commanders in the middle of a campaign would be "a grievous thing," but he acknowledged that perhaps it had to be done. As for Hood, Lee offered this evaluation: "a good fighter very industrious on the battlefield, careless off." "I have had no opportunity of judging of his action, when the whole responsibility rested upon him"—Hood had only served as division commander in the Army of Northern Virginia. Then, quite without any presidential coaxing, he added, "Genl Hardee has more experience in managing an army."[41]

The next day, July 13, the president replied to Lee's advice, acknowledging that relieving Johnston would be a "sad alternative." "But the case seems hopeless in present hands," he added. Johnston himself was doing nothing to reassure the government. His telegram of July 12 merely stated that enemy troops were crossing the river and digging in; "elsewhere everything quiet." Meanwhile negative word was spreading in Richmond. "Everybody has at last come to the conclusion that Johnston has retreated far enough," recorded Colonel Josiah Gorgas, the army's chief of ordnance, in his journal on the thirteenth. Even though the situation before Atlanta was becoming more critical with every day, Davis still chose not to act quickly. On the morning of July 13, General Bragg arrived in Atlanta. In the president's words, Bragg was to "promote the ends and objects which have been discussed between us," which can only be taken to mean preventing Sherman from capturing the city. Yet Bragg's first telegram was anything but reassuring. Arriving at the downtown depot, he could see panicked citizens boarding trains to flee the city; Johnston's retreat across the Chattahoochee had sent the populace into a tailspin. "Indications seem to favor an entire evacuation of this place," he wired even before he had met with Johnston. Then, after his meeting, Bragg sent further depressing details: Johnston was not contesting the enemy's river crossing; two Federal corps were already on the south bank; the strength of the army had been reduced by ten thousand men in the past month.[42]

General Bragg sent no telegrams on July 14, which he spent conferring further with Johnston and his corps commanders, including Hood. Davis was busy, too, meeting with his cabinet. (War Bureau chief Kean recorded in his diary on the fourteenth that "the retreats of Johnston" were "the present excitements . . . with the Cabinet.") The day before, Seddon had written out a long memorandum addressed to Senator Hill "in order to have the basis on which to found an official recommendation to the president"—the cabinet would soon be meeting to discuss Johnston. In his memo Seddon recapped all that he had heard from Hill on the tenth. Especially important was the senator's statement that "with the army and means at his [Johnston's] command he was unable to repel the enemy from Georgia or prevent his advance." According to Kean, Hill found Seddon's report "not strong enough," so he composed his own statement. The senator spent a good deal of time writing it, emphasizing his main point: "General Johnston distinctly stated that the only way to get Sherman's army out of the country was by an attack in his rear—by cutting the railroad and destroying his supplies, &c."

Either Davis or Seddon invited Hill to attend the cabinet meeting, at which Hill could amplify the points in his memorandum or answer questions. Besides, by this time the Georgia senator had been swung over to Seddon's opinion that Johnston had to go. According to Colonel Gorgas, Hill "urged a change of commanders, having ascertained to his entire satisfaction that Johnston would not fight even for Atlanta but would continue the retrograde under the flanking movements of Sherman."

Present at the meeting were the president, Senator Hill, Secretary Seddon, Secretary of State Judah P. Benjamin, Postmaster General John H. Reagan, and Naval Secretary Stephen R. Mallory. Seddon and Benjamin took the lead. In 1872 Seddon recalled that to Davis "I recommended removal"; Johnston "did not intend to fight a battle for the relief of Atlanta, but was already arranging, by another disastrous retreat, to abandon his position there." Likewise, Benjamin affirmed in 1879, "I was most anxious and urgent that he shd. be replaced by some other commander." Benjamin had once held Johnston in high esteem, "but from a close observation of his career I became persuaded that his nervous dread of *losing a battle* would prevent at all times his ability to cope with an enemy of nearly equal strength." Mallory recorded in his diary how Benjamin asserted, "Johnston is determined not to fight, it is of no use to re-enforce him, he is not going to fight." In 1878 Reagan also remembered the meeting, recalling to Davis, "I know you were urged by letters and telegrams and by deputations sent to Richmond, in the most earnest manner to make the change." At some point a vote was taken, and it was unanimous for relieving Johnston of command. "The whole Cabinet concurred," Seddon remembered. A number of historians, even of the Atlanta campaign, tend to overlook this momentous cabinet meeting. James McPherson at least observes the unanimity of the vote against Johnston.[43]

The president, however, was still not prepared to act. After the war, former Confederate congressman James Lyons of Richmond recalled that on the night of the cabinet meeting Ben Hill had dinner with him. "He said he was admitted to the session of the cabinet," Lyons wrote to W. T. Walthall in June 1878. After the vote, Hill told Lyons, the president voiced opposition, saying, "Gentlemen it is very easy to remove the Genl. But when he is removed his place must be filled and where will you find a man to fill it?" Apparently there was some talk of whom that man would be. General Hardee, senior corps commander in the army, would have been a logical choice to succeed Johnston, but the cabinet remembered that the previous December, after Bragg's resignation, Hardee had agreed to step in only as a temporary successor, not a permanent one. According to Seddon, "Genl. Hardee, from his connection with and repute in the Army, seemed a natural appointment, and the Cabinet and President would have preferred him had he not on a previous occasion when temporarily succeeding Gen. Bragg, declared conviction of his own incompetency to such command."[44]

William J. Hardee might not have wanted army command, but John B. Hood did. The corps commander apparently spent a good deal of time on July 14 in private conversation with Bragg. Apparently at the latter's suggestion, Hood wrote a long letter addressed to Bragg, in which he expressed regret that Johnston had passed up "several chances to strike the enemy a decisive blow." Hood added a thinly veiled promise that if he were given the chance, he would attack Sherman "even if we should have to recross the river to do so." Hood knew that his meaning would be understood. "Please say to the President," he closed, "that I shall continue to do my duty cheerfully and faithfully."[45]

Bragg spent most of the fifteenth in town; he did not visit Johnston that day. In telegrams to Richmond he explained, "I cannot learn that he [Johnston] has any more plan for the future than he has had in the past." Bragg did acknowledge, though, "the impression prevails that he is more inclined to fight." "The morale of our army," he added, "is still reported good." Bragg also wrote a long letter to the president, explaining fully what he had concluded from his visit. "As far as I can learn, we do not propose any offensive operations"; Johnston seemed content to await the enemy's advance. To this Bragg clearly objected. "There is but one remedy," he concluded: "offensive action." Bragg did not advocate relieving Johnston, but "if any change is made, Lieutenant-General Hood would give unlimited satisfaction." Bragg was very clear in expressing his opinion that Hood would make a better successor than Hardee. "General Hood has been in favor of giving battle," he affirmed, whereas "General Hardee generally favored the retiring policy." (Bragg's statements were not quite true: Hood at Cassville had argued for the army to retreat and Hardee had not.) The general telegraphed the president to expect his report, then packed his and Hood's letters together and gave them to a staff officer, Lieutenant Colonel H. W. Walter. Walter left Atlanta on the fifteenth for at least a two-day train trip to the capital. Bragg left the city that evening for Alabama on an extended tour of inspection.[46]

In the end, Bragg's letter, which probably arrived in Richmond on July 17 or 18, proved inconsequential. President Davis felt he had to act. He had decided as early as the twelfth that Johnston would have to be relieved and was thinking of appointing Hood as his replacement. His cabinet had unanimously voted to back him on at least the former action, if not the latter. But his most trusted (and successful) general, Robert E. Lee, seemed reluctant to endorse a change in army commanders and was decidedly lukewarm toward Hood. Obviously, Lee could not be ignored. On the very morning after the cabinet meeting, Secretary Seddon boarded a 5:00 a.m. train from Richmond to Petersburg to meet with Lee. He conferred with the general, probably informing him of the cabinet vote and continuing to ask his opinion. According to Major General Wade Hampton, Lee advised that Johnston not be fired; if he could not lead an army successfully, "we had no one who could." Seddon returned to the capital right after his meeting, arriving around 11:00 a.m. He made his way straight to the president's office and met with him for at least an hour.[47]

Possibly because of Lee's misgivings, the president decided to give General Johnston one last chance to save his job. On July 16 he telegraphed a very pointed message. "I wish to hear from you as to present situation, and your plan of operations so specifically as will enable me to anticipate events." General Johnston could have figuratively heard a bomb dropping upon him when the Confederate president requested information as to his plans. He could not have been unaware of all that was going on in Richmond, at least because of the telegram Senator Hill sent him on the fourteenth (probably after the cabinet meeting): "You must do the work with your present force. For God's sake do it." Nevertheless, Johnston decided to respond to the president's telegram in a most negative, or at least nebulous, manner. The enemy outnumbered him two to one, he answered late on the sixteenth: "My plan of operations, must, therefore, depend upon that of the enemy. It is mainly to watch for an opportunity to fight to advantage. We are trying to put Atlanta in condition to be held for a day or two by the Georgia militia, that army movements may be freer and wider." "This was the clincher," as historian Steven Woodworth has written. And indeed it was, as remembered by the president's cabinet members. "The answer was deemed evasive and unsatisfactory," remembered Secretary Seddon, "and then and not till then, under the belief that Genl.

J. really meant to abandon Atlanta without decisive engagement[,] did the President finally decide and authorize his removal." Postmaster Reagan said the same. "The change was not finally made," he wrote in 1878, "until . . . General Johnston would not give the Secretary of War to understand certainly whether he would give battle rather than uncover Atlanta."[48]

And what did "freer and wider" mean, anyway? Johnston argued after the war that he intended for Major General Gustavus W. Smith's militia to hold the fortified city while he took his infantry in an attacking battle against Sherman. To Hood and his friends this notion appeared ludicrous. One of them was General Smith himself. "I wonder if old Joe did intend to leave my little band in charge of Atlanta whilst the three corps and the cavalry were hunting for Sherman's right of left flank," he wrote Hood in 1879. "Carrumba! Wouldn't that have been a kettle of fish?"[49]

With the "clincher" in hand, the administration acted swiftly. Adjutant General Samuel Cooper wired Johnston on the seventeenth that he was being relieved of command of the Army of Tennessee, "as you have failed to arrest the advance of the enemy to the vicinity of Atlanta, far in the interior of Georgia, and express no confidence that you can defeat or repel him." General Hood was being promoted to full general; Johnston was to turn the army over to him.[50]

Braxton Bragg hit the nail on the head in his characterization of John Bell Hood. "Do not understand me as proposing him as a man of genius, or a great general," he had written Davis on July 15, "but as far better in the present emergency than any one we have available."[51] That "far better," as we know, proved very much wanting in Hood's six months in command of the Army of Tennessee. To be sure, he probably held Atlanta against Sherman longer than Johnston would have. But in that month and a half before the city's fall, the Army of Tennessee lost at least 13,000 casualties. (Some historians estimate Confederate forces suffered around 35,000 officers and men lost in the Atlanta campaign, about half under Johnston, half under Hood.)[52] The real consequence of Hood's appointment lay in his disastrous Tennessee campaign of November–December 1864, leading to the destruction of the Army of Tennessee. Two weeks before the army crossed the Tennessee River at the start of its campaign, returns posted 35,662 officers and men. Two weeks after its retreat ended at Tupelo, the army had only 18,708 present for duty.[53]

President Davis and his cabinet could not have foreseen, of course, such a calamitous consequence of their decision in July 1864 to fire Johnston and replace him with Hood. And while they did not make this decision rashly or without much agonizing deliberation, their action nonetheless constituted a turning point in Confederate military history as it led to the fall of Atlanta. Sherman's capture of the city, Albert Castel astutely concludes, "destroyed the South's hope, its last realistic one, that it could gain its independence by depriving the North of its will to go on with the war. This is why the Atlanta Campaign was the final, decisive turning point of the Civil War: it assured Northern victory by defeating the South's attempt to win by not losing."[54]

Editors' Notes

1. Joseph E. Johnston, *Narrative of Military Operations: Directed, during the Late War between the States* (New York: D. Appleton, 1874), 290.
2. Ibid., 296.
3. Mary Chesnut, *A Diary from Dixie, as Written by Mary Boykin Chesnut*, ed. Isabella D. Martin and Myrta Lockett Avary (New York: D. Appleton, 1905), 248.
4. *OR*, vol. 24, pt. 3, 884.
5. Ibid., 888.
6. Frank E. Vandiver, ed., *The Civil War Diary of General Josiah Gorgas* (Tuscaloosa: University of Alabama Press, 1947), 50.
7. Sam Watkins, *Co. Aytch, or a Side Show of the Big Show*, ed. Philip Leigh (Yardley, Pa.: Westholme, 2013), 134–35.
8. Ulysses S. Grant, *The Personal Memoirs of Ulysses S. Grant* (Hartford, Conn.: Charles Webster, 1885; New York: Library of America, 1990), 505.
9. Ibid., 632.
10. William T. Sherman, *Memoirs of General W. T. Sherman*, ed. Charles Royster (New York: Library of America, 1990), 354.
11. Johnston, *Narrative*, 461.
12. Grant, *Personal Memoirs*, 632.

Contributor's Notes

13. A standard work on this topic remains T. Harry Williams, *Lincoln and His Generals* (New York: Alfred A. Knopf, 1952).
14. Stanley F. Horn, *The Army of Tennessee: A Military History* (Indianapolis: Bobbs-Merrill, 1941), 155–56, 305–6, 339–40; Thomas Lawrence Connelly, *Army of the Heartland: The Army of Tennessee, 1861–1862* (Baton Rouge: Louisiana State University Press, 1967), 180–81; Thomas Lawrence Connelly, *Autumn of Glory: The Army of Tennessee, 1862–1865* (Baton Rouge: Louisiana State University Press, 1971), 277, 421–23; Steven E. Woodworth, *Jefferson Davis and His Generals: The Failure of Confederate Command in the West*

(Lawrence: University Press of Kansas, 1990), 106–7, 253–54, 282–86.

15. James M. McPherson, "American Victory, American Defeat," in *Why the Confederacy Lost*, ed. Gabor S. Boritt (New York: Oxford University Press, 1992), 41.

16. Herman Hattaway, *General Stephen D. Lee* (Jackson: University Press of Mississippi, 1976), 146; James Lee McDonough, *Nashville: The Western Confederacy's Final Gamble* (Knoxville: University of Tennessee Press, 2004), 274; Willey Sword, *Embrace an Angry Wind: The Confederacy's Last Hurrah; Spring Hill, Franklin, and Nashville* (New York: HarperCollins, 1992), 426; John D. Fowler, *Mountaineers in Gray: The Nineteenth Tennessee Volunteer Infantry Regiment, C.S.A.* (Knoxville: University of Tennessee Press, 2004), 174–75; Horn, *Army of Tennessee*, 421.

17. Jeff'n Davis to James Phelan, March 1, 1865, *OR*, vol. 47, pt. 2, 1304–11; Gilbert E. Govan and James W. Livingood, *A Different Valor: The Story of General Joseph E. Johnston, C.S.A.* (Indianapolis: Bobbs-Merrill, 1956), 345, 347; Craig L. Symonds, *Joseph E. Johnston: A Civil War Biography* (New York: W. W. Norton, 1992), 342.

18. Stephen Davis, "Gen. John Bell Hood," in *Kentuckians in Gray: Confederate Generals and Field Officers of the Bluegrass State*, ed. Bruce S. Allardice and Lawrence Lee Hewitt (Lexington: University Press of Kentucky, 2008), 152–54.

19. Stephen Davis, *Atlanta Will Fall: Sherman, Joe Johnston, and the Yankee Heavy Battalions* (Wilmington, Del.: Scholarly Resources, 2001), 27–32.

20. Richard M. McMurry, *John Bell Hood and the War for Southern Independence* (Lexington: University Press of Kentucky, 1982), 95–97; Hood to Davis, March 7, 1864, Hood to Bragg, March 10, Hood to Seddon, March 10, and Hood to Bragg, April 13, *OR*, vol. 32, pt. 3, 606–8, 781; Hood to Bragg, April 3, Braxton Bragg Papers, Western Reserve Historical Society, Manuscript Collection No. 2000, Cleveland, Ohio (microfilm at John C. Hodges Library, University of Tennessee, Knoxville).

21. The best history of the Atlanta campaign remains Albert Castel, *Decision in the West: The Atlanta Campaign of 1864* (Lawrence: University Press of Kansas, 1992). Richard M. McMurry, *Atlanta 1864: Last Chance for the Confederacy* (Lincoln: University of Nebraska Press, 2000), is a more concise but equally sound survey. The Cassville incident is treated in pp. 195–206 and 79–83, respectively.

22. Davis to Johnston, May 18, 1864, *OR*, vol. 38, pt. 4, 725.

23. Edward Younger, ed., *Inside the Confederate Government: The Diary of Robert Garlick Hill Kean* (New York: Oxford University Press, 1957), 151.

24. Hood to Davis, May 21, 1864, in Ellsworth Eliot Jr., *West Point in the Confederacy* (New York: G. A. Baker, 1941), 100–101; C. Vann Woodward, ed., *Mary Chesnut's Civil War* (New Haven: Yale University Press, 1981), 616 (entry of June 4).

25. Bragg to Davis, June 4, 1864, *OR*, vol. 38, pt. 4, 762.

26. Bragg to Johnston, June 7, 1864, ibid.; Richard M. McMurry, "The Mackall Journal and Its Antecedents," typescript courtesy of the author (entry of June 9); Johnston to Bragg, June 11, 1864, *OR*, vol. 38, pt. 4, 769.

27. Mackall to wife, April 29, 1864, and Manning to mother, June 8, in Richard M. McMurry, "'The Enemy at Richmond': Joseph E. Johnston and the Confederate Government," in *Conflict and Command*, ed. John T. Hubbell (Kent, Ohio: Kent State University Press, 2012), 219–20.

28. Davis to Lee, June 9, 1864, in *The Papers of Jefferson Davis*, 14 vols. to date, ed. Lynda Lasswell Crist et al. (Baton Rouge: Louisiana State University Press, 1971–), 10:458.

29. Johnston to Bragg, June 16, 1864, *OR*, vol. 38, pt. 4, 777; Johnston to Bragg, June 27, ibid., 796.

30. Johnston to Bragg, June 16, 1864, ibid.; S. Davis, *Atlanta Will Fall*, 70; Johnston to Bragg and to S. D. Lee, both June 3, *OR*, vol. 38, pt. 4, 756.

31. Russell W. Blount Jr., *Clash at Kennesaw, June and July 1864* (Gretna, La.: Pelican, 2012), 70 (Hood as "presidential tattler"); Hardee to Davis, June 22, 1864, Jefferson Davis Collection, MSS 22, box 1, folder 40, Manuscript, Archives, and Rare Book Library, Emory University, Atlanta.

32. Alvy L. King, *Louis T. Wigfall: Southern Fire-Eater* (Baton Rouge: Louisiana State University Press, 1970), 196.

33. Wheeler to Bragg, July 1, 1864, Bragg Papers.

34. Brown to Davis, June 28, 1864, and Davis to Brown, June 29, *OR*, vol. 52, pt. 2, 680–81.

35. Ezra J. Warner and W. Buck Yearns, *Biographical Register of the Confederate Congress* (Baton Rouge: Louisiana State University Press, 1975), 118–19; Govan and Livingood, *Different Valor*, 299–301; Benjamin H. Hill to W. T. Walthall, October 12, 1878, in Jefferson Davis, *The Rise and Fall of the Confederate Government*, 2 vols. (New York: D. Appleton, 1881), 2:559; Hill to Seddon, July 14, 1864, *OR*, vol. 52, pt. 2, 706.

36. S. Davis, *Atlanta Will Fall*, 92–95; Johnston to Bragg, July 5, 1864, Davis to Johnston, July 7, and Johnston to Davis, July 8, *OR*, vol. 38, pt. 5, 865, 867, 869.

37. Davis to Bragg, July 9, *OR*, vol. 52, pt. 2, 695–96.

38. Castel, *Decision in the West*, 339–40.

39. Johnston to Bragg, July 10, 1864, *OR*, vol. 38, pt. 5, 873; Davis to Phelan, March 1, 1865, ibid., vol. 47, pt. 2, 1310.

40. Hill to Walthall, October 12, 1878, in J. Davis, *Rise and Fall of the Confederate Government*, 2:559–60; Brian Steel Wills, *A Battle from the Start: The Life of Nathan Bedford Forrest* (New York: HarperCollins, 1992), 217–19; Cecil Fletcher Holland, *Morgan and His Raider: A Biography of the Confederate General* (New York: Macmillan, 1942), 326–27.

41. J. Davis, *Rise and Fall*, 2:560–61; Johnston to Bragg, July 11, 1864, *OR*, vol. 38, pt. 5, 876; Davis to Lee, July 12, *OR*, vol. 52, pt. 2, 692; Lee to Davis, July 12, 1864, in *Lee's Dispatches: Unpublished Letters of General Robert E. Lee, C.S.A. to Jefferson Davis and the War Department of the Confederate States of America 1862–1865*, ed. Douglas Southall Freeman and Grady McWhiney (New York: G. T. Putnam Sons, 1957), 282–84.

42. Here and the next two paragraphs: Davis to Lee, July 13, 1864, *OR*, vol. 52, pt. 2, 692; Johnston to Bragg, July 12, 1864, ibid., vol. 38, pt. 5, 877; Sarah Woolfolk Wiggins, ed., *The Journals of Josiah Gorgas, 1857–1878* (Tuscaloosa: University of Alabama Press, 1995), 121; Davis to Bragg, July 9, 1864, *OR*, vol. 39, pt. 2, 695; Judith Lee Hallock, *Braxton Bragg and Confederate Defeat*, vol. 2 (Tuscaloosa: University of Alabama Press, 1991), 191–93; Bragg to Davis, July 13, 1864, *OR*, vol. 38, pt. 5, 878.

43. S. Davis, *Atlanta Will Fall*, 109–12; Younger, *Inside the Confederate Government*, 165–66; Seddon to Hill, July 13, 1864, *OR*, vol. 52, pt. 2, 694; Hill to Seddon, July 14, 1864, *OR*, vol. 52, pt. 2, 705; Wiggins, *Journals of Josiah Gorgas*, 123; Seddon to Davis, June 17, 1872, in *Jefferson Davis, Constitutionalist: His Letters, Papers and Speeches*, 10 vols., ed. Dunbar Rowland (Jackson: Mississippi Department of Archives and History, 1923), 7:320; Benjamin to Davis, February 15, 1879, in *Jefferson Davis, Constitutionalist*, 8:356; Bruce Catton, *Never Call Retreat* (New York: Doubleday, 1965), 330 (quoting Mallory's diary); Reagan to Davis, February 7, 1878, and Seddon to W. T. Walthall, Feb. 10, 1879, in *Jefferson Davis, Constitutionalist*, 8:79, 349; James M. McPherson, *Embattled Rebel: Jefferson Davis as Commander in Chief* (New York: Penguin, 2014), 199.

44. Lyons to Walthall, June 10, 1878, and Seddon to Walthall, February 10, 1879, in *Jefferson Davis, Constitutionalist*, 8:215–16, 349.

45. Hood to Bragg, July 14, 1864, *OR*, vol. 38, pt. 5, 879–80.

46. Bragg to Davis, July 15, 1864, ibid., 879–81; S. Davis, *Atlanta Will Fall*, 113; Bragg to Davis, July 15, 1864, *OR*, vol. 39, pt. 2, 713.

47. Younger, *Inside the Confederate Government*, 166–67; Hampton to Johnston, undated, in Joseph E. Johnston, "Opposing Sherman's Advance," in *Battles*

& Leaders (Yoseloff, 1956) 4:277; Robert M. Hughes, *General Johnston* (New York: G. Appleton, 1893), 252 ("beyond question . . . General Lee advised against it").

48. Davis to Johnston and Johnston to Davis, July 16, 1864, *OR*, vol. 38, pt. 5, 882–83; Hill to Johnston, July 14, 1864, ibid., 879; Steven E. Woodworth, "How to Lose a City," *Civil War* 9, no. 1 (January–February 1991): 33; Seddon to Walthall, February 10, 1879, and Reagan to Davis, February 7, 1878, in *Jefferson Davis, Constitutionalist*, 8:78, 353.

49. Johnston, *Narrative of Military Operations*, 350; Stephen M. Hood, ed., *The Lost Papers of Confederate General John Bell Hood* (El Dorado Hills, Calif.: Savas Beatie, 2015), 71.

50. Cooper to Johnston, July 17, 1864, *OR*, vol. 38, pt. 5, 885.

51. Bragg to Davis, July 15, 1864, ibid., vol. 39, pt. 2, 714.

52. Army of Tennessee abstracts, July 10, 1864, ibid., vol. 38, pt. 5, 679; September 10, 1864, ibid., vol. 39, pt. 2, 829; McMurry, *Atlanta 1864*, 197.

53. Abstracts, November 6, 1864, and January 20, 1865, *OR*, vol. 45, pt. 1, 664, 681.

54. Albert Castel, "The Atlanta Campaign and the Presidential Election of 1864: How the South Almost Won by Not Losing," in *Winning and Losing in the Civil War: Essays and Stories* (Columbia: University of South Carolina Press, 1996), 29–30.

9. ❄ The Election of 1864

Editors' Introduction

"War is a continuation of politics by other means," Prussian general Carl von Clausewitz once said.[1]

For Abraham Lincoln, in the summer of 1864, the two could not have been more inextricably linked. *The failure of politics to resolve Northern and Southern differences had led to secession, which then led to war; later, the Emancipation Proclamation radically and irrevocably changed the war's political dimensions. Now, with the fall election looming before him, Lincoln faced a subtle twist to von Clausewitz's dictum: he needed success in war in order to continue his politics.*

"I confess that I desire to be re-elected," he told Republican leaders in early August. "I have the common pride of humanity to wish my past four years['] administration endorsed. . . . I want to finish this job of putting down the rebellion, and restoring peace and prosperity to the country."[2]

But his prospects looked grim. *"The tide is setting strongly against us,"* Republican strategist Henry Raymond advised in an August 22 letter. Indiana, New York, Pennsylvania, and even Lincoln's home state of Illinois were all lining up against Lincoln's reelection. *"Nothing but the most resolute and decided action on the part of the government and its friends, can save the country from falling into hostile hands,"* Raymond said. *"Two special causes are assigned to this great reaction in public sentiment—the want of military successes, and the impression in some minds, the fear and suspicion in others, that we are not to have peace in any event under this administration until Slavery is abandoned."*[3]

The lack of military success across the board vexed Lincoln, but the Confederate strategy of prolonging the war came as no surprise. *"Every bullet we can send against the Yankees is the best ballot that can be deposited against Lincoln's election,"* the Augusta Constitutionalist proclaimed in January 1864. *"The battlefields of 1864 will hold the polls of the momentous decision."*[4]

Confederate lieutenant general James Longstreet echoed similar sentiments from eastern Tennessee in a March letter to the Confederacy's quartermaster general:

A troubled Lincoln faced a complicated political and military scenario going into the election of 1864. This statue, sculpted by Daniel Chester French and on display at Lincoln's tomb in Springfield, Illinois, depicts a contemplative Lincoln; the original stands outside the statehouse in Lincoln, Nebraska. *Photo by Chris Mackowski*

If we can make a telling campaign early in the spring we may be able to get an honorable peace in a short time; if we do not, the war will in all probability be prolonged, and no one call tell what may result.

An effective campaign, early in the season will have greater effect upon our people and upon our cause than anything that may happen at a later day. If we can break up the enemy's arrangements early, and throw him back, he will not be able to recover his position nor his morale until the Presidential election is over, and we shall then have a new President to treat with. If Lincoln has any success early he will be able to get more men and may be able to secure his own reelection. In that event the war must go on for four years longer.[5]

By August 1864, Ulysses S. Grant had bogged down outside Petersburg after an especially brutal spring campaign; William T. Sherman had done likewise outside Atlanta after cat-and-mousing all spring with Joe Johnston and then vainly slugging it out with Johnston's successor, John Bell Hood. Nathaniel Banks had been turned back on the Red River in Louisiana. Benjamin Butler had been bottled up at Bermuda Hundred, Virginia. David Hunter had been turned back in the Shenandoah Valley of Virginia, and Confederates were once again running rampant there. Lincoln might win the war of attrition that Grant had proposed in the spring of 1864, but if Lincoln wanted to win reelection, he needed to win a war of annihilation.

Raymond's other point, abandoning slavery as a war aim, also weighed on Lincoln. He briefly toyed with the idea, assuming that he could reimpose it as a war aim once reelected, but he realized that doing so would appear to be an act of desperation—not to mention a morale crusher for freed and enslaved black people everywhere. He recognized how irrevocable abolition truly was and so resolved to stick to his original course, no matter where it might lead.

On the morning of August 23, Lincoln took a sheet of paper from his desk and scribbled a note to himself, his cabinet, and the nation—and ultimately posterity itself: "This morning, as for some days past, it seems exceedingly probable that this Administration will not be re-elected. Then it will be my duty to so co-operate with the President elect, as to save the Union between the election and the inauguration; as he will have secured his election on such ground that he can not possibly save it afterwards."[6] *Lincoln folded the page, slid it into an envelope and sealed it, and then presented the sealed envelope to his cabinet at a meeting. He asked everyone to sign the envelope, memo unseen, and then he tucked it away: his solemn oath that, no matter the outcome of the election, he would work to his fullest capacity to prosecute the war as vigorously as possible so long as he stayed in office—even if that meant only until March.*

If Lincoln somehow won the election, no one doubted he would carry on the war as long as necessary. If he lost, as even he expected, he would try to wrap up the war before the new president took office. Confederates rested their hopes on the fact that he would not be able to do so.

As Rea Andrew Redd explains in the following essay, those clashing expectations created a tense context for the election, which played out as a twisting series of political and military events, North and South. Lincoln's resolve inextricably wove politics and war together for one final push. The election of 1864, then, became not a turning point but rather the point of no return.

The Point of No Return: Turning Points within the 1864 Presidential Election and the Doom of the Confederacy

Rea Andrew Redd

In mid-January 1865, some White House callers expressed anxiety to the president about the military situation. Lincoln went to a map and showed them how Lieutenant General Ulysses S. Grant had Lee trapped at Petersburg, and how Major General William T. Sherman was moving through the Carolinas. As historian Michael Burlingame relates, Lincoln remarked that his own situation, after being elected twice to the presidency, called to mind

> an old fellow in the early days of Indiana who had been a wicked and lascivious sinner but he had joined the church and was getting baptized. The preacher dipped him in a river, and he came up gasping and rubbing his face. Then began calling on the preacher to dip him again and baptize him once more. The preacher said once was enough. The old fellow insisted. So the preacher dunked him again. As he came up and rubbed the water out of his eyes and mouth and got his breath, the old man blurted out, "Now I've been baptized twice and the Devil can kiss my ass." Lincoln pointed to a spot on the map and said that when Sherman's army got to that place where Grant was the war would be ended. "And then," said Lincoln, "the Southern Confederacy can kiss my ass."[7]

The Assumptions

Was Lincoln's second election to the American presidency a turning point in the Union's quest for victory during the war?[8] If so, did this particular

UNION AND LIBERTY!   AND   UNION AND SLAVERY!

Republican campaign propaganda from the 1864 election portrayed Lincoln as pro-Union and antislavery while depicting his Democratic opponent, George McClellan, as pro-Union and proslavery. *Library of Congress*

turning point doom the Confederacy's odds of gaining independence? Often repeated are the assertions that a George B. McClellan victory would in some way ensure a victory for the Confederacy and a Lincoln victory would be a crushing defeat for the Confederacy.

During October and November 1864, Northern voters went to the polls and faced a distinct choice. Casting a ballot for the Union Party, which was organized by Republicans, was a vote to continue the war until certain victory. A victory, not an armistice, would be achieved. Casting a ballot for the Democratic Party was a vote to settle the war through an armistice designed in part by European arbitrators.

Lincoln won about 55 percent of the popular vote with, for the first time in American history, thousands of furloughed soldiers casting ballots or voting while on campaign. Three out of four soldier votes were cast for the Republican ticket; it is possible that soldiers who were Democrats crossed party lines to vote for Lincoln. He also garnered 212 electoral votes. George B. McClellan and Thomas Pendleton received only 21 electoral votes coming from Delaware, New Jersey, and Kentucky.[9]

The renomination and reelection of Lincoln were not foregone conclusions. No sitting president had received renomination since 1840; none had been reelected since Andrew Jackson's second victory in 1832. Within the

Republican Party were former candidates from 1860 who were willing to challenge Lincoln in 1864. In particular, Ohio senator and U.S. treasury secretary Salmon P. Chase believed that he could oust Lincoln as head of the Republican ticket. Ambitious and skilled, Chase used his four years of federal patronage appointments to build a national base. Others, such as John C. Frémont and Horace Greeley, were disappointed by being left in military and political backwaters. They angled to gather support from those Republicans who were disenchanted with Lincoln and those who were War Democrats.

Meeting in Baltimore during the second week of June 1864, the Republican Party rebranded itself as the National Union Party in order to attract War Democrats and Union sympathizers living in the border states. The convention organizers brought forth a platform that committed the party to accepting the unconditional surrender of Confederate armies and an amendment to the U.S. Constitution that would make slavery illegal throughout the land. Also, delegations from the president's reconstructed states of Louisiana and Tennessee were admitted to the convention, and Andrew Johnson, Tennessee senator who had not seceded from the U.S. Senate, was added to the ticket.

But within two months of the convention's meeting, Radical Republicans Benjamin Wade and Henry Davis let loose a salvo against Lincoln. Presidential Reconstruction should cease and Congressional Reconstruction should hold sway. This endeavor, along with Confederate raids into Maryland and Pennsylvania, which resulted in a brief assault on Washington, D.C., and the burning of Chambersburg, Pennsylvania, showed many that Lincoln might be losing the war and likely losing the election.[10]

During the spring and summer of 1864, war weariness and the lengthening of battlefield casualty lists revived the prospects of Peace Democrats. Clement Vallandigham, a leading Copperhead, had returned from a yearlong, presidentially ordered exile in the Confederacy. He was allowed to speak out against the war and call for an armistice and European arbitration. After Lincoln requested another five hundred thousand volunteers on July 18, Horace Greeley, the quixotic and influential editor of the *New York Tribune*, wrote to Lincoln on August 8, 1864, that "our bleeding, bankrupt and almost dying country . . . longs for peace—shudders at the prospect of fresh conscriptions, of other wholesale devastations, and of new rivers of human blood." Greeley forecasted that if Lincoln did not do something to meet this longing, then Lincoln and the Republicans would "be beaten out of sight next November."[11]

During the summer of 1864, Lincoln's own speculations included the notion that Greeley may be right. In August, a warning came from Henry J.

Raymond, chairman of the Republican National Committee, that the tides in Pennsylvania and Indiana were running against the Republican presidential ticket. Also Thurlow Weed, a close friend and political confidant of William Seward, put Lincoln on guard by remarking that voters were clamoring for peace and that his reelection may be an impossibility. While reflecting on 1864 in later years, Alexander McClure, editor, politician, and active in Pennsylvania Republican Party politics, recalled that at no time from January to September 3 was there a time that McClellan would have *not* defeated Lincoln.[12]

The Republican Party's Previous Victories

Founded during 1854, the Republican Party began fielding political candidates during the 1856 election. Remnants of the Whig, Know-Nothing, and Free-Soil Parties joined with disaffected Democrats and unaffiliated abolitionists. Their cri de coeur included opposition to the late 1854 release of the Ostend Manifesto in which three U.S. State Department ambassadors described the rationale for the purchase of Cuba from Spain while implying a declaration of war if Spain refused. The first Republican state convention was organized in Pittsburgh, Pennsylvania, in 1855, and in the next year a national organizing convention was held again in Pittsburgh while the 1856 Kansas-Nebraska Act was being hotly debated in Congress. The meeting attracted delegates from twenty-four states and established a national executive committee to organize their first nominating convention to be held in Philadelphia. In the presidential election of 1856, with John C. Frémont as a candidate, the party captured a bit more than 60 percent of the popular vote in the North. Young, unorganized, and labeled "black" and "disunion," the party was six years old when it offered Abraham Lincoln as a candidate for the presidency in 1860.[13]

The November 1860 Republican victories in the White House and Congress were the immediate cause for South Carolina's December 1860 secession. The presidential campaign in the South had pitted Constitutional Unionist against Southern rights candidates, while in the North, Stephen Douglas and Abraham Lincoln contested for votes. Victory required 152 of 303 electoral votes. Lincoln won 180 votes in the North and Pacific Coast; John Bell won 39 from Virginia, Kentucky, and Tennessee; John C. Breckinridge won 72 in the South and New Jersey and Delaware. Douglas won Missouri's 9 votes. These figures would inform political party strategies during the elections of 1862 and 1864.[14]

The midterm election of 1862 was significant as the first national congressional contest during the war. It revealed erosion of the Republican power at national and state levels. Also, it indicated to a degree the unpopularity of some presidential policies and actions. The war closed the Mississippi River and hindered trade between the Midwest and the South. Agricultural produce traveled eastward on the Great Lakes instead of southward on the river. The Morrill Tariff of 1861 gave northwestern Democrats an issue, as did the increase in railroad charges on goods shipped. Additionally, the arrests of dissidents in the border states and the intimidation by the military of some newspaper editors alarmed voters who feared the expansion of political authority against state political power. Yet as important at these issues were, another was greater.

The Republican Party was committed to ending slavery. The 1861 and 1862 Confiscation Acts and the 1862 Militia Act angered Democrats and others. The use of black soldiers in noncombat roles was becoming a reality. The preliminary Emancipation Proclamation of September 1862 altered the character of the war at its foundation. Bundled together, these legislative acts and the proclamation gave notice that the Lincoln administration was conducting the war in a manner that was not foreseen in early 1861. Frustration and war-weariness with failed battlefield strategy and tactics and high casualty rates underscored that sacrifices of treasure, blood, and social norms were required by Lincoln and his political party.

The election returns of 1862 informed Lincoln that the 1864 election must include the active duty soldiers' votes. Few if any provisions were made in 1862 to gather votes from those on military campaigns. Between late 1862 and the 1864 autumn elections, states made liberal provisions for gathering the votes of soldiers either by giving them furlough from camps or by allowing voting in camp or on the march.[15]

Citizens were highly politicized during the war, and the issues were constantly debated in homes and before the public. Most wished to have the Union restored. The leaders and members of each political party debated the measures that would bring about the restoration and under what conditions the so-called Confederate states would reenter the Union. In general, Democrats blamed Republicans for the war and the ensuing destruction of property and property rights. They believed that, by these acts and policies, the Republicans had engendered animosity so deep that a harmonious solution was unlikely. Republicans doubted the loyalty of those who questioned the policies and military actions necessary to reunite the Union.

Despite the Republican Party's domination of Congress during the war, the states that remained in the Union were divided politically. During the 1860 election, Lincoln garnered 39.8 percent of the popular vote while Douglas, along with Breckinridge, gathered 47.6 percent. Bell, the Constitutional Union candidate, picked up 12.6 percent. Lincoln did very well in the upper North, New England, and those regions to which New Englanders had moved. The lower North gave the Republicans a much lower majority. The Republican Party was very weak in the border states, which were almost evenly divided between the Constitutional Union and Democratic Parties.

Within the border states, a possible determining factor was seen to be those Southern-sympathizing Democrats who had joined the Confederate armies. They would not be present to cast a ballot in the 1864 election. But among those remaining and those in the lower North, the issues of emancipation, individual liberties, and loss of political power to a central authority were hotly engaged.

Nevertheless, 1854 to 1864 was a decade of enormous growth for the Republicans. During the 1863 state elections, Democrats faced charges of pro-Confederate sympathies and flagrant disloyalty. These perceptions damaged the Democratic Party's reputation. In no statewide contest did the Democratic candidate prevail. For the upcoming 1864 congressional and executive elections, Republicans understood that the lower North was essential for control of the House of Representatives and the White House. For both parties, the key to success was not to change opponents' minds but to get the party faithful to the ballot box. A brief coalition of prowar Democrats, Unionists, and Republicans was viewed as essential for Lincoln's victory. Building this coalition required emphasizing the common goal of a restored Union with a limited reconstruction of the South and no discussion of contrabands' political attributes after the war. Lincoln's December 1863 Proclamation of Amnesty and Reconstruction anticipated the message of the 1864 campaign. In that proclamation, the president described how the Confederate states and their citizens would be restored to the Union.[16]

Reconstruction as a Campaign Issue

Issued on December 8, 1863, the Proclamation of Amnesty and Reconstruction applied to all lands currently occupied by Union forces. Lincoln would pardon almost any Confederate who swore loyalty to the U.S. Constitution and the Union. Individuals who would be excluded from the pardon would be high-ranking civil and military leaders and those convicted of war crimes. Once 10 percent of voters in a Confederate state took the oath of allegiance and organized a government that abolished slavery, that state could elect new representatives and Lincoln would recognize the state government as legitimate.[17]

The president's outlined policy was intended to placate the desired brief coalition of prowar Democrats, Unionists, and Republicans. But the "Ten Percent Plan" deeply agitated those Republicans who wanted a much slower process for the restoration of disloyal states with a redistribution of plantation lands and civil rights protections for former slaves. This heavy disappointment prompted Radical Reconstruction Republicans to begin a conversation regarding a candidate other than Lincoln for the 1864 presidential campaign. These individuals noted that since the presidency of Andrew Jackson, no sitting president had won a second term. Both the 1856 candidate, John C. Frémont, and Salmon P. Chase, who had sought the 1860 nomination, discussed this possibility during 1863 and 1864. Early endorsements of Frémont came from Wendell Phillips, abolitionist orator and lawyer, and Frederick Douglass, noted African American public speaker. In the course of 1863 and 1864, Radical Republicans promoted amendments that would limit the presidency to one term and abandon the electoral college. These Radical Republicans supported constitutional amendments that would abolish slavery, confiscate slaveholder lands, and establish race and gender equality.

During mid-1864, Benjamin F. Butler, a Massachusetts lawyer, politician, soldier, former Democrat, and friend of the Radical Republicans, suggested that he would be available if prevailed upon as a compromise candidate to unify the Republican camps. That was proved to be unnecessary because Lincoln used party machinery to dominate the nominating convention meeting in Baltimore during June.

Conservative Republicans rebranded the party for the 1864 presidential effort. They campaigned by promoting it as the National Union Party and accepting Andrew Johnson, a loyal Unionist, as Lincoln's vice president. Johnson displaced Hannibal Hamlin, a Radical Republican representing Maine. Radical Republicans were also angered by the presence at the convention of delegates from Tennessee and from the reconstructed state governments of Louisiana and Arkansas.

Radicals were present during the creation of the party's 1864 platform document, which blamed slavery for the war and gave accolades to the Emancipation Proclamation, African American soldiers, and the possibility of the passage of an amendment to abolish slavery. Additionally, the platform endorsed new western homesteads, continental railroad subsidies, and immigration. France was condemned for its intervention in the current Mexican civil war.

After the convention, doubts lingered regarding Lincoln's success at the polls in November. Secretary Chase and John C. Frémont became restless and continued to promote themselves as third-party candidates. In due course after the close of the convention, Lincoln accepted Chase's resignation and then promoted him to the position of chief justice of the United States a few months after the October death of Roger Taney. Lincoln held the timing of Chase's nomination close to his chest. Friends of Lincoln were not sure whether it was to keep Chase's lust for the presidency at bay or whether it was a delayed reward so as not to appear to be a corrupt bargain.

Radical Republicans in Congress pushed forward the Wade-Davis Bill, which posited congressional authority over the readmission of Southern states. Upon Lincoln's pocket veto of the legislation, both Senators Wade and Davis declared Lincoln to be dictatorial and on the verge of usurping authority. Pledging themselves to the cause, but not to their political comrade, their conversation turned to nominating Ulysses S. Grant as a third party candidate at a second convention. Friends of Grant avowed that he did not desire in the least bit to become president in 1864 and made the point to Lincoln. To a few Radical Republicans, who were of the "anyone but Lincoln" camp, Grant may have been the least acceptable candidate because of his determination to end the war with the nearly unconditional surrender of the Confederacy. Lincoln's friends polled the Republican governors, who endorsed Lincoln for a second term.

Meanwhile, the Democratic Party's nominating convention placed George B. McClellan on the top of the presidential ticket. His running mate, Representative George H. Pendleton of Ohio, was offered as a peace candidate. The party's platform was widely perceived as a peace-by-armistice document, with African Americans being returned as property to the South. "The Union is the one condition of peace. We ask no more," stated McClellan in his nomination acceptance letter.[18]

At this point, Radical Republicans understood that the loss of the White House to the Democratic Party would set back the clock to 1860. To them Lincoln began to appear as the lesser of two evils. When encouraged to consider the postponement of the presidential election of 1864, Lincoln vowed that the normal constitutional and democratic process would not be interrupted by the war.[19]

War Views and Copperheads

Within nearly every citizen's grasp were daily or weekly newspapers. The electoral handiwork of both the Democratic and Republican candidates would rest upon the actual military situations in Virginia, Tennessee, Georgia,

Louisiana, and Texas. The news favored Republicans during the summer of the nominating conventions, but each story also had disappointing elements.

By the end of May, Major General Nathaniel Banks's Red River campaign in Louisiana was an obvious failure. By the end of June, the Army of the Potomac had suffered almost catastrophic losses of more than 39,000, but so had the Army of Northern Virginia, with about 33,600 killed, wounded, and missing. At that point, Lieutenant General Jubal Early's segment of the Army of Northern Virginia was in the northern end of the Shenandoah Valley, entering Maryland with Washington, D.C., as its destination.

Just two weeks later, Early's troops were retreating out of Maryland, back into the Shenandoah. On the second-to-last day of July, Major General George Meade's army suffered a dramatic, heartrending defeat at the battle of the Crater in the siege lines of Petersburg. Meanwhile on July 20, Brigadier General William T. Sherman's armies were preparing for the battle of Peachtree Creek, with Atlanta nearly within artillery range. On July 30, a large portion of Chambersburg, Pennsylvania, was burned on orders from rebel brigadier general John McCausland for failing to provide a ransom of $500,000 in U.S. currency or $100,000 in gold.

That August in Chicago, the Democratic Party's convention nominated McClellan for president and Pendleton for vice president. The party was bitterly split between the War Democrats, Moderate Peace Democrats, and Radical Peace Democrats. War Democrats supported the war but resisted Lincoln's use of presidential powers. Moderate Peace Democrats wished to pursue a negotiated armistice that would secure a Union victory and reunification. They believed that an armistice could finish the war without destroying the South in the way that Sherman and Major General Philip H. Sheridan would do during the late autumn of 1864. Radical Peace Democrats, commonly labeled Copperheads, declared the war to be a failure and favored an immediate end to hostilities without securing either reunification or emancipation.[20]

Pendleton was a close associate of the Copperhead Clement Vallandigham. On May 5, 1863, Vallandigham was arrested for violation of General Orders No. 38. Tried by a military court on May 6 and 7, he was charged with "publicly expressing . . . sympathy for those in arms against the Government of the United States, and declaring disloyal sentiments and opinions, with the object and purpose of weakening the power of the Government in its efforts to suppress an unlawful rebellion." On June 2, the military court banished him to the Confederacy, but, after touring the rebel states, Vallandigham escaped to Canada. As a delegate from Ohio, he openly attended the 1864 Democratic

National Convention in Chicago and contributed thoughts and text to the party's platform. The platform consisted of five paragraphs, of which the third is both representative and striking:

> Resolved, That the aim and object of the Democratic party is to preserve the Federal Union and the rights of the States unimpaired, and they hereby declare that they consider that the administrative usurpation of extraordinary and dangerous powers not granted by the Constitution—the subversion of the civil by military law in States not in insurrection; the arbitrary military arrest, imprisonment, trial, and sentence of American citizens in States where civil law exists in full force; the suppression of freedom of speech and of the press; the denial of the right of asylum; the open and avowed disregard of State rights; the employment of unusual test-oaths; and the interference with and denial of the right of the people to bear arms in their defense is calculated to prevent a restoration of the Union and the perpetuation of a Government deriving its just powers from the consent of the governed.[21]

The phrase "is to preserve the Federal Union and the rights of the States unimpaired" was the most difficult plank in the platform for McClellan to stand on. The war and emancipation impaired states' rights. A New York critic of Lincoln, J. W. Rathbone, revealed his own sentiments to Manton Marble, proprietor and editor of the *New York World* and a Lincoln antagonist whose offices were not attacked as others were during the New York City Draft Riots of 1863: "I admire McClellan & should vote for him but cannot swallow Pendleton & that Chicago platform." Lincoln understood the dilemma that McClellan was in. He told Solomon Pettis, a Pennsylvania Republican leader, that "after the expenditure of blood and treasure that has been poured out for the maintenance of the government and the preservation of the Union, the American people were not prepared to vote the war a failure." Even Radical Republicans softened their sentiments a bit toward Lincoln. They thought that Lincoln's reelection might bring about a disaster but that the election of McClellan would bring damnation.[22]

By late September, the Democratic Party was weakened by both its emphasis on peace by armistice and its fearmongering threats of renegade African Americans wandering through both the South and the North. The Republicans charged the Democrats with disloyalty, abandonment of the Union, and not considering an armistice until they saw they were losing the war.

News from the battlefield in late summer and autumn also encouraged Northern voters to finish the war with Lincoln. Sherman's armies captured Atlanta, Georgia; Admiral David Farragut's fleet captured Mobile, Alabama; Sheridan's troops nearly destroyed Early's army at Winchester and Fisher's Hill, Virginia, and finally did destroy it at Cedar Creek, Virginia, in late October. John Nicolay, one of the president's several secretaries, explained to his fiancée in mid-September that the situation had not been hopeful for months but, especially in the wake of news from Georgia, there was now "a perfect revolution in feeling. Three weeks ago, our friends everywhere were despondent, almost to the point of giving up the contest in despair. Now they are hopeful, jubilant, hard at work and confident of success."[23]

Since states controlled elections and had a variety of polling practices, returns came in as early as mid-September. They showed Republicans doing marginally well in all regions but weakest in the border states. When voting was completed in November, Lincoln won all but Delaware, Kentucky, and McClellan's home state of New Jersey. He received 55 percent of the popular vote. The next House of Representatives would contain 149 Republicans and 42 Democrats; the Senate would have 42 Republicans and 10 Democrats. For Republicans, the election of 1864 was more successful than the election of 1860. The best hope for the Democrats was to bring the Southern states quickly back into the Union and thereby gain representatives and senators.

The Confederacy Views the 1864 Election

Within the Confederacy, response to the Northern election fell into two camps. Confederate vice president Alexander Stephens believed that the Copperhead movement was in the ascent during the election year. The Northern Copperheads desired a negotiated peace because the North was itself divided. The Confederate vice president promoted peace societies in the North and advanced a series of peace proposals that were intended to show that Lincoln would not negotiate. The *Augusta Chronicle and Sentinel* echoed Stephens's sentiments.

The Confederate vice president believed that Jefferson Davis had lost the focus on state sovereignty and that both sides had nearly lost their will to continue the destructive war. He faulted raids such as Early's and McCausland's for being too aggressive, leading Northerners to rally around Lincoln. He wanted the Confederacy to choose a defensive strategy that would thwart military invasions.

Stephens also believed that the Democratic platform crafted by Vallandigham and assorted Copperheads was the first real ray of light for the

Southern states. If an armistice could be negotiated, he hoped it would lead to permanent peace and to reunion on the South's terms.[24] He suggested in a published letter that his government would likely be willing to open negotiations. *New York Tribune* editor Horace Greeley was enticed by Confederate agents located across the Niagara River who were rumored to be waiting for the Lincoln administration to open peace talks with them.[25]

Conversely, Jefferson Davis's dilemma was that he overestimated his ability to influence public opinion in both the South and the North regarding the Union's 1864 presidential election. The opportunities for doing so were apparent to him, but he lacked the political skills to develop and enact a plan to capitalize on those opportunities. For Davis, peace without independence was failure, so an armistice could not be an objective. The *Charleston Mercury* followed Davis's interpretation of events. His overt policy was to strengthen the Copperheads and resist any military incursions of the North. He believed too that Early's raid into Maryland and McCausland's razing of Chambersburg, Pennsylvania, would elicit Northern disgust toward Lincoln.

He also favored terrorism to encourage urban violence and reap social chaos among Northern voters. Occurring during the middle of the voting season, the St. Albans, Vermont, raid of October 19, 1864, was a sudden attack from Canada by former Confederate soldiers meant to plunder banks, raise money, and trick the Union army to divert troops to defend their northern border against further raids. Leaving one citizen dead, another wounded, and one shed burned, the band managed to steal more than $208,000 (a bit over $3 million in 2016 dollars). In New York City, agents of the Confederacy operated throughout the war, and some planned an act of terrorism for Election Day, November 1864. While that day passed without incident, on November 25 the saboteurs set fires at several hotels and P. T. Barnum's museum. Their four-ounce "Greek Fire" recipe was faulty, and closed rooms did not contain enough oxygen for them to explode properly. Firefighters extinguished the smoldering sheets even as the conspirators returned to Canada. Comparisons between the terroristic raids and Colonel Ulric Dahlgren's raid on Richmond during March 1864 were made, but the alleged death threat against President Davis was a significant difference in the three events.

Davis attempted to weaken the North by other clandestine efforts from Canada, as well. His government funded secret societies with gold dollars to advance agents' plots, such as raiding federal prisoner-of-war camps and arming the escapees. His agents promoted rumors of gold-hoarding in an effort to bring about rampant speculation in Northern financial markets.

Davis, wanting the 1864 Northern election to be attended by violence, refused the Democratic peace effort, believing his endorsement would taint the Northern Copperheads. Davis and like-minded Confederates believed that the Democratic Party could not be relied upon for the protection of Southern liberties. McClellan was a War Democrat whose postconvention letter repudiated secession and parts of the 1864 Democratic platform. Davis correctly believed that McClellan, for the sake of soldiers already slain, would not accept a peace without reunion.[26]

McClellan's acceptance of the Democratic Party's nomination letter restated what he had been saying since 1861. All efforts of statesmanship should be made "to secure such peace, reestablish the Union, and guarantee for the future the Constitutional rights of every State." If the war had been conducted in such a manner, then reconciliation "would have been easy, and we might have reaped the benefits of our many victories on land and sea." Gaining peace with honor intact would make reunion possible. Manton Marble's *New York World* believed that upon McClellan's election to the presidency, the South would come to understand that "submission to the Union does not involve the overthrow of their institutions, the destruction of their property, . . . social chaos, negro equality, and the nameless horrors of a servile war. . . . On the election of General McClellan . . . a peace party will spring, as if by magic, in every part of the South." Regarding the magic needed for a peace party to be generated in the South, Confederate ordnance chief Josiah Gorgas stated that with any cessation of hostilities "our armies would dissolve like frost before the rising sun."[27]

Additionally, Lee requested during September 1864 "immediate and vigorous measures to increase the strength of our armies. . . . As matters now stand, we have no troops disposable to meet movements of the enemy or strike where opportunity presents without taking them from the trenches and exposing some important point." Davis's response on November 7 included the understanding that if Lincoln was indeed reelected, then new enlistments must be forthcoming. The Confederate Congress had passed "a bill allowing the president to secure the services of blacks for combat duty but made emancipation contingent upon the consent of the owners and the states involved." Davis then sent an emissary to Europe to inform "Confederate diplomats that the Confederacy was willing to offer emancipation of the slaves" in return for diplomatic recognition. By the latter months of 1864, in Davis's mind Confederate independence trumped the peculiar institution of slavery.[28]

Generally speaking, there were four possibilities on the table during the 1864 presidential election: (1) reunion with slavery; (2) reunion without slavery;

(3) independence with slavery; (4) independence without slavery. To these four options, two more may be added for clarity: (5) perpetual resistance after the armies' surrenders and the capture of the Confederacy's executives; and (6) submission of all armed resistance.

Both Lincoln and McClellan were prowar and accepted a core principle: only battlefield victories would win Southern independence. Davis's solution was to stoke the fires of Confederate will and increase enlistments by highlighting rumors of Federal atrocities and demonizing Federal generals and soldiers. Such an emphasis, Davis believed, would bring deserters back into Confederate armies. He wanted every able Southern man at the front, deserters included. He portrayed Yankees as vicious dogs that must be whipped by masters. Each military defeat should be a political defeat for the Federals.

In a November 5, 1864, letter, Stephens stated that Davis was in favor of Lincoln's election. Davis repudiated Stephens's claim, saying there was no functional difference between the Northern parties and that he had never been interested in the 1864 election. But Davis believed that Lincoln was the devil he knew and that the election of McClellan might breed renewal of Federal resolve. Confederate newspapers advanced the notion that the Northern election was a fraud organized by abolitionists and their mobs. Lincoln, they claimed, would not permit a fair election and filled Northern newspapers with false charges of rebel battlefield atrocities in order to denigrate Southern honor and unite Northerners against the Confederacy. They predicted that Lincoln's election fraud would backfire and finally remove the North from Lincoln's thrall. As the peace movement in the North stumbled, Davis's faith in increased sacrifices and covert actions came to dominate popular opinion.[29]

In addition to these two competing Southern strategies for Confederate influence on the Northern election, there was a third. Some Southerners rejected the Confederacy and saw Lincoln's reelection as essential to their future. Anti-Davis individuals and loyal Unionists were attracted to the Lincoln ticket in part because Andrew Johnson was on it. In *The South versus the South*, William Freeling calculates that the slave states added approximately 450,000 troops to the Union army. Of those 450,000, about 200,000 came from the Southern border states of Delaware, Maryland, Kentucky, and Missouri. African Americans troops from the South numbered 150,000, while 100,000 were white men from the Confederate states. These figures were important because white Southern Unionism was at the heart of the Lincoln campaign.[30]

The popular understanding of Andrew Johnson contains both a stereotype and an enigma. Lincoln picked Johnson, a War Democrat and the most prominent Southern Unionist, to legitimize his reconstruction policy. The "Ten Percent Plan," which required a tenth of the citizens of a seceded state to take the oath of allegiance to the United States before it could be readmitted to the Union, laid out the president's policy for readmission. Lincoln's generous terms may be seen as the bait for Southerners to support their state's withdrawal from the Confederacy. Countering Lincoln's plan was the Wade-Davis Bill, which moved Lincoln's 10 percent up to 50 percent in order to secure the rights and privileges of the Union. Johnson's vice presidency was intended to create a truly Union party of Republicans aligned with War Democrats. Choosing a border state War Democrat for a high executive office would prove that loyal Unionists could be rewarded and relied upon.[31]

Born into poverty, Johnson apprenticed as an itinerant tailor. He eventually settled in Greeneville, Tennessee, where he served as an alderman and mayor before becoming a member of the Tennessee House of Representatives and the Tennessee Senate. In 1843, he was elected to the federal House of Representatives for the first of five two-year terms. Johnson then served four years as governor of Tennessee, after which the state legislature elected him to the U.S. Senate in 1857.

In 1861, Johnson made a courageous choice. He argued that, based on the Constitution, secession was lawlessness. He did not leave the U.S. Senate when his state left the Union. As a result, his family was driven into exile from Tennessee and his image was hung in effigy. In his congressional service, he sought passage of the Homestead Bill. This was passed in 1862, soon after he left his Senate seat to receive Lincoln's appointment as the military governor of Union-occupied Tennessee.

During the course of the war, Johnson came to embrace emancipation as a wartime measure. In 1863, he lobbied Lincoln to exempt Tennessee from the Emancipation Proclamation so he could work for emancipation from inside the state and not have it imposed from Washington. As he pressed for abolition, he freed his own slaves. His speeches labeled slavery a cancer. Lincoln watched Johnson work this issue throughout Tennessee, and in 1864 Tennessee delegates at the Union Party convention put forth Johnson's name for the office of vice president. Johnson was a stark contrast to the Democratic Party vice presidential candidate, the Copperhead Pendleton. In 1864, Johnson, as a War Democrat and Southern Unionist, was a logical choice as running mate for Lincoln, who wished to campaign on a message of national unity.[32]

The Soldiers' Vote

Lincoln blamed reverses in the 1862 elections partly on the fact that many Republicans were on active duty in the military. Since that election, nineteen states had adopted legislation that allowed troops to cast ballots while in the field or by proxy. Those states not enacting such laws were Delaware, Illinois, Indiana, Massachusetts, New Jersey, and Oregon. Lincoln requested William Chandler of New Hampshire to write a political tract accusing Democrats of trying to prevent soldiers from voting. Indiana Republicans warned Lincoln that their state might tip to the Democratic Party unless the most recent military draft was delayed and Indiana soldiers on campaign were furloughed.[33]

Lincoln communicated to Sherman that Indiana's October 11 election was the only one that month that prevented troops from voting in the field. He stated, "Anything you can safely do to let her soldiers, or any part of them, go home and vote at the State election will be greatly in point." Sherman, though not a Lincoln admirer, furloughed nine thousand sick and wounded Indiana soldiers. Additionally, Brigadier General John A. Logan of Illinois and Major General Carl Schurz of New York sought and obtained furloughs, allowing them to leave the field to campaign for Lincoln. Logan journeyed to Illinois, and Schurz met with his fellow German Americans in several states.[34]

McClellan's campaign was a dismal failure among the soldiers, who loathed the Democratic platform. He disavowed that platform in a public letter, but even strong McClellan supporters from 1862 deserted him in 1864. "The nomination of McClellan is not well received in army, from the fact that they put that abominable traitor, Pendleton[,] on as Vice President. The ticket has no chance here. McClellan's friends have abandoned him," a colonel in the Army of the Potomac wrote to his wife in August 1864. By early October, he reported to her that he had not come across an officer or man who would vote for McClellan and Pendleton. "Why, we won't touch the Chicago platform," they had told him. Later that month he told her that in his division the vote was running seven to one in favor of Lincoln. And although his corps consisted largely of Democrats, voter sentiment there was ten to one in favor of Lincoln.[35]

Most historians agree that two factors carried Lincoln to victory. The first was the progress of the Union military in 1864, especially General Sherman's capture of Atlanta. The second was that Lincoln's supporters conducted a campaign that successfully portrayed the Democratic platform as the work of traitors. Of the total 150,635 soldier votes cast and counted, Lincoln gathered

116,887 and McClellan 33,784.[36] Historian Jonathan White believes that about 20 percent of the troops did not cast a ballot in the election of 1864.[37]

Alternatively, did Lincoln's reelection ensure a Northern victory? In a way, John Wilkes Booth supplied an answer.

The Turning Point

Would the defeat of Lincoln have led to Southern independence? Historian Elizabeth Varon's answer is no.[38] Lincoln, Grant, and Sherman would have done everything to ensure victory before the March 4, 1865, presidential inauguration. McClellan would not have called an armistice when a victory was within his armies' grasp. Davis's understanding appears to be based on the fact that with food stores and railroads nearly not existing, the armies of the South faced battlefield extinction or surrender en masse.

The autumn 1864 Federal victories crushed Confederate hopes for foreign recognition. However, the 1864 election did not crush Jefferson Davis's morale because the margin of Lincoln's victory—while sobering to the Southern president—was not a landslide. Yet others in the Confederate government realized that they were hopelessly outmanned and outsupplied. As John B. Jones noted in his *Rebel War Clerk's Diary*, there was the rumor that Lincoln would call for a million-man draft. Even if that rumor was untrue, Jones wrote, he was certain that Lincoln could get the troops if he needed to.[39]

A pillar of Davis's creed was that if the manpower would come back to the armies and hold out a little longer, then help would come from overseas. He was certain that the overwhelming resources and manpower of the Union could not beat the courage and stamina of the Confederate army and that Europe would recognize the Confederacy.

But European powers were unwilling to challenge a popular president who had already demonstrated his vast resources. Without the prospect for help from the outside, the Confederate republic was doomed. Thus, Lincoln's victory in 1864 was a catastrophic setback from which the Confederacy could not recover. As the war ground on, the might of Union bullets and ballots would eventually triumph over states' rights. Lincoln's reelection was the last pound of weight pressed upon the chest of the Confederacy before its surrender. Then, as the story goes, the so-called Confederacy could kiss Lincoln's derriere.

Editors' Notes

1. Carl von Clausewitz, *On War*, ed. Anatol Rapoport (New York: Penguin Books, 1982), 119.

2. John Nicolay, *An Oral History of Abraham Lincoln: John G. Nicolay's Interviews and Essays*, ed. Michael Burlingame (Carbondale: Southern Illinois University Press, 2006), 78.

3. See http://memory.loc.gov/mss/mal/mal1/354/3547800/.

4. *Augusta Constitutionalist*, January 22, 1864, quoted by Gordon Rhea, *The Battle of the Wilderness* (Baton Rouge: Louisiana State University Press, 1994), 18.

5. James Longstreet to Alexander Lawton, March 5, 1864, *OR*, vol. 32, pt. 3, 588.

6. The text of the letter, a facsimile of the original, and more at the Library of Congress: http://blogs.loc.gov/loc/2014/08/abraham-lincolns-blind -memorandum/.

Contributor's Notes

7. Michael Burlingame, *Abraham Lincoln: A Life* (Baltimore: Johns Hopkins University Press, 2008), 2:752.

8. James B. McPherson considers the turning point theses in both *Battle Cry of Freedom: The Civil War Era* (New York: Oxford University Press, 1988) and *Ordeal by Fire: The Civil War and Reconstruction* (New York: Alfred A. Knopf, 1982). He understands that there were three turning points in the war: (1) the battle of Antietam and, coming on its heels, the Emancipation Proclamation; (2) the Pennsylvania campaign of 1863; and (3) the reelection of Lincoln. Others for consideration may be the creation of the Joint Committee on the Conduct of the War, the creation of the Army of the Potomac by George B. McClellan, and other topics included in this volume.

9. Gary Gallagher and Joan Waugh, *The American War: A History of the Civil War Era* (State College, Pa.: Flip Learning, 2015), 180–81.

10. McPherson, *Battle Cry of Freedom*, 713–17.

11. Quoted in McPherson, *Ordeal by Fire*, 387.

12. Allen C. Guelzo, *Fateful Lightning: A New History of the Civil War and Reconstruction* (New York: Oxford University Press, 2012), 462–63.

13. Christopher Bates, "Election of 1858," in *Encyclopedia of the American Civil War*, ed. David S. Heidler and Jeanne T. Heidler (New York: W. W. Norton, 2000), 634–35.

14. Mark Lause, "Election of 1860," in ibid., 636–39.

15. Bruce Tap, "Election of 1862," in ibid., 639–40.

16. Phyllis Field, "Election of 1864," in ibid., 640–42.

17. Transcription, Abraham Lincoln, Proclamation of Amnesty and Reconstruction, December 8, 1863, http://hd.housedivided.dickinson.edu/node/40452.

18. Stephen W. Sears, *George B. McClellan: The Young Napoleon* (New York: Ticknor and Fields, 1988), 375–76.

19. John C. Waugh, *Reelecting Lincoln: The Battle for the 1864 Election* (New York: Da Capo, 1997), 270–72; Michael Burlingame, 631–32, 666–67.

20. Michael Burlingame, 675–676, 681–684, 688–690.

21. *National Party Conventions, 1831–2004*, CQ Press Inc. (Washington, D.C., 2005), 61–62.

22. Michael Burlingame, *Abraham Lincoln*, 682–83.

23. Nicolay to Therena Bates, September 11, 1864, in *With Lincoln in the White House*, ed. Michael Burlingame (Carbondale: Southern Illinois University Press, 2000), 158.

24. Lincoln understood the Confederate terms well—though after the election and during January 1865 at the Hampton Roads peace initiative, Lincoln appears to have a settled opinion on the lack of legitimacy of the Confederate government.

25. "Confederate View of 1864 Election," Elizabeth Varon, November 8, 2014, https://www.c-span.org/video/?322673-2/discussion-confederate-view-1864 -election.

26. Larry E. Nelson, *Bullets, Ballots, and Rhetoric: Confederate Policy for the United States Presidential Contest of 1864* (Tuscaloosa: University of Alabama Press, 1980), 61, 110–15.

27. Sears, *George B. McClellan*, 376–77.

28. Nelson, *Bullets, Ballots, and Rhetoric*, 167–69.

29. Ibid., 27–29, 46–47.

30. A discussion of Freeling's work is in "Confederate View of 1864 Election."

31. Ibid.

32. Waugh, *Reelecting Lincoln*, 197–201.

33. Ibid., 339–40.

34. Burlingame, *Abraham Lincoln*, 711–15.

35. Quoted in Waugh, *Reelecting Lincoln*, 342–344.

36. Ibid., 353–54.

37. Jonathan W. White, *Emancipation: The Union Army and the Reelection of Abraham Lincoln* (Baton Rouge: Louisiana State University Press, 2014), 12.

38. A discussion of J. B. Jones's diary is in "Confederate View of 1864 Election."

39. Ibid.

The Gun That Killed Abraham Lincoln

With a single shot John Wilkes Booth changed the course of American history. The gun he chose was a .44-caliber pistol, made by Henry Deringer of Philadelphia. One shot was all that Booth had.

A modern version of a .44-caliber lead ball

The gun was favored for its small size—it could easily be concealed inside a pocket. It fired a single, round lead ball, weighing nearly an ounce—and was most accurate at close range.

John Wilkes Booth's single-shot pistol serves as the focal point of a large display at Ford's Theatre, in the basement museum. *Photo by Chris Mackowski*

Conclusion

Chris Mackowski

In the days before her husband's death, Mary Todd Lincoln claimed to have a premonition. "Mr. Lincoln's life is always exposed," she told a confidant, Elizabeth Keckly, a freed slave who worked as one of Washington's most popular dressmakers. "Ah, no one knows what it is to live in constant dread of some fearful tragedy," Mrs. Lincoln added. "I have a presentiment that he will meet with a sudden and violent end. I pray God to protect my beloved husband from the hands of the assassin."[1]

Mrs. Lincoln's fears came to pass just a few days later as she and her husband attended a performance of *Our American Cousin* at Ford's Theatre in downtown Washington, D.C. During one of the play's best laugh lines, John Wilkes Booth shot Abraham Lincoln in the back of the head with a derringer.

"Just now, after his generous dealings with Lee, I should have said the danger was past," lamented New York diarist George Templeton Strong after hearing the news.[2] He echoed a belief overheard on the street "fifty times at least": Booth had murdered the best friend the South had in the world. Gone was any "talk of concession and conciliation." Public opinion suddenly deemed "Grant's generous dealing with Lee . . . a blunder," Strong added. "Let us henceforth deal with rebels as they deserve. The rose-water treatment does not meet their case."[3]

Strong's April 15 diary entry captured a widespread sentiment across the North. "This atrocity has invigorated national feeling," Strong noted. "People who pitied our misguided brethren yesterday, and thought they had been punished enough already, and hoped there would be a general amnesty . . . talk approvingly today of vindictive justice and favor."[4] A sharp turn, indeed.

Lincoln's assassination is most often seen as the tragic postscript to the end of the Civil War in those heady days after Appomattox, which itself is commonly seen as the end of the war. However, it took Confederate forces more than two more months to fully lay down arms—and all the way to November, if one includes the CSS *Shenandoah*'s eventual surrender—but Appomattox's ceremonial stacking of arms presents the sort of narrative neat-and-tidiness we culturally tend to prefer in our storytelling.

But Union soldiers understood at the time that "if anything, Appomattox was halftime," says historian Brian Matthew Jordan. Jordan writes extensively about their perspective in his Pulitzer-finalist book *Marching Home: Union Veterans and Their Unending Civil War*. As Jordan explained in a 2015 interview, the veterans' postwar writings clearly indicated that "this thing wasn't over." "Yes, they were on the right side and, yes, they had won a military triumph on the battlefield," Jordan said, "but even that military triumph on the battlefield hadn't settled all the issues, and they were keenly aware of the unfinished social and political work of this war."[5]

Seen in this context, Lincoln's assassination is not merely the shift from America's "Civil War" narrative to America's "Reconstruction" narrative—as the general public today commonly understands it—but a turning point of the conflict itself, which Union veterans saw as ongoing, albeit in a different form.

An authority no less than Ulysses S. Grant, general-in-chief of the U.S. army, understood it in the same way. Responding to a letter from his friend Lieutenant General William T. Sherman, who expressed concern about "ugly questions left by the war," Grant explained his decision to eventually accept a nomination for president.[6] "It is [an office] I would not occupy for any mere personal consideration, but, from the nature of the contest since the close of active hostilities, I have been forced into it," he conceded. "I could not back down without, as it seems to me, leaving the contest for power over the next four years between mere trading politicians, the elevation of whom, no matter which party won, would lose to us, largely, the results of the costly war which we have gone through."[7]

Note Grant's use of phrases like "the contest" and "active hostilities." He still recognized a struggle, which had evolved from armed resistance into something different. He did not want to lose the peace after winning the war. He also wanted to do so in a way that would carry on Lincoln's legacy. "I knew his goodness of heart, his generosity, his yielding disposition, his desire to have everybody happy, and above all his desire to see all the people of the United States enter again upon the full privileges of citizenship with equality among all," Grant explained in his memoirs.[8] While Lincoln never left a record of his exact plans for Southerners during Reconstruction, he had made it clear to Grant, Sherman, and others that "if I were in your place, I'd let 'em up easy." "All he wanted of us," Sherman recalled, "was to defeat the opposing armies, and to get the men composing the Confederate armies back to their homes, at work at their farms and in their shops."[9]

Grant believed Andrew Johnson had abdicated on Lincoln's vision and that "reconstruction had been set back, no telling how far."[10] "I feared that his course towards them would be such as to repel, and make them unwilling citizens; and if they became such they would remain so for a long time," Grant prophesied.[11] "They surely would not make good citizens if they felt that they had a yoke around their necks."[12] Yet Johnson vehemently repeated an ever-ready rejoinder—"Treason is a crime and must be made odious"—that "did engender bitterness of feeling," Grant said, and "with no assurances of safety, many Southerners were driven to a point almost beyond endurance."[13]

It could have all worked out so differently, Grant mused: "But for the assassination of Mr. Lincoln, I believe the great majority of the Northern people, and the soldiers unanimously, would have been in favor of a speedy reconstruction on terms that would be the least humiliating to the people who had rebelled against their government."[14]

* * *

Grant is not the only one, of course, to wonder what might have been. As we have looked back on this essay collection, we have seen much to consider, ourselves. "For want of a nail," right?

While explorations of "what if" doubtless prove entertaining, they are often fruitless exercises. More fascinating are explorations of what *did* happen and the consequences thereof. And just as crucial are explorations of why we remember things as we do—a confounding process that often obscures larger and more meaningful understandings. Our own cultural tendency toward a narrative structure that favors rising action forces an artificially contrived climax that, in essence, dismisses the second half of the war as relatively unimportant. We argue, instead, that you consider an ongoing, intertwined flow.

For instance: the Union defeat at First Manassas led to the appointment of George B. McClellan, which in turn led to the rise of the North's preeminent army. But even as McClellan built that army, he had to begin looking over his shoulder at the political environment, made more volatile by the congressional second-guessing of the Joint Committee on the Conduct of the War, which arose following the loss at Ball's Bluff. The committee's scrutinous eye would inflict every army commander in the East with career-ending cases of caution until Grant finally arrived. Hampered more by political intrigues in the West than by coherent Confederate resistance, his string of victories made him impossible for Lincoln to ignore, particularly in the face of growing pressure exerted by Robert E. Lee's own string of victories in the East. Yet Lee's rise to command came with its own cost for the Confederacy—a grim arithmetic Grant immediately understood and exploited, beginning in the Wilderness. Those same numbers worked against John Bell Hood when he assumed command of the Confederate Army of Tennessee and also had a negative impact on Lincoln's prospects for reelection. But battlefield victories cemented the president's prospects, which in turn ensured that those Confederate casualties would be for naught. It also ensured that the promise of freedom he made with the Emancipation Proclamation—redefining the war as well as the subsequent peace—would carry forward. That peace, however, was preempted by an assassin's bullet, which carried conflict onward from the field of battle into the political and social spheres.

Told this way, Gettysburg need not even show up as a key event in the overall narrative of the war. It was, as some historians already suggest, just a notch in the Federal "win" column during an otherwise long back-and-forth sequence in the East that generally favored the Confederates.

Lincoln offered an account of sorts of what he thought the great events of the war were. In a cabinet meeting on April 14, 1865, he told his assembled counselors—including Grant—that he had had a dream the previous evening, and it led him to expect great news that day from Sherman. The dream was, he explained with a kind of "poetic mysticism . . . his usual dream which preceded great events." As his clerks John Hay and John G. Nicolay recounted years later, Lincoln "seemed to be, he said, in a singular and indescribable vessel, but always the same, moving with great rapidity towards a dark and indefinite shore; he had had this dream before Antietam, Murfreesboro, Gettysburg, and Vicksburg."[15]

"'Murfreesboro' was no victory," Grant countered, "and had no important results." Lincoln did not argue the point, although he had, just the previous August, characterized the battle as "a hard earned victory which, had there been a defeat instead, the nation could scarcely have lived over."[16] Rather, Lincoln returned to his point that the dream served as a premonition for great news from Sherman, "as he knew of no other important event which was likely at present to occur."[17]

During that meeting—"the last day of Lincoln's firm and tolerant rule," Nicolay and Hay said—Lincoln laid out "words of clemency and good-will."[18] "He was particularly desirous to avoid the shedding of blood, or any vindictiveness of punishment," the secretaries recounted. "Enough lives have been sacrificed," Lincoln said; "we must extinguish our resentments if we expect harmony and union."[19] Of note: "he was anxious to close the period of strife without overmuch discussion."[20]

Five days after Appomattox, Lincoln did not see things as neatly tidied up but, rather, still as a "period of strife." He himself saw the work ongoing. The narrative of the war continued. The pages of history, still being written, continued still to turn.

Notes

1. Quoted in Elizabeth Keckly, *Behind the Scenes, or, Thirty Years a Slave, and Four Years in the White House* (New York: G. W. Carleton, 1868), 178.

2. George Templeton Strong, "George Templeton Strong: Diary, April 15, 1865," in *The Civil War: The Final Year as Told by Those Who Lived It*, ed. Aaron Sheehan-Dean (New York: Library of America, 2014), 684.

3. Ibid., 686.

4. Ibid., 685.

5. Brian Matthew Jordan, interview with Chris Mackowski, April 19, 2016. Full transcript of the interview available online at https://emergingcivil war.com/tag/jordan-pulitzer-finalist/.

6. William T. Sherman to Grant, June 7, 1868, in *The Papers of Ulysses S. Grant*, ed. John Y. Simon, vol. 18 (Carbondale: Southern Illinois University Press, 1991), 293n.

7. Grant to Sherman, June 21, 1868, ibid., 292.

8. Ulysses S. Grant, *The Personal Memoirs of Ulysses S. Grant* (Hartford, Conn.: Charles Webster, 1885; New York: Library of America, 1990), 750–51.

9. William Tecumseh Sherman, *Memoirs of General W. T. Sherman*, ed. Charles Royster (New York: Library of America, 1990), 326.

10. Grant, *Personal Memoirs*, 751.

11. Ibid.

12. Ibid., 752.

13. Ibid., 751.

14. Ibid., 752.

15. John G. Nicolay and John Hay, from *Abraham Lincoln: A History*, quoted in *President Lincoln Assassinated!! The Firsthand Story of the Murder, Manhunt,*

Trial, and Mourning, ed. Harold Holzer (New York: Library of America, 2014), 396.

16. Ibid.; Roy P. Basler, ed., *The Collected Works of Abraham Lincoln* (New Brunswick, N.J.: Rutgers University Press, 1953), 6:424–25.

17. Holzer, *Lincoln Assassinated!!*, 396.

18. Ibid., 396, 398.

19. Ibid., 397–98.

20. Ibid., 397.

Contributors

Index

Contributors

A number of this volume's contributors are involved with Emerging Civil War (www.emergingcivilwar.com), a collaborative public history initiative cofounded by Chris Mackowski and Kristopher D. White that features more than two dozen historians and invites participation by other Civil War scholars and researchers.

Daniel T. Davis is the managing editor of Emerging Civil War. He has worked as a historian at both Appomattox Court House National Historic Site and at Fredericksburg and Spotsylvania National Military Park, as well as for the U.S. Army. His interest in the American Civil War, which focuses on cavalry operations in the Eastern Theater, stems from weekend battlefield trips with his dad. He is the coauthor of six titles in the Emerging Civil War Series and has coauthored articles for *Hallowed Ground*, *Civil War Times*, and *Blue and Gray Magazine*.

Stephen Davis, of Atlanta, wrote a feature article about fighting around Atlanta for a special issue of *Blue and Gray Magazine* in August 1989. His book *Atlanta Will Fall: Sherman, Joe Johnston, and the Heavy Yankee Battalions* (2001) is a campaign narrative. His *What the Yankees Did to Us: Sherman's Bombardment and Wrecking of Atlanta* (2012) chronicles the city's encounter with war and enemy occupation. Davis is the author of two books on the Atlanta campaign for the Emerging Civil War Series, as well as a study of John B. Hood's generalship in 1864.

Thomas A. Desjardin is the author of several books on the Civil War, including *These Honored Dead: How the Story of Gettysburg Shaped American Memory* (2003), and his work has twice been nominated for the Lincoln Prize. A former historian at Gettysburg National Military Park, Desjardin has served since 2014 as the state of Maine's commissioner of education.

Ryan Longfellow works as a history teacher, chairs the social studies department at Spotsylvania (Virginia) Middle School, and facilitates the World History Learning Community. In 2015 he was chosen as the Spotsylvania County mentor teacher of the year. For more than fifteen years, Ryan has worked as a park guide at Fredericksburg and Spotsylvania National

Military Park, interpreting the battlefields of central Virginia, including the Wilderness.

Chris Mackowski is a writing professor in the Jandoli School of Communication at St. Bonaventure University. He serves as the editor in chief of *Emerging Civil War* and is the editor of the Emerging Civil War Series and a coeditor of the Engaging the Civil War series. He has written or cowritten more than a dozen books about the Civil War, and his work has appeared in all the major Civil War magazines. Mackowski is also the historian-in-residence at Stevenson Ridge, a historic property and inn on the Spotsylvania battlefield.

Gregory A. Mertz has worked for the National Park Service for thirty-five years and is currently the supervisory historian at Fredericksburg and Spotsylvania National Military Park. As a boy growing up in what is now Wildwood, Missouri, he traveled with his Boy Scout troop to the Shiloh battlefield every spring to hike one of the six trails there. He has written several articles for *Blue and Gray Magazine*, is the founding president of the Rappahannock Valley Civil War Round Table, and is a former vice president of the Brandy Station Foundation.

A former U.S. Marine, **James A. Morgan** is a volunteer guide at the Ball's Bluff battlefield for the Northern Virginia Regional Park Authority and the author of *A Little Short of Boats: The Battles of Ball's Bluff and Edwards Ferry, October 21–22, 1861* (2011). He is a past president of the Loudoun County Civil War Roundtable and a member of the Loudoun County Civil War Sesquicentennial Committee.

A native Virginian, **Robert Orrison** serves as the historic site operations supervisor for Prince William County. He also leads tours with Civil War Excursion Tours and is a coauthor of *A Want of Vigilance: The Bristoe Station Campaign* (2015) and *A Long Road North: A Guide to the Gettysburg Campaign* (2016). Orrison serves as the treasurer of the Historic House Museum Consortium of Washington, D.C., sits on the boards of directors of the Mosby Heritage Area Association and Virginia Civil War Trails, and is the vice president of the Virginia Association of Museums.

Kevin Pawlak is the education specialist for the Mosby Heritage Area Association and is a licensed battlefield guide at Antietam National Battlefield. He previously worked at Harpers Ferry National Historical Park and interned with the Papers of Abraham Lincoln at the Abraham Lincoln Presidential Library in Springfield, Illinois. Pawlak serves on the boards of directors of the Shepherdstown Battlefield Preservation Association and the Save Historic Antietam Foundation and is on the advisory board for the George Tyler

Moore Center for the Study of the Civil War at Shepherd University. He is the author of *Shepherdstown in the Civil War: One Vast Confederate Hospital* (2015).

Rea Andrew Redd is the director of Eberly Library and an adjunct instructor in history at Waynesburg University in Pennsylvania. He is the author of *The Gettysburg Campaign Study Guide*, volumes 1 and 2, and of a blog, *Civil War Librarian*. He frequently speaks to groups about Abraham Lincoln, Civil War–era medicine, Pennsylvania's Civil War history, and Gettysburg, the aftermath and the address. He teaches U.S. history survey courses, the Civil War and Reconstruction, U.S. environmental history, Pennsylvania history, and American wars. He also teaches a service and learning course on the battle of Gettysburg, which includes leading student volunteers on service projects for Gettysburg National Military Park and the Gettysburg Battlefield Preservation Association.

Kristopher D. White is a cofounder and the chief historian of Emerging Civil War. He is also the education manager at the Civil War Trust. He was a staff military historian at Fredericksburg and Spotsylvania National Military Park and is a former member of the Association of Licensed Battlefield Guides at Gettysburg. He serves as the historical content editor of the Emerging Civil War Series.

Index

Page numbers in italics indicate illustrations.

ENGAGING
─── *the* ───
CIVIL WAR

Engaging the Civil War, a series founded by the historians at the blog Emerging Civil War (www.emergingcivilwar.com), adopts the sensibility and accessibility of public history while adhering to the standards of academic scholarship. To engage readers and bring them to a new understanding of America's great story, series authors draw on insights they gained while working with the public—walking the ground where history happened at battlefields and historic sites, talking with visitors in museums, and educating students in classrooms. With fresh perspectives, field-tested ideas, and in-depth research, volumes in the series connect readers with the story of the Civil War in ways that make history meaningful to them while underscoring the continued relevance of the war, its causes, and its effects. All Americans can claim the Civil War as part of their history. This series helps them engage with it.

Chris Mackowski and Brian Matthew Jordan, Series Editors

Queries and submissions
emergingcivilwar@gmail.com